ON FREUD'S "THE UNCONSCIOUS"

CONTEMPORARY FREUD
Turning Points and Critical Issues

Series Editor: Gennaro Saragnano

On Freud's "Analysis Terminable and Interminable"
edited by Joseph Sandler

On Freud's "On Narcissism: An Introduction"
edited by Joseph Sandler, Ethel Spector Person, Peter Fonagy

On Freud's "Observations on Transference-Love"
edited by Ethel Spector Person, Aiban Hagelin, Peter Fonagy

On Freud's "Creative Writers and Day-Dreaming"
edited by Ethel Spector Person, Peter Fonagy, Sérvulo Augusto Figueira

On Freud's "A Child Is Being Beaten"
edited by Ethel Spector Person

On Freud's "Group Psychology and the Analysis of the Ego"
edited by Ethel Spector Person

On Freud's "Mourning and Melancholia"
edited by Leticia Glocer Fiorini, Thierry Bokanowski, Sergio Lewkowicz

On Freud's "The Future of an Illusion"
edited by Mary Kay O'Neil and Salman Akhtar

On Freud's "Splitting of the Ego in the Process of Defence"
edited by Thierry Bokanowski and Sergio Lewkowicz

On Freud's "Femininity"
edited by Leticia Glocer Fiorini and Graciela Abelin-Sas

On Freud's "Constructions in Analysis"
edited by Thierry Bokanowski and Sergio Lewkowicz

On Freud's "Beyond the Pleasure Principle"
edited by Salman Akhtar and Mary Kay O'Neil

On Freud's "Negation"
edited by Mary Kay O'Neil and Salman Akhtar

On Freud's "On Beginning the Treatment"
edited by Christian Seulin and Gennaro Saragnano

On Freud's "Inhibitions, Symptoms and Anxiety"
edited by Samuel Arbiser and Jorge Schneider

ON FREUD'S "THE UNCONSCIOUS"

Edited by

Salman Akhtar & Mary Kay O'Neil

Series Editor

Gennaro Saragnano

CONTEMPORARY FREUD
Turning Points and Critical Issues

LONDON AND NEW YORK

First published 2013 by Karnac Books Ltd.

Published 2018 by Routledge
2 Park Square, Milton Park, Abingdon, Oxon OX14 4RN
711 Third Avenue, New York, NY 10017, USA

Routledge is an imprint of the Taylor & Francis Group, an informa business

British Library Cataloguing in Publication Data

A C.I.P. for this book is available from the British Library

ISBN 9781782200277 (pbk)

Edited, designed and produced by The Studio Publishing Services Ltd
www.publishingservicesuk.co.uk
e-mail: studio@publishingservicesuk.co.uk

CONTENTS

CONTEMPORARY FREUD
IPA Publications Committee vii

ACKNOWLEDGEMENTS ix

EDITORS AND CONTRIBUTORS xi

Introduction
Salman Akhtar 1

PART I
"The unconscious" (1915e)
Sigmund Freud 21

PART II
Discussion of "The unconscious" 79

1 Metapsychology and clinical practice: lessons from Freud's "The unconscious"
Peter Wegner 81

2 “The unconscious” in psychoanalysis and neuropsychology
Mark Solms 101

3 Freud’s “The unconscious”: can this work be squared with a biological account?
Linda Brakel 119

4 A Hindu reading of Freud’s “The unconscious”
Madhusudana Rao Vallabhaneni 132

5 The repressed maternal in Freud’s topography of mind
Kenneth Wright 160

6 Complementary models of the mind in Freud’s “The unconscious”?
Bernard Reith 179

7 The unconscious in work with psychosomatic patients
Marilia Aisenstein 203

8 The unconscious and perceptions of the self
Ira Brenner 216

9 “In spite of my ego”: problem solving and the unconscious
Stefano Bolognini 234

EPILOGUE
Mary Kay O’Neil 254

REFERENCES 270

INDEX 289

CONTEMPORARY FREUD

IPA Publications Committee

This significant series was founded by Robert Wallerstein and subsequently edited by Joseph Sandler, Ethel Spector Person, Peter Fonagy, and, lately, by Leticia Glocer Fiorini. Its important contributions have always greatly interested psychoanalysts of different latitudes. It is therefore my great honour, as the new Chair of the Publications Committee of the International Psychoanalytical Association, to continue the tradition of this most successful series.

The objective of this series is to approach Freud's work from a present and contemporary point of view. On the one hand, this means highlighting the fundamental contributions of his work that constitute the axes of psychoanalytic theory and practice. On the other, it implies the possibility of getting to know and spreading the ideas of present psychoanalysts about Freud's *oeuvre*, both where they coincide and where they differ.

This series considers at least two lines of development: a contemporary reading of Freud that reclaims his contributions, and a clarification of the logical and epistemic perspectives from which he is read today.

Freud's theory has branched out, and this has led to a theoretical, technical, and clinical pluralism that has to be worked through. It has, therefore, become necessary to avoid a snug and uncritical co-existence of concepts in order to consider systems of increasing complexities that take into account both the convergences and the divergences of the categories at play.

Consequently, this project has involved an additional task—that is, gathering psychoanalysts from different geographical regions representing, in addition, different theoretical stances, in order to be able to show their polyphony. This also means an extra effort for the reader that has to do with distinguishing and discriminating, establishing relations or contradictions that each reader eventually will have to work through.

Being able to listen to other theoretical viewpoints is also a way of exercising our listening capacities in the clinical field. This means that the listening should support a space of freedom that would allow us to hear what is new and original.

In this spirit, we have brought together authors deeply rooted in the Freudian tradition and others who have developed theories that had not been explicitly taken into account in Freud's work.

"The unconscious" is one of the most important and well known of Freud's essays on metapsychology. Written in 1915, it contains and describes the basic concepts of what is known as the Freudian topographic model of the mind. Salman Akhtar and Mary Kay O'Neil have now collected here a series of essays written by very distinguished analysts who approach and comment on this text of Freud's in the light of contemporary psychoanalysis and from different points of view, including recent studies in neurophysiology and ethology. This renders the readers updated on one of the core concepts of our discipline. Special thanks are, therefore, due to the editors and to the contributors to this volume, which enriches the Contemporary Freud series.

Gennaro Saragnano
Series Editor
Chair, IPA Publications Committee

ACKNOWLEDGEMENTS

We are deeply grateful to the distinguished colleagues who contributed to this volume. We appreciate their efforts, their sacrifice of time, and their patience with our requirements, reminders, and requests for revisions. We are also grateful to Dr Joseph Slap for his help with one of the chapters in this book. We acknowledge with sincerity the guidance of the members of the IPA Publications Committee, especially its Chair, Genaro Saragnano. We are also thankful to Jan Wright for her skillful help in preparing parts of the manuscript, to Frederick Lowy for his insightful comments and translation of parts of the German text, and to Rhoda Bawdekar for keeping track of all sorts of matters during the book's production. Finally, we wish to express our gratitude to Oliver Rathbone of Karnac Books who shepherded this project to its completion and to the team at The Studio Publishing Services for their meticulous copy-editing and typesetting.

Salman Akhtar & Mary Kay O'Neil

EDITORS AND CONTRIBUTORS

Marilia Aisenstein is a training analyst of the Hellenic Psychoanalytical Society and the Paris Psychoanalytical Society. She has been president of the Paris Society and of the Paris Psychosomatic Institute, a member of the editorial board of the *Revue Française de Psychanalyse*, and co-founder and editor of the *Revue Française de Psychosomatique*. She has been Chair of the IPA's International New Groups, and is the European representative to the IPA's Executive Committee. She presently works in private practice and gives seminars in both the Hellenic and the Paris Societies, and is the President of the Executive Board of the Paris Society's Psychoanalytical Clinic. She has contributed chapters and written books on psychosomatics and hypochondria and numerous (130) papers in French and international reviews. She received the Maurice Bouvet prize in 1992.

Salman Akhtar is a Professor of Psychiatry at Jefferson Medical College, and Training and Supervising Analyst at the Psychoanalytic Center of Philadelphia. He has served on the Editorial Boards of the *International Journal of Psychoanalysis* and *Journal of the American Psychoanalytic Association*, and is currently the Book Review Editor of the *International Journal of Applied Psychoanalytic Studies*. His sixty-four books include *Broken Structures* (1992), *Quest for Answers* (1995), *Inner Torment* (1999), *Immigration and Identity* (1999), *New Clinical Realms* (2003), *Objects of Our Desire* (2005), *Regarding Others* (2007), *The Damaged Core* (2009), *Turning Points in Dynamic Psychotherapy* (2009), *The Comprehensive Dictionary of Psychoanalysis* (2009), *Immigration and Acculturation* (2011), *Matters of Life and Death* (2011), *Psychoanalytic Listening* (2012), and *Good Stuff* (2013), as well as thirty-eight edited books in the realm of culture and psychoanalysis, including *Freud along the Ganges* (2005), *The Crescent and the Couch* (2008), *Freud and the Far East* (2009), and *The African American Experience: Psychoanalytic Perspectives* (2012), which deal with India, the Islamic world, the Far Eastern culture, and the African-American population of the USA, respectively. Dr Akhtar is the recipient of the Best Paper of the Year Award from the *Journal of American Psychoanalytic Association* (1995), the Edith Sabshin Award (2000) from the American Psychoanalytic Association, the Kun Po Soo Award (2004), the Irma Bland Award (2005) from the American Psychiatric Association, the Sigmund Freud Award for Distinguished Contribution to Psychoanalysis from the American Society of Psychoanalytic Physicians (2000), and the Robert Liebert Award (2003) for distinguished contributions to Applied Psychoanalysis from the Columbia University Center for Psychoanalytic Training and Research and, most recently, the highly prestigious Sigourney Award (2012) for outstanding contributions to the field of psychoanalysis. Dr Akhtar has delivered invited lectures at academic institutions in countries around the world, including Australia, Belgium, Brazil, Canada, Chile, China, the UK, France, Germany, Italy, Japan, Mexico, Peru, Serbia, and Turkey. His books have been translated into many languages, including German, Rumanian, Spanish, and Turkish. He has also published seven volumes of poetry and is a Scholar-in-Residence at the Inter-Act Theatre Company in Philadelphia.

Stefano Bolognini is a psychiatrist, training and supervising psychoanalyst of the SPI. He was the national scientific director and then the president of the Italian Psychoanalytic Society, and IPA Board Representative 2003–2007. He was co-founder of the "Serious Pathologies Committee" of his Society, and he works as supervisor in psychiatric public services and in day-hospitals for borderline and psychotic adolescents. He was co-Chair of the IPA CAPSA and Chair of the 100th Anniversary IPA Committee. A member of the European Board of the *International Journal of Psychoanalysis* from 2002 to 2012, he has published papers in the most important international journals and in many international collective books. His books *Psychoanalytic Empathy* (2002) and *Secret Passages. Theory and Practice of the Interpsychic Dimension* (2008) have been published in the main international languages from several publishers. He also published *Like Wind, Like Wave* (2006, Other Press, New York), a collection of amusingly told personal anecdotes, each with its concluding considerations from a psychoanalytic perspective; he also publishes articles on newspapers and actively participates in public mediatic debates. He is now the president-elect of the International Psychoanalytic Association. He lives and works in Bologna, Italy.

Linda Brakel is an Adjunct Associate Professor in Psychiatry at the University of Michigan Medical School, a Faculty Associate in the Philosophy Department at the University of Michigan, and a Faculty Member of the Michigan Psychoanalytic Institute. She is the author of articles that range widely—from empirical research on psychoanalytic theory, to philosophical matters best considered within the realm of the philosophy of mind and action, to straightforward clinical topics, and, perhaps of most note, thoroughly interdisciplinary projects, including her two recent volumes: *Philosophy, Psychoanalysis, and the A-Rational Mind* (Oxford, 2009) and *Unconscious Knowing and Other Essays in Psycho-Philosophical Analysis* (Oxford, 2010).

Ira Brenner is Clinical Professor of Psychiatry at Jefferson Medical College in Philadelphia and Training and Supervising Analyst at the Psychoanalytic Center of Philadelphia, where he is also Director Emeritus of the Adult Psychotherapy Training Program. He has a special interest in the area of psychological trauma and is the author of over eighty publications, including co-editing two special issues of *The International Journal of Applied Psychoanalytic Studies* and writing four books: *The Last Witness: The Child Survivor of the Holocaust,* co-authored with Judith Kestenberg (1996), *Dissociation of Trauma: Theory, Phenomenology, and Technique* (2001), *Psychic Trauma: Dynamics, Symptoms, and Treatment* (2004), and *Injured Men: Trauma, Healing, and the Masculine Self* (2009). A member of Phi Beta Kappa and the Alpha Omega Alpha medical honor society, he has received a number of awards for his work, including the Gratz Research Prize from Jefferson for work on the Holocaust, the Piaget Writing Award for his 2001 book, the Gradiva Award for his 2009 book, the Bruno Lima Award for his work in disaster psychiatry, and Practitioner of the Year Award from the Philadelphia Psychiatric Society. He has lectured nationally and internationally, and is in private practice, treating people of all ages, in the greater Philadelphia area.

Mary Kay O'Neil is a supervising and training psychoanalyst who has recently moved from Montreal to Toronto, where she is in private practice. She is the past Director of the Canadian Institute of Psychoanalysis (Quebec, English) and a North American Representative on the Board of the International Psychoanalytical Association. In addition, she has served on a number of IPA committees, including ethics committees at the local, national, and international levels, and on the editorial Board of the *International Journal of Psychoanalysis*. Dr O'Neil received a PhD from the University of Toronto, where she was an Assistant Professor in the Department of Psychiatry. She completed her psychoanalytic training at the Toronto Institute of Psychoanalysis and is a Registered Psychologist in both Quebec and Ontario. The author of *The Unsung Psychoanalyst: The Quiet Influence of Ruth Easser*, she co-authored/edited five other books and has contributed numerous professional journal articles as well as chapters and book reviews. Her publications and research include depression and young adult development, emotional needs of sole support mothers, post termination analytic contact, and psychoanalytic ethics. Her research activities have been funded by foundations in Toronto and Montreal.

Bernard Reith is a member of the Swiss Psychoanalytical Society and works as psychoanalyst in private practice in Geneva, Switzerland. He is Chairman of the Working Party on Initiating Psychoanalysis (WPIP) of the European Psychoanalytic Federation since 2004 and Board Member of the Analyst at Work Section of the International Journal of Psychoanalysis since 2012. He was Secretary of the Swiss Psychoanalytical Society from 2009 to 2012 and is Chairman of its Commission on Research in Psychoanalysis since 2012. Originally trained as a psychiatrist and psychotherapist, he is also founding member and past president of the Suisse Romande branch of the

European Federation for Psychoanalytic Psychotherapy in the Public Sector, co-founder and past co-director of the Continuous Education Program in Psychoanalytic Psychotherapy at the University of Geneva and Consultant with the Geneva University Hospitals. He has co-edited the book *Initiating Psychoanalysis: Perspectives*. His main current fields of interest are qualitative clinical research in psychoanalysis, grounded dialogue between different psychoanalytic models and the understanding of the psychoanalyst's position as seen from within these different models.

Mark Solms is best known for his discovery of the forebrain mechanisms of dreaming, and for his pioneering integration of psychoanalytic theories and methods with those of modern neuroscience. Currently, he holds the Chair of Neuropsychology at the University of Cape Town and Groote Schuur Hospital (Departments of Psychology and Neurology). His other current positions include: Honorary Lecturer in Neurosurgery at St Bartholomew's & Royal London School of Medicine, and Director of the Arnold Pfeffer Center for Neuropsychoanalysis at the New York Psychoanalytic Institute. He was awarded Honorary Membership of the New York Psychoanalytic Society in 1998. Other awards include the George Sarton Medal of the Rijksuniversiteit Gent (1996) and the Sigourney Prize (2012). He has published widely in both neuroscientific and psychoanalytic journals, and has authored five books. His latest book (with Oliver Turnbull), *The Brain and the Inner World* (2002), is a best-seller and has been translated into twelve languages. He is the authorised editor and translator of the forthcoming *Revised Standard Edition of the Complete Psychological Works of Sigmund Freud* (twenty-four volumes), and the *Complete Neuroscientific Works of Sigmund Freud* (four volumes). He is a member of the British Psychoanalytical Society and the South African Psychoanalytical Association (of which he is President).

Madhusudana Rao Vallabhaneni obtained his medical degree from Guntar Medical College in India. Following that, he trained in psychiatry at the Queen's University in Belfast, Northern Ireland, at the St Louis University, St Louis, MO, in the USA, and at Dalhousie University in Canada. He trained in psychoanalysis at the St Louis Psychoanalytic Institute. Dr Vallabhaneni is a Fellow of the Royal

College of Physicians and Surgeons in Canada and a full member of the International Psychoanalytic Association, the American Psychoanalytic Association, and the Canadian Psychoanalytic Society. He serves on the teaching faculty of the Toronto Psychoanalytic Institute and the Department of Psychiatry at the University of Toronto. He is the Chair of the Curriculum Committee of the Advanced Training Program in Psychoanalytic Psychotherapy, sponsored by the Toronto Psychoanalytic Society. Dr Vallabhaneni is a serious scholar of Hindu scriptures and has written significantly on the views of self in Advaitic Vedantism and psychoanalysis. He is also an attending psychiatrist at the Mt Sinai Hospital in Toronto and maintains a private practice of psychiatry and psychoanalysis in Toronto, Canada.

Peter Wegner is a training and supervising analyst of the German Psychoanalytical Association since 1995 and is in private practice in Tübingen, Southwest Germany. He was born in 1952 in Berlin and studied Psychology from 1972 to 1978 at the University of Tübingen, followed by a training in psychodrama (1982) and psychoanalysis (1986). From 1978 to 1982, he was employed at two centres for counselling (children and adults) and from 1982 to 1995 was assistant lecturer at the Department for Psychoanalysis, Psychotherapy and Psychosomatic, University of Tübingen. He was Chair of the training committee of the Institute for Psychoanalysis Stuttgart/Tübingen (2000–2006) and member of the Publication Committee of the IPA (2001–2005). From 2006 to 2012 he was Vice-President and President of the European Psychoanalytical Federation (EPF). He has specialised in clinical questions of long-term and high frequency psychoanalysis and has published numerous papers in this field on the subjects of opening scene, initial interviews and initiating psychoanalysis, silence and free association, timelessness and external reality, transference and precedence of the countertransference, enactment and performance, three modes of psychoanalytic work and uncertainty, and on Freud's "The future prospects of psycho-analytic therapy" (see all publications under www.drpeterwegner.de).

Kenneth Wright is a British psychoanalyst well known for his work on Winnicott. He trained with the Independent Group of the BPS and as marital and individual psychotherapist at the Tavistock Clinic. He has lectured widely, both in the UK and abroad, and written extensively on creativity and art. His widely acclaimed book, *Vision and Separation: Between Mother and Baby* (Free Association Books, 1991) won the 1992 Mahler Literature Prize. His most recent book is *Mirroring and Attunement: Self-realisation in Psychoanalysis and Art* (Routledge, 2009). He is a Patron of the Squiggle Foundation and practises in Suffolk.

ON FREUD'S "THE UNCONSCIOUS"

Introduction

Salman Akhtar

Of the five papers—"Instincts and their vicissitudes" (1915c), "Repression" (1915d), "The unconscious" (1915e), "A metapsychological supplement to the theory of dreams" (1917d), and "Mourning and melancholia" (1917e)—that Freud had originally intended to publish in a book titled "Preliminaries to a Metapsychology", none stands out more in theoretical weight and clinical significance than "The unconscious". Laplanche and Pontalis's (1973) declaration that if Freud's discoveries "had to be summed up in a single word, that word without doubt would have to be 'unconscious'" (p. 474), though not directed specifically to this paper, might as well have been so aimed. Indeed, this forty-nine page essay covers a wide terrain of ontogenesis, clinical observation, linguistics, neurophysiology, spatial metaphor, phylogenetic schemata that manifest through primal phantasies, the nature of thinking, latent affect, and the mental life of instincts. Freud intended this paper (along with the other four mentioned above) to clarify and deepen the "psychoanalytic system" (1917d, p. 222). And it does.

A careful reading of it nearly 100 years after its publication, however, reveals more. Equipped with the psychoanalytic knowledge accrued over a century, one assesses the paper afresh and discovers the different "fates" its various contents have met. Some have become so well accepted as to be commonplace. On top of the list of such ideas is the very proposal of an unconscious part of the mind. This is so fundamental to the psychoanalytic viewpoint as to render a re-hash of Freud's "justification" of it entirely unnecessary. There are, however, other widely accepted contents of this paper of Freud's that might benefit from some explication. Then there are those ideas that have been elaborated upon and modified by subsequent analysts. Still other ideas have undergone a sort of "dis-use atrophy". And finally, there are passages that, to this day, remain unappreciated and are not fully mined for their heuristic potential. I will now select twelve major propositions from Freud's (1915e) "The unconscious", in order to illustrate how they have become (i) canonised, (ii) embellished, (iii) shelved, or (iv) overlooked.

Canonised

Proposition 1: There is more to the unconscious than the repressed

This proposal is stated by Freud in the following words: "The repressed does not cover everything that is unconscious. The unconscious has the wider compass: the repressed is a part of the unconscious" (p. 166). Freud repeated this in *The Ego and the Id*, saying that "all that is repressed is *Ucs*, but not all that is *Ucs* is repressed" (1923b, p. 18). These passages permit a view of the other contents of the unconscious: (i) the material accrued due to "primal repression" (Freud, 1895a, 1926d; Kinston & Cohen, 1986) and what Frank (1969) termed "the unrememberable and the unforgettable" residues of preverbal childhood, (ii) instinctual representatives, and (iii) the "primal phantasies" (Freud, 1915f) of parental sexual intercourse, seduction by an adult, and castration. The last mentioned are all related to the origin of things (i.e., of the subject, of sexuality, of distinctions between sexes, respectively) and, though shaped by environmental cues, are basically the phylogenetically transmitted memories of corresponding events in man's pre-history.

More was added to the list of what the unconscious contains later. Freud's (1923b) own "structural theory" suggested that not only id (the cauldron of "instinctual representatives" mentioned above) but also portions of ego and superego were unconscious. Ego's defence mechanisms, for instance, functioned entirely out of the subject's awareness. The same was largely true for its synthetic function (Hartmann, 1939). Many superego dictates also existed as contents of the unconscious. And, with further development of psychoanalytic theory, it became clear that ego-dystonic and/or unmentalised self- and object-representations made their home in the unconscious as well. Not surprisingly then, the fact that the contents of the unconscious exceed the repressed material has now become an integral aspect of the psychoanalytic canon.

Mention should also be made here of Bollas's (1992) suggestion that just as there are repression-derived unconscious elements, there are reception-based unconscious elements. The aim of such "reception" is to allow the unconscious development of ideas without the impingement of consciousness. With reception,

> the ego understands that unconscious work is necessary to develop a part of the personality, to elaborate a phantasy, to allow for the evolution of a nascent emotional experience, and ideas or feelings and words are sent to the system unconscious, not to be banished but to be given a mental space for development which is not possible in consciousness. Like the repressed ideas, these ideas, words, images, experiences, affects, etc., constellate into mental areas and then began to scan the world of experience for phenomena related to such inner work. Indeed, they may possibly seek precise experiences in order to nourish such unconscious constellations. The contents of the received are then the nuclei of genera which, like the repressed, will return to consciousness, but in the case of genera as acts of self-enrichment rather than paroled particles of the incarcerated. (p. 74)

This touches upon the issue of unconscious problem solving, which I address later in this discourse. At this point, I wish to move on to the second proposition in Freud's "The unconscious" that has become fully and widely accepted in psychoanalysis.

Proposition 2: the system Ucs operates in ways that are different from the system Cs

Having divided the mind into three topographical sectors, which are the systems *Cs*, *Pcs*, and *Ucs*, Freud noted that the first two of these operate on a logical basis. Events are temporally ordered, contradictions exist, and secondary process thinking predominates. In contrast, the operating principles of the unconscious were "*exemption from mutual contradiction*, *primary process* (mobility of cathexis), *timelessness*, and *replacement of external by psychical reality*" (1915e, p. 187, italics in the original). These ideas have been universally accepted in psychoanalysis and the mechanisms of displacement, condensation, and symbolism have become integral to the psychoanalytic way of thinking. This has facilitated not only the understanding of the neurotic symptomatology and dreams, but also of prejudicial stereotypes, animistic iconography of certain religions, perspectival juxtapositions of modern art, and the audacious leaps of the creative mind. Indeed, the entire psychoanalytic understanding of what is superficially illogical and absurd rests upon the grasp of the fact that a strikingly different methodology is followed by a sector of the mind that remains hidden from the naked eye.

Proposition 3: simply informing the patient of his unconscious content does not effect change

Having distinguished the operating principles of the systems *Cs* and *Ucs*, Freud became aware that a simple transposition of ideas existing in the former to the latter would alter nothing. He explained this in some detail:

> If we communicate to a patient some idea which he has at one time repressed but which we have discovered in him, our telling him makes at first no change in his mental condition. Above all, it does not remove the repression nor undo its effects, as might perhaps be expected from the fact that the previously unconscious idea has now become conscious. On the contrary, all that we shall achieve at first will be a fresh rejection of the repressed idea. But now the patient has in actual fact the same idea in two forms in different places in his mental apparatus: first, he has the conscious memory of the auditory trace of the idea, conveyed in what we told him; and secondly, he also has – as we know for certain – the unconscious memory of his experience as it was in its earlier form. (1915e, p. 175)

Such understanding has also become commonplace, especially in the chamber of clinical discourse. The over-enthusiastic experimentations of "direct analysis" (Rosen, 1947, 1953) notwithstanding, all contemporary psychoanalysts have come to appreciate Freud's sage counsel regarding interpretative technique. Merely telling the patient what something (e.g., a dream, a parapraxis, a symptom, a transference yearning) means is hardly helpful when its essence is veiled by forceful operations of the defensive ego. All one can achieve under such circumstances is intellectualised compliance; the patient might parrot the interpretation back, but shows little change in dynamics and behaviour. Recognising this, Anna Freud (1936) originated the term "defence analysis" and set into motion the idea that defences should be analysed before addressing the drives they hide or oppose. Fenichel (1941) emphasised that "analysis starts always from the surface of the present" (p. 19), and Loewenstein (1951) laid down a detailed "hierarchy of interpretation". None of this was to be followed in a cartoonish manner, however. One also hinted at the instinctual derivatives being warded off while interpreting a defensive operation. Brenner (1976) and, more recently, Ross (2003) have elucidated this matter further. Feldman's (2007) insightful essay about addressing (or not addressing) sequestered parts of the self also deals with it, though from a perspective other than that of the modern ego psychology. Freud's warning that in making the unconscious conscious one must not disregard the patient's need to not know is heeded by psychoanalysts of all persuasions.

Embellished

Proposition 4: there might exist an unlimited number of mutually independent psychic states in the mind

Freud spoke of "different latent mental processes [that] enjoy a high degree of mutual independence, as though they have no connection with one another, and know nothing of one another" (1915e, p. 170). He added that "we must be prepared, if so, to assume the existence in us not only of a second consciousness, but of a third, fourth, perhaps of an unlimited number of states of consciousness, all unknown to us and to one another" (1915e, p. 170).

These assertions are appealing to intuition, but turn out to be confusing and contradictory upon careful consideration. In talking of "latent mental processes" that "know nothing of one another",

Freud implies a compartmentalisation of the unconscious. This goes against the absence of contradictions and the great mobility of cathexis he otherwise assigned to this system. How can various latent processes remain unaware of each other if there are no barriers *within* the unconscious? Further conundrum results when Freud talks of "states of consciousness" that are unknown to each other. To begin with, a "state of consciousness", by definition, is not a "latent mental process", and yet Freud seems to be using the two interchangeably. Moreover, what the psychic location is of a state of consciousness when it is "unknown to us" (1915e, p. 170) is left unanswered. Can a state of consciousness exist on an unconscious level and still be called a state of consciousness?

This issue of mutually independent psychic states within the mind became even more complicated with the introduction of the term "ego", which we know has two implications: "one in which the term distinguishes a person's self as a whole (including, perhaps, his body) from other people, and the other in which it denotes a particular part of the mind characterized by special attributes and functions" (editor's introduction, Freud, 1923b, p. 7). The "states of consciousness" mentioned in "The unconscious" most probably correspond to the first meaning of the term "ego". Hartmann's (1950) distinction of the "self" from the "ego" went along similar lines and Jacobson's (1964) refinement of it by calling it "self-representation" brought it back into the realm of psychic reality.

A consequence of such theoretical convolutions was that Freud's original proposal of many "latent mental processes" and "states of consciousness" existing autonomously in the mind was clinically accepted but investigatively carried in different directions. Prominent outcomes of such exposition include the proposals that (i) if the early care-takers of a child were too numerous and too contradictory in their personalities, then "different identifications seize hold of consciousness in turn" (Freud, 1923b, p. 30), which, in the setting of severe trauma, can lead to dissociative conditions (Brenner, 1994, 2001; Kluft, 1985, 1986); (ii) if early exposure to female genitals and to the primal scene was excessive, the intensified castration anxiety led to the mind's holding two contradictory attitudes: women do and do not have a penis (Freud, 1927e); (iii) if constitutionally excessive aggression is fuelled by severe early frustration, the hatred of reality becomes great and splits the mind into co-existing psychotic and non-psychotic parts (Bion, 1957); (iv) less severe forms of the aforementioned background result in "borderline personality organization" (Kernberg, 1975); (v) lack of mirroring of archaic grandiosity by the child's parents can lead to a "vertical split" in the psyche, whereby a narcissistic sector operates independently from an object-related one (Kohut, 1971); (vi) even a well-adjusted and well-functioning self is hardly monolithic; it is comprised of many subsets of self-representations, some of which are closer to actions and others to contemplation (Eisnitz, 1980); (viii) there might also exist "cultural conflicts" (Akhtar, 2011) which express ill-fitting mentalities within an immigrant's mind, and "state-dependent self-representations" (Ghorpade, 2009) which reflect the selective activation of self-states under highly specific environmental cues. Clearly, Freud's 1915e proposal of independent psychic states within the mind has been given much thought and texture with the passage of time.

Proposition 5: system Cs contains word and thing presentations while system Ucs contains only the latter

Freud's lifelong interest in language led to his tracing the genealogy of words in Appendix C of his paper, "The unconscious" (1915e). In it, he offered a meticulous description of how sounds and perceptions (both external and internal) give rise to denotative labels, which can progress to connotations and, still later, to more complex lexical structures such as similes and metaphors. Freud emphasised that such "higher" lexical forms populate only the system *Cs*. The currency of system *Ucs* continues to be concrete and sensual, or what Freud called "thing-presentations". He stated that

> We now seem to know all at once what the difference is between a conscious and an unconscious presentation. The two are not, as we supposed, different registrations of the same content in different psychical localities, not yet different functional states of cathexis in the same locality; but the conscious presentation compromises the presentation of the thing plus the presentation of the word belonging to it, while the unconscious presentation is the presentation of the thing alone. (1915e, p. 201)

Freud's distinction of the languages of the system *Cs* (containing both thing and word presentations) and system *Ucs* (containing only the former) was anticipated, though without such terminology, by Ferenczi (1911), who noted that uttering obscene words in one's mother tongue evokes greater moral retribution than saying the same things in a later acquired language, because the originally acquired obscene words (i.e., those of the mother tongue) stay close to the acts and things they describe; the word becomes the thing or the act. Ferenczi's antecedent insight notwithstanding, the fact is that Freud's ideas on thing and word presentations have had a rich yield over the course of time. Arieti's (1974) and Searles' (1965) painstaking observations on the paleologic and concretised language in schizophrenia and Amati-Mehler, Argentieri, and Canestri's (1993) magisterial treatise on polylingualism and polyglotism in psychoanalysis owe their origins to Freud's (1915e) keen observations. The same is true of my own contribution to the understanding of technical dilemmas when the analyst or analysand or both are bilingual (Akhtar, 1999, 2011). Pine's (1997) developmentally orientated reminder that the analyst must help to name affects and assist the patient in finding words for inner experiences when the latter fails to do so is in the same spirit. Transforming the patient's unthinkable mental thoughts into thinkable thoughts (Bion, 1962a), helping the patient "mentalise" (Fonagy & Target, 1997), and, paradoxically at times, first paying attention to "things" (since they carry more psychological weight) before they can be rendered into words (Bolognini, 2011) are other elaborations of Freud's original ideas in this regard.

Proposition 6: dynamic, topographic, and economic principles form the tripod of metapsychology

Freud declared that "when we have succeeded in describing a psychical process in its dynamic, topographic, and economic aspects, we should speak of it as a *metapsychological* presentation" (1915e, p. 181, italics in the original). Now, the fact is that Freud (1898, 1901b) had used the expression "metapsychology" long before writing "The unconscious", but that use was linked to "metaphysics" (e.g., speculations about life after death, out-of-body existence, nature's hints for humans to behave in this or that way) since he regarded such ideas to be "nothing but psychology projected into the external world" (1901b, p. 258). In "The unconscious" (1915e), however, the expression "metapsychology" appeared in a far more nuanced manner. Freud proposed that in order to evolve a deeper understanding of mental phenomena, one must go beyond what is conscious and view the underlying material from many different angles. This multi-faceted viewpoint constituted "metapsychology" and consisted of dynamic, topographic, and economic perspectives.

- *Dynamic perspective* sought to explain mental phenomena in terms of the interaction of forces. Such forces could be contradictory or collaborative, infantile or contemporary, and progressive or regressive. They can be instinctual in nature and have specific aims and objects (Freud, 1915c), or may represent the moral imperatives of the superego (Freud, 1923b). Interaction between such forms results in intrapsychic conflict. A variety of outcomes are then possible, including compromise formations, deflected and disguised gratifications, or stalemates, inhibitions, and psychic paralysis (Freud, 1926d).
- *Topographic perspective* led to viewing mental phenomena in terms of their being *Cs*, *Pcs*, or *Ucs*. This not only meant their psychic location, but also involved their operational characteristics. The conscious and organised subjective experience represented only one aspect, since a stream of unknown and "illogical" material invariably hid underneath it. There existed censorships between *Cs* and *Pcs*, and between *Pcs* and *Ucs*, and the material had to alter its form (i.e., from thing to word presentation) as it travelled across these barriers. *Cs* "derivatives" were, thus, traceable to forceful and direct *Ucs* claims and impulses. With the introduction of the "tripartite model" of the mind (Freud, 1923b), defensive operations of the ego and the moral injunctions of the superego also became traceable to the deeper layers of the *Ucs*. Talking of the latter, Freud declared that "the normal man is not only far more immoral than he believes but also far more moral than he knows" (1923b, p. 52).
- *Economic perspective* dealt with the energy of the forces behind mental phenomena. It assumed that psychic energy determined the nature of mental processes; easy mobility and low discharge threshold characterised "primary process", and stability and high discharge threshold characterised "secondary process". The

quantity of energy was also deemed critical; a certain amount of energic investment was essential for an organisation to be feasible. The concerns of such "economics" included intensity of drives, strength of countercathexis, degrees of excitement, tension discharge, and quantum of affect. The ultimate goal of these forces was not to eliminate energic tension altogether, but to maintain a certain level of tension that was characteristic for the individual. This view changed with Freud's (1920g) proposal of a "death instinct", which sought to reduce animate to inanimate, and return the organism to inertia. None the less, the energic play of forces and quantities remained central to the "economic principle".

Freud's metapsychology became a revered centrepiece of psychoanalytic theory. More "perspectives" were added later. Rapaport's (1960) seminal synthesis of the pertinent literature from 1915 to 1960, listed six metapsychological perspectives: (i) topographic, (ii) dynamic, (iii) economic, (iv) genetic, (v) structural, and (vi) adaptive. The first three replicated those of Freud. Others were fresh additions. The "genetic perspective" facilitated enquiry about the childhood origins of (or contributions to) a particular current experience or behaviour. The "structural perspective" dealt with abiding psychological configurations ("structures") involved in mental phenomena. While id, ego, and superego were readily recognised as "structures", memory traces, self-representations, object-representations, and even certain fixed relational scenarios could also be subsumed under this concept. The "adaptive perspective" stated that all psychological experience is of some use to the subject and is serving some beneficial purpose. Rapaport's scheme became widely accepted and is reflected in the glossaries of psychoanalysis (e.g., Akhtar, 2009a; Moore & Fine, 1990). Those who felt unease with the rigours of metapsychology found solace in Waelder's (1962) reminder that psychoanalytic observation existed on many levels of abstraction, with clinical material representing one and metapsychological deconstruction the other end of this spectrum. The two hardly contradicted each other.

The heuristic backbone of psychoanalysis, metapsychology continued to attract a steady flow of publications over the ten decades following its introduction by Freud (PEP Web reveals that of the 163 papers with the word "metapsychology" in their titles, 132 appeared between 1942 and 1999, and thirty-one since 2000). This, of course, does not eliminate the harsh criticism of metapsychology by some (Grunbaum, 1998; G. Klein, 1976; Rodrigué, 1969; Schafer, 1976) and an equally ardent defence of it by others (Lothane, 2001; Modell, 1981). Critics regard it as a historical vestige, an experience-distant pseudo-explanation, an untenable reification and concretisation of mental operations, and an unnecessary distraction from clinical immersion. They also consider Freudian metapsychology to be unduly biological and less humane than narrative-based and hermeneutically orientated psychoanalytic perspectives. Supporters find it to be a theoretically anchoring and conceptually enriching foundation that allows for psychoanalytic psychology to remain (and become) a ubiquitous and scientific enterprise. Modell (1981) reminds the profession that metapsychology serves three important functions:

> first, a selection of psychological phenomena could be termed universal in the sense that they are characteristic of the human species; secondly, a set of assumptions upon which a psychological system can be founded and made explicit; and, thirdly, metapsychology functions as a modeling device, an imaginary entity, and experimental thinking. (p. 400)

He concludes that "metapsychology needs to be modified but not abandoned" (p. 400).

In a careful assessment of the two sides of this debate over metapsychology, Frank (1995) came to the following wise conclusion:

> Whether Freud's metapsychology will continue in its present form constitutes no argument; either it will go on changing in response to an evolving science, or it will fall by the wayside in favor of a more appropriate epistemological organization. But any investigative and therapeutic endeavor such as psychoanalysis must inevitably give rise to theorization based on certain assumptions. One is only deluding oneself if one requires that the propositions involved be independent of meta-theoretical assumption. (pp. 519–520)

It is interesting in this context to note that while some contemporary theorists, for instance, the latter-day Kohut (1977, 1982), abandoned metapsychology altogether, others (e.g., Kernberg, 1975, 1976,

1992, 1995) and Green (1982, 1993, 2001) have consistently linked their phenomenological observations to a deeper metapsychological base.

Proposition 7: the unconscious can yield solutions to intellectual problems

In the beginning section of "The unconscious", Freud (1915e) included many observations that would justify the concept of the unconscious. Among these were parapraxes, dreams, puzzling symptoms of psychopathology, and "ideas that come into our head we do not know from where, and with *intellectual conclusions* arrived at we do not know how" (pp. 166–167, italics added). Thus, Freud set the groundwork for discovering a "problem-solving function" of the unconscious. Numerous recorded accounts of sudden insight into the solution of an intellectual riddle stand in support of Freud's implicit proposal. These range from the prototypical "Eureka!" scream of Archimedes (ca 210 BC) upon discovering the relationship between volume and density to Sir Alec Jeffrey's joyous realisation in 1984 of the scope of DNA fingerprinting for identifying individuals for forensic purposes. Books by Koestler (1964) and Rugg (1963) describe in detail the unpredictable moment that ensues when a creative individual has turned away from the problem at hand and is in a psychic state that can hardly be called fully alert.

What also became known was that many creative individuals were intuitively familiar with such workings of the unconscious and relied upon it quite faithfully. An especially beautiful description of such unconscious creativity comes from Ian McEwan's (2005) novel, *Amsterdam*, which delineates a gifted musician's struggle to find the right coda for a symphony he is working on.

> He had no preliminary sketch of an idea, not a scrap, not even a hunch, and he would not find it by sitting at the piano and frowning hard. It could only come in its own time. He knew from experience that the best he could do was relax, step back, while remaining alert and receptive. He would have to take a long walk in the country, or even a series of long walks. He needed mountains, big skies. The Lake District, perhaps. The best ideas caught him by surprise at the end of twenty miles when his mind was elsewhere. (p. 24)

Psychoanalysts after Freud regarded the idea of unconscious problem solving with ambivalence. The preoccupation with pathogenic fantasy and repressed impulses distracted them from viewing the unconscious in a positive light. Not a single publication with the words "unconscious problem solving" in its title appeared in the (just about) hundred years after Freud's initial proposal. None the less, the concept kept resurfacing in one form or the other in our literature. Alexander (1947) mentioned "dreams of the problem solving type" and Rangell (1971) spoke of "unconscious decision making". Evoking Piaget's (1970) term, "cognitive unconscious", Rangell stated the following:

> Just as secondary elaboration works over a latent dream into an integrated manifest product (Freud, 1900), so does thinking of an elaborate and accurate nature with the equivalent of secondary-process decision-making as a final outcome take place completely at unconscious levels. Indeed, problem-solving of a highly sophisticated nature, on an unconscious or preconscious level (Kris, 1952), is known to take place in acts of discovery and creativity, wherein dreams or reverie states impinge on consciousness. (pp. 438–439)

A few years later, Weiss and Sampson (1986) declared that the patient's "unconscious plan" in seeking treatment was to have the therapist disconfirm his pathogenic beliefs. Weiss (1988) later proposed an "unconscious control hypothesis", which stated that

> the patient may unconsciously use his higher mental functions and that he exerts a certain degree of control over his unconscious mental life. He uses this control to develop goals, to test the therapist (and, at time same time, his own pathogenic beliefs), and to regulate the coming forth of the repressed mental contents, bringing them forth when he unconsciously decides that he could safely experience them. (p. 94)

More recently, Casement (1991) has elucidated the concept of "unconscious hope", which propels the search for development-facilitating objects and experiences and undergirds the optimistic dimension of repetition compulsion. Finally, Heijn (2005) has demonstrated the unconscious processes involved in the phenomena of foresight, planning, and discovery.

Shelved

Proposition 8: mental processes are reflective of energic shifts in the mind

This line of thinking on Freud's part is exemplified by the following passage in "The unconscious":

> Anticathexis is the sole mechanism of primary repression; in the case of repression proper ('after-pressure'), there is 'an additional withdrawal' of the *Pcs* cathexis. It is very possible that it is precisely the cathexis that is withdrawn from the idea that is used for anticathexis. (1915e, p. 181)

Over time, however, such "hydraulic" conceptualisation lost its appeal. Expressions associated with economic perspective (e.g., hypercathexis, force, quantity, constancy principle, impetus of the instinct, bound and free energy, level of excitement, pressure, after-pressure, discharge, quantum of affect) began to appear less and less often in psychoanalytic discourse. The post-Freudian rise of "alternative" psychologies of psychoanalysis (e.g., object-relations theory, self psychology, interpersonal psychoanalysis, relational and intersubjective perspectives), with their emphasis upon the dynamics of the clinical "here-and-now", contributed to the demise of the economic perspective. The shift of psychoanalytic theorising from an empirical science model to a hermeneutic paradigm also facilitated this trend.

It is not that analysts no longer talk of "over-reaction", "too-muchness", and "deficit", etc., but the rigour of theorising *vis-à-vis* such concepts has waned. Bion's (1963, 1965) grid was perhaps the last candle in the darkness around the economic perspective of metapsychology. Otherwise, the profession has become silent on this topic. Yesterday's economic principle was a measuring tape of forces and energies; today's economic principle is a barometer of the patient's ego capacities and the analyst's countertransference burdens. The whole situation brings to mind the following wry quip by an analytic patient who had read much of my writings: "You used to be a scholar and now you are merely an intellectual!"

Proposition 9: affects cannot be unconscious

Freud emphasised that one can only speak of unconscious ideas and not of unconscious emotions, since the latter, by definition, constitute the felt experience of drive discharge. He said that "although no fault can be found with their linguistic usage, there are no unconscious affects as there are no unconscious ideas" (1915e, p. 178). This fitted the topographic model well. However, with the advent of structural theory (Freud, 1923b), the field became muddled. For instance, if "signal anxiety" (Freud, 1926d) was unconscious, how did one know that it was anxiety? What about unconscious guilt? How should one label the sadness and/or paranoid fear that hid behind "manic defense" (Klein, 1935)? Attempts to answer such questions resulted in a controversy. Some theorists (e.g., Blau, 1955; Fenichel, 1945; Moore & Fine, 1968) sided with Freud's earlier assertion that there was no such thing as unconscious affect. Others (Eissler, 1953; Joffe & Sandler, 1968; Pulver, 1971) took the opposite stance. This debate lost its impetus over time, especially since affect theory itself underwent revision, with primitive affects being regarded as primary communicative pathways for the relationship between self and its objects (Krause & Merten, 1999; Mahler, Pine, & Bergman, 1975; Spitz, 1965; Stern, 1985) and viewed even as the building blocks of drives themselves (Kernberg, 1975). Rangell's (1995) reminder that Freud himself was "inconsistent" (p. 382) with regard to affects—stating at one place (Freud, 1915e) that they cannot be unconscious and the exact opposite another place (Freud, 1937d)—also led to a diminution of interest in such dichotomisation. Clinicians continued to hold that interpretative resolution of defences (regardless of whether these centred around repression or splitting) often results in the patient's experiencing affects not otherwise felt. They stopped fretting over whether these affects existed as such in the unconscious, or whether the availability of new ideas, memories, and impulses resulted in their being felt for the first time. The suggestion by some investigators (Talvitie & Ihanus, 2002, 2003) that the latter is true of all unconscious "content" further lessened the preoccupation with the existence of unconscious affects. A metapsychological concern was thus transformed into a clinical one.

Proposition 10: inherited mental functions form the bedrock of the Ucs

This proposal has been relegated to remote corners of psychoanalytic theorising. Freud (1915e) had declared that "if inherited mental functions exist in the human beings – being analogous to instinct in animals – these constitute the nucleus of the *Ucs*" (p. 195). Freud's failed Lamarkian trajectory and psychoanalysts' sentimental antipathy towards Jung (whose 1916 concept of "collective unconscious" came suspiciously close to Freud's notion of "inherited mental functions") caused inattention to this realm. Freud (1916–1917) did state that "primal phantasies" were "simply filling in the gaps in individual truth with pre-historic truth" (p. 371) and Laplanche and Pontalis (1973) iterated that "structures exist in the phantasy dimension (*la fantasmatique*) which are irreducible to the contingencies of the individual's lived experience" (p. 333). In practice, however, only the Kleinians continued to assume an inherent knowledge of gender differences and parental sexual intercourse. The idea of psychic inheritance might have been reincarnated as "transgenerational transmission" of trauma (elucidated extensively in the Holocaust studies) and "chosen traumas" (Volkan, 1987) of large groups, but the latter are not quite in the spirit of Freud's "inherited mental functions" (1915e, p. 195), which referred to the instinctual substrate of the mind.

Overlooked

Proposition 11: the systems Cs and Ucs can exchange their content and characteristics

Freud stated that "we must be prepared to find possible pathological conditions under which the two systems [*Cs* and *Ucs*] alter, or even exchange, both their content and their characteristics" (1915e, p. 189). To be sure, the flooding of conscious awareness, in psychotic states, with primitive fantasies and concretised language (see, especially, Arieti, 1974) does attest to the veracity of Freud's suggestion that the system *Cs* can acquire the characteristics of system *Ucs*, but what about the flow of traffic in the opposite direction? This remains largely unexplored. In other words, what might be the circumstances when the system *Ucs* acquires the characteristics of system *Cs*? Could Arlow's (1969) proposal of a highly organised and behaviourally relevant "unconscious fantasy" illustrate such transposition? And, does the exchange of characteristics between the two systems have to be pathological? What about the birth of metaphor and the writing of poetry? Do we not see the operational characteristics of the system *Ucs* deftly blended with those of the system *Cs* here? Conversely, in unconscious problem solving (see above), can we deny that the system *Ucs* is working in a logical manner akin to that of the system *Ucs*? There are other questions, as well, to raise here. For instance, does the exchange of formal characteristics between the system *Cs* and *Ucs* always occur involuntarily? Or, can one actively cause such an exchange? And, when the exchange of characteristics happens, is it *in toto* or can it be partial? If so, what determines the choice of the formal operations that are relocated? Clearly, more thought is needed here.

Proposition 12: Under certain psychic circumstances, perfect functioning is possible

There is another intriguing passage in "The unconscious" that, I believe, has remained unappreciated. Before I go into its diverse and profound implications, allow me to quote this passage in its entirety.

> Co-operation between a preconscious and an unconscious impulse, even when the latter is intensely repressed, may come about if there is a situation in which the unconscious impulse can act in the same sense as one of the dominant trends. The repression is removed in this instance, and the repressed activity is admitted as a reinforcement of the one intended by the ego. The unconscious becomes ego-syntonic in respect of this single conjunction without any change taking place in its repression apart from this. In this co-operation, the influence of the *Ucs* is unmistakable: the reinforced tendencies reveal themselves as being different nevertheless different from the normal; they make specially perfect functioning possible, and they manifest a resistance in the face of opposition . . . (Freud, 1915e, pp. 194–195).

What Freud is proposing here is that when the conscious aims coincide with unconscious aims, repression is lifted and impulses from these two sources combine and gain strength. Up to this point, there is little novelty of thought. Three qualifiers offered by Freud, however, give this passage its uniqueness: (i) the reinforced tendencies are "different from the normal", (ii) they make "specially perfect functioning" possible, and (iii) they manifest "resistance in the face of opposition". The first two of these can be condensed into each other;

in other words, such reinforced tendencies are different from the normal because they make specially perfect functioning possible. But is it not amazing to witness Freud mention the possibility of "perfect functioning" after having declared that the best one can hope for in life is a transformation of "hysterical misery into common unhappiness" (1895a, p. 305)? A charitable compromise is to suggest that moments of "perfect functioning" might exist in the overall setting of "common unhappiness", sort of like days of good weather in an otherwise harsh season. But what is this "perfect functioning" in the first place? Could it be akin to Winnicott's (1960) "true self", the essence of which lies in seamless psychosomatic confluence and unperturbed "going-on-being"? Does Freud's assertion approximate the Buddhist aphorism of "one thought-one action" here?

The addition of "resistance in the face of opposition" (offered by such "specially perfect functioning") opens up the topic of courage which until recently had not been adequately addressed in psychoanalytic literature. And even those authors who have written on courage (Coles, 1965; Glover, 1941; Kohut, 1985; Levine, 2006; O'Neil, 2009) do not link their postulates with this particular statement of Freud's. Sheepishly, I admit that I, too, have overlooked it in my recent essay on the phenomena of courage, counterphobia, and cowardice (Akhtar, 2013). That being said, I assert that both parts of Freud's statement ("specially perfect functioning" and "resistance in the face of opposition") leave much more to be discovered.

Concluding remarks

In this breathless sprint through the pages of Freud's 1915e paper, "The unconscious", I have attempted to demonstrate that some of its contents have been canonised, others embellished or shelved, and still others are only now being truly appreciated. My coverage has been wide-ranging and yet it is not exhaustive. I have not addressed Freud's (1915e) notions of (i) "first and second censorships" (pp. 190–195), (ii) "organ speech" (pp. 197–201), and (iii) "psycho-physical parallelism" (pp. 206–208). These topics have been elaborated upon, respectively, in a remarkable essay by Sandler and Sandler (1983), in contemporary French studies of psychosomatics (e.g., Aisenstein, 1993, 2008, 2010a; Marty, 1980; Marty, de M'Uzan, &

David, 1963; McDougall, 1974), and in the emergent sub-speciality of neuropsychoanalysis (e.g., Bernstein, 2011; Schore, 2002; Solms, 2003; Solms & Turnbull, 2000). I have not discussed these themes due to a lack of deeper knowledge of literature pertaining to them.

The book in your hands not only fills this lacuna, it goes much further, beyond what I have been able to elucidate. The book includes sophisticated essays on the biological and neurophysiological correlates of Freud's system *Ucs* (Brakel, Solms) and on the dynamic underbelly of psychosomatic conditions (Aisenstein). It also contains evocative and meaningful pieces on metapsychology, ontogenesis, and clinical technique (Wegner, Wright), Hinduism and the Freudian unconscious (Vallabhaneni), the seeds of more recent analytic paradigms in this particular paper of Freud (Reith), and unconscious influences upon self-perception, especially when the self is cleaved into dissociated fragments (Brenner). The last chapter of the book is a charming and witty piece on unconscious problem solving (Bolognini). A thoughtful epilogue by my co-editor and good friend, Mary Kay O'Neil, anchors us back to Freud while keeping an eye on contemporary developments and future possibilities. Eloquently and soberly, she weaves the contents of this book into a rich tapestry of psychoanalytic thought and praxis. To say anything further about our book runs the risk of immodesty, even though what is said might actually be true.

PART I

"The unconscious" (1915e)

Sigmund Freud

EDITOR'S NOTE

DAS UNBEWUSSTE

(*a*) German Editions:

1915 *Int. Z. Psychoanal.*, **3** (4), 189–203 and (5), 257–69.
1918 *S.K.S.N.*, **4**, 294–338. (1922, 2nd ed.)
1924 *G.S.*, **5**, 480–519.
1924 *Technik und Metapsychol.*, 202–41.
1931 *Theoretische Schriften*, 98–140.
1946 *G.W.*, **10**, 264–303.

(*b*) English Translation:

'The Unconscious'

1925 *C.P.*, **4**, 98–136. (Tr. C. M. Baines.)

The present translation, though based on that of 1925, has been very largely rewritten.

This paper seems to have taken less than three weeks to write—from April 4 to April 23, 1915. It was published in the *Internationale Zeitschrift* later in the same year in two instalments, the first containing Sections I–IV, and the second Sections V–VII. In the editions before 1924 the paper was not divided into sections, but what are now the section-headings were printed as side-headings in the margin. The only exception to this is that the words 'The Topographical Point of View', which are now part of the heading to Section II, were originally in the margin at the beginning of the second paragraph of the section at the words 'Proceeding now . . .' (p. 172). A few minor changes were also made in the text in the 1924 edition.

If the series of 'Papers on Metapsychology' may perhaps be regarded as the most important of all Freud's theoretical writings, there can be no doubt that the present essay on 'The Unconscious' is the culmination of that series.

The concept of there being unconscious mental processes is of course one that is fundamental to psycho-analytic theory. Freud was never tired of insisting upon the arguments in support of it and combating the objections to it. Indeed, the very last unfinished scrap of his theoretical writing, the fragment written by him in 1938 to which he gave the English title 'Some Elementary Lessons in Psycho-Analysis' (1940*b*), is a fresh vindication of that concept.

It should be made clear at once, however, that Freud's interest in the assumption was never a philosophical one—though, no doubt, philosophical problems inevitably lay just round the corner. His interest was a *practical* one. He found that without making that assumption he was unable to explain or even to describe a large variety of phenomena which he came across. By making it, on the other hand, he found the way open to an immensely fertile region of fresh knowledge.

In his early days and in his nearest environment there can have been no great resistance to the idea. His immediate teachers—Meynert, for instance[1]—in so far as they were interested in psychology, were governed chiefly by the views of J. F. Herbart (1776–1841), and it seems that a text-book embodying the Herbartian principles was in use at Freud's secondary school (Jones, 1953, 409 f.). A recognition of the existence of unconscious mental processes played an essential part in Herbart's system. In spite of this, however, Freud did not immediately adopt the hypothesis in the earliest stages of his psychopathological researches. He seems from the first, it is true, to have felt the force of the argument on which stress is laid in the opening pages of the present paper—the argument, that is, that to restrict mental events to those that are conscious and to intersperse them with purely physical, neural events 'disrupts psychical continuities' and introduces unintelligible gaps into the chain of observed phenomena. But there were two ways in which this difficulty could be met. We might disregard the physical events and adopt the hypothesis that the gaps are filled with unconscious mental ones; but, on the other hand, we might disregard the conscious mental events and construct a purely physical chain, without any breaks in it, which would cover all the facts of observation. To Freud, whose early scientific career had been entirely concerned with physiology,

[1] The possible influence on Freud in this respect of the physiologist Hering is discussed below in Appendix A (p. 205).

this second possibility was at first irresistibly attractive. The attraction was no doubt strengthened by the views of Hughlings-Jackson, of whose work he showed his admiration in his monograph on aphasia (1891*b*), a relevant passage from which will be found below in Appendix B (p. 206). The neurological method of describing psychopathological phenomena was accordingly the one which Freud began by adopting, and all his writings of the Breuer period are professedly based on that method. He became intellectually fascinated by the possibility of constructing a 'psychology' out of purely neurological ingredients, and devoted many months in the year 1895 to accomplishing the feat. Thus on April 27 of that year (Freud, 1950*a*, Letter 23) he wrote to Fliess: 'I am so deep in the "Psychology for Neurologists" that it quite consumes me, till I have to break off really overworked. I have never been so intensely preoccupied by anything. And will anything come of it? I hope so, but the going is hard and slow.' Something *did* come of it many months later—the torso which we know as the 'Project for a Scientific Psychology', despatched to Fliess in September and October, 1895. This astonishing production purports to describe and explain the whole range of human behaviour, normal and pathological, by means of a complicated manipulation of two material entities—the neurone and 'quantity in a condition of flow', an unspecified physical or chemical energy. The need for postulating any unconscious mental processes was in this way entirely avoided: the chain of physical events was unbroken and complete.

There were no doubt many reasons why the 'Project' was never finished and why the whole line of thought behind it was before long abandoned. But the principal reason was that Freud the neurologist was being overtaken and displaced by Freud the psychologist: it became more and more obvious that even the elaborate machinery of the neuronic systems was far too cumbersome and coarse to deal with the subtleties which were being brought to light by 'psychological analysis' and which could only be accounted for in the language of mental processes. A displacement of Freud's interest had in fact been very gradually taking place. Already at the time of the publication of the *Aphasia* his treatment of the case of Frau Emmy von N. lay two or three years behind him, and her case history was written more than a year before the 'Project'. It is in a footnote to that case history (*Standard Ed.*, **2**, 76) that his first published use of the term 'the unconscious' is to be found; and though the *ostensible* theory underlying his share in the *Studies on Hysteria* (1895*d*) might be a neurological one, psychology, and with it the necessity for unconscious mental processes, was steadily creeping in. Indeed, the whole basis of the repression theory of hysteria, and of the cathartic method of treatment, cried out for a psychological explanation, and it was only by the most contorted efforts that they had been accounted for neurologically in Part II of the 'Project'.[1] A few years later, in *The Interpretation of Dreams* (1900*a*), a strange transformation had occurred: not only had the neurological account of psychology completely disappeared, but much of what Freud had written in the 'Project' in terms of the nervous system now turned out to be valid and far more intelligible when translated into mental terms. The unconscious was established once and for all.

But, it must be repeated, what Freud established was no mere metaphysical entity. What he did in Chapter VII of *The Interpretation of Dreams* was, as it were, to clothe the metaphysical entity in flesh and blood. He showed for the first time what the unconscious was like, how it worked, how it differed from other parts of the mind, and what were its reciprocal relations with them. It was to these discoveries that he returned, amplifying and deepening them, in the paper which follows.

At an earlier stage, however, it had become evident that the term 'unconscious' was an ambiguous one. Three years previously, in the paper which he wrote in English for the Society for Psychical Research (1912*g*), and which is in many ways a preliminary to the present paper, he had carefully investigated these ambiguities, and had differentiated between the 'descriptive', 'dynamic' and 'systematic' uses of the word. He repeats the distinctions in Section II of this paper (p. 172 ff.), though in a slightly different form; and he came back to them again in Chapter I of *The Ego and the Id* (1923*b*) and, at even greater length, in Lecture XXXI of the *New Introductory Lectures* (1933*a*). The untidy way in which the contrast between 'conscious' and 'unconscious' fits the differences between the various systems of the mind is already stated clearly below (p. 192); but the whole

[1] Oddly enough it was Breuer, in his theoretical contribution to the *Studies*, who was the first to make a reasoned defence of unconscious ideas (*Standard Ed.*, **2**, 222 f.).

position was only brought into perspective when in *The Ego and the Id* Freud introduced a new structural picture of the mind. In spite, however, of the unsatisfactory operation of the criterion 'conscious or unconscious?', Freud always insisted (as he does in two places here, pp. 172 and 192, and again both in *The Ego and the Id* and in the *New Introductory Lectures*) that that criterion 'is in the last resort our one beacon-light in the darkness of depth psychology'.[1]

[1] The closing words of Chapter I of *The Ego and the Id*.—For English readers, it must be observed, there is a further ambiguity in the word 'unconscious' which is scarcely present in the German. The German words '*bewusst*' and '*unbewusst*' have the grammatical form of passive participles, and their usual sense is something like 'consciously known' and 'not consciously known'. The English 'conscious', though it *can* be used in the same way, is also used, and perhaps more commonly, in an *active* sense: 'he was conscious of the sound' and 'he lay there unconscious'. The German terms do not often have this active meaning, and it is important to bear in mind that 'conscious' is in general to be understood in a passive sense in what follows. The German word '*Bewusstsein*', on the other hand (which is here translated 'consciousness'), *does* have an active sense. Thus, for instance, on page 173 Freud speaks of a psychical act becoming 'an object of consciousness'; again, in the last paragraph of the first section of the paper (page 171) he speaks of 'the perception [of mental processes] by means of consciousness'; and in general, when he uses such phrases as 'our consciousness' he is referring to our consciousness *of* something. When he wishes to speak of a mental state's consciousness in the *passive* sense, he uses the word '*Bewusstheit*', which is translated here 'the attribute of being conscious', 'the fact of being conscious' or simply 'being conscious'—where the English 'conscious' is, as almost always in these papers, to be taken in the passive sense.

THE UNCONSCIOUS

We have learnt from psycho-analysis that the essence of the process of repression lies, not in putting an end to, in annihilating, the idea which represents an instinct, but in preventing it from becoming conscious. When this happens we say of the idea that it is in a state of being 'unconscious',[1] and we can produce good evidence to show that even when it is unconscious it can produce effects, even including some which finally reach consciousness. Everything that is repressed must remain unconscious; but let us state at the very outset that the repressed does not cover everything that is unconscious. The unconscious has the wider compass: the repressed is a part of the unconscious.

How are we to arrive at a knowledge of the unconscious? It is of course only as something conscious that we know it, after it has undergone transformation or translation into something conscious. Psycho-analytic work shows us every day that translation of this kind is possible. In order that this should come about, the person under analysis must overcome certain resistances—the same resistances as those which, earlier, made the material concerned into something repressed by rejecting it from the conscious.

I. Justification for the Concept of the Unconscious

Our right to assume the existence of something mental that is unconscious and to employ that assumption for the purposes of scientific work is disputed in many quarters. To this we can reply that our assumption of the unconscious is *necessary* and *legitimate*, and that we possess numerous proofs of its existence.

It is *necessary* because the data of consciousness have a very large number of gaps in them; both in healthy and in sick people psychical acts often occur which can be explained only by presupposing other acts, of which, nevertheless, consciousness affords no evidence. These not only include parapraxes and dreams in healthy people, and everything described as a psychical symptom or an obsession in the sick; our most personal daily experience acquaints us with ideas that come into our head

[1] [See Editor's Note, p. 165 footnote.]

we do not know from where, and with intellectual conclusions arrived at we do not know how. All these conscious acts remain disconnected and unintelligible if we insist upon claiming that every mental act that occurs in us must also necessarily be experienced by us through consciousness; on the other hand, they fall into a demonstrable connection if we interpolate between them the unconscious acts which we have inferred. A gain in meaning is a perfectly justifiable ground for going beyond the limits of direct experience. When, in addition, it turns out that the assumption of there being an unconscious enables us to construct a successful procedure by which we can exert an effective influence upon the course of conscious processes, this success will have given us an incontrovertible proof of the existence of what we have assumed. This being so, we must adopt the position that to require that whatever goes on in the mind must also be known to consciousness is to make an untenable claim.

We can go further and argue, in support of there being an unconscious psychical state, that at any given moment consciousness includes only a small content, so that the greater part of what we call conscious knowledge must in any case be for very considerable periods of time in a state of latency, that is to say, of being psychically unconscious. When all our latent memories are taken into consideration it becomes totally incomprehensible how the existence of the unconscious can be denied. But here we encounter the objection that these latent recollections can no longer be described as psychical, but that they correspond to residues of somatic processes from which what is psychical can once more arise. The obvious answer to this is that a latent memory is, on the contrary, an unquestionable residuum of a *psychical* process. But it is more important to realize clearly that this objection is based on the equation—not, it is true, explicitly stated but taken as axiomatic—of what is conscious with what is mental. This equation is either a *petitio principii* which begs the question whether everything that is psychical is also necessarily conscious; or else it is a matter of convention, of nomenclature. In this latter case it is, of course, like any other convention, not open to refutation. The question remains, however, whether the convention is so expedient that we are bound to adopt it. To this we may reply that the conventional equation of the psychical with the conscious is totally inexpedient. It disrupts psychical continuities, plunges us into the insoluble difficulties of psycho-physical parallelism,[1] is open to the reproach that for no obvious reason it over-estimates the part played by consciousness, and that it forces us prematurely to abandon the field of psychological research without being able to offer us any compensation from other fields.

It is clear in any case that this question—whether the latent states of mental life, whose existence is undeniable, are to be conceived of as conscious mental states or as physical ones—threatens to resolve itself into a verbal dispute. We shall therefore be better advised to focus our attention on what we know with certainty of the nature of these debatable states. As far as their physical characteristics are concerned, they are totally inaccessible to us: no physiological concept or chemical process can give us any notion of their nature. On the other hand, we know for certain that they have abundant points of contact with conscious mental processes; with the help of a certain amount of work they can be transformed into, or replaced by, conscious mental processes, and all the categories which we employ to describe conscious mental acts, such as ideas, purposes, resolutions and so on, can be applied to them. Indeed, we are obliged to say of some of these latent states that the only respect in which they differ from conscious ones is precisely in the absence of consciousness. Thus we shall not hesitate to treat them as objects of psychological research, and to deal with them in the most intimate connection with conscious mental acts.

The stubborn denial of a psychical character to latent mental acts is accounted for by the circumstance that most of the phenomena concerned have not been the subject of study outside psycho-analysis. Anyone who is ignorant of pathological facts, who regards the parapraxes of normal people as accidental, and who is content with the old saw that dreams are froth ['*Träume sind Schäume*'][2] has only to ignore a few more problems of the psychology of consciousness in order to spare himself any need to assume an unconscious mental activity. Incidentally, even before the time of psycho-analysis, hypnotic experiments, and especially post-hypnotic suggestion, had tangibly demon-

[1] [Freud seems himself at one time to have been inclined to accept this theory, as is suggested by a passage in his book on aphasia (1891*b*, 56 ff.). This will be found translated below in Appendix B (p. 206).]

[2] [Cf. *The Interpretation of Dreams* (1900*a*), *Standard Ed.*, **4**, 133.]

strated the existence and mode of operation of the mental unconscious.[1]

The assumption of an unconscious is, moreover, a perfectly *legitimate* one, inasmuch as in postulating it we are not departing a single step from our customary and generally accepted mode of thinking. Consciousness makes each of us aware only of his own states of mind; that other people, too, possess a consciousness is an inference which we draw by analogy from their observable utterances and actions, in order to make this behaviour of theirs intelligible to us. (It would no doubt be psychologically more correct to put it in this way: that without any special reflection we attribute to everyone else our own constitution and therefore our consciousness as well, and that this identification is a *sine qua non* of our understanding.) This inference (or this identification) was formerly extended by the ego to other human beings, to animals, plants, inanimate objects and to the world at large, and proved serviceable so long as their similarity to the individual ego was overwhelmingly great; but it became more untrustworthy in proportion as the difference between the ego and these 'others' widened. To-day, our critical judgement is already in doubt on the question of consciousness in animals; we refuse to admit it in plants and we regard the assumption of its existence in inanimate matter as mysticism. But even where the original inclination to identification has withstood criticism—that is, when the 'others' are our fellow-men—the assumption of a consciousness in them rests upon an inference and cannot share the immediate certainty which we have of our own consciousness.

Psycho-analysis demands nothing more than that we should apply this process of inference to ourselves also—a proceeding to which, it is true, we are not constitutionally inclined. If we do this, we must say: all the acts and manifestations which I notice in myself and do not know how to link up with the rest of my mental life must be judged as if they belonged to someone else: they are to be explained by a mental life ascribed to this other person. Furthermore, experience shows that we understand very well how to interpret in other people (that is, how to fit into their chain of mental events) the same acts which we

[1] [In his very last discussion of the subject, in the unfinished fragment 'Some Elementary Lessons in Psycho-Analysis' (1940*b*), Freud entered at some length into the evidence afforded by post-hypnotic suggestion.]

S.F. XIV—M

refuse to acknowledge as being mental in ourselves. Here some special hindrance evidently deflects our investigations from our own self and prevents our obtaining a true knowledge of it.

This process of inference, when applied to oneself in spite of internal opposition, does not, however, lead to the disclosure of an unconscious; it leads logically to the assumption of another, second consciousness which is united in one's self with the consciousness one knows. But at this point, certain criticisms may fairly be made. In the first place, a consciousness of which its own possessor knows nothing is something very different from a consciousness belonging to another person, and it is questionable whether such a consciousness, lacking, as it does, its most important characteristic, deserves any discussion at all. Those who have resisted the assumption of an unconscious *psychical* are not likely to be ready to exchange it for an unconscious *consciousness*. In the second place, analysis shows that the different latent mental processes inferred by us enjoy a high degree of mutual independence, as though they had no connection with one another, and knew nothing of one another. We must be prepared, if so, to assume the existence in us not only of a second consciousness, but of a third, fourth, perhaps of an unlimited number of states of consciousness, all unknown to us and to one another. In the third place—and this is the most weighty argument of all—we have to take into account the fact that analytic investigation reveals some of these latent processes as having characteristics and peculiarities which seem alien to us, or even incredible, and which run directly counter to the attributes of consciousness with which we are familiar. Thus we have grounds for modifying our inference about ourselves and saying that what is proved is not the existence of a second consciousness in us, but the existence of psychical acts which lack consciousness. We shall also be right in rejecting the term 'subconsciousness' as incorrect and misleading.[1] The well-known cases of '*double conscience*' [2] (splitting of consciousness) prove

[1] [In some of his very early writings, Freud himself used the term 'subconscious', e.g. in his French paper on hysterical paralyses (1893*c*) and in *Studies on Hysteria* (1895), *Standard Ed.*, **2**, 69 *n.* But he disrecommends the term as early as in *The Interpretation of Dreams* (1900*a*), *Standard Ed.*, **5**, 615. He alludes to the point again in Lecture XIX of the *Introductory Lectures* (1916–17), and argues it a little more fully near the end of Chapter II of *The Question of Lay Analysis* (1926*e*).]

[2] [The French term for 'dual consciousness'.]

nothing against our view. We may most aptly describe them as cases of a splitting of the mental activities into two groups, and say that the same consciousness turns to one or the other of these groups alternately.

In psycho-analysis there is no choice for us but to assert that mental processes are in themselves unconscious, and to liken the perception of them by means of consciousness to the perception of the external world by means of the sense-organs.[1] We can even hope to gain fresh knowledge from the comparison. The psycho-analytic assumption of unconscious mental activity appears to us, on the one hand, as a further expansion of the primitive animism which caused us to see copies of our own consciousness all around us, and, on the other hand, as an extension of the corrections undertaken by Kant of our views on external perception. Just as Kant warned us not to overlook the fact that our perceptions are subjectively conditioned and must not be regarded as identical with what is perceived though unknowable, so psycho-analysis warns us not to equate perceptions by means of consciousness with the unconscious mental processes which are their object. Like the physical, the psychical is not necessarily in reality what it appears to us to be. We shall be glad to learn, however, that the correction of internal perception will turn out not to offer such great difficulties as the correction of external perception—that internal objects are less unknowable than the external world.

[1] [This idea had already been dealt with at some length in Chapter VII (F) of *The Interpretation of Dreams* (1900*a*), *Standard Ed.*, **5**, 615–17.]

II. Various Meanings of 'the Unconscious'—The Topographical Point of View

Before going any further, let us state the important, though inconvenient, fact that the attribute of being unconscious is only one feature that is found in the psychical and is by no means sufficient fully to characterize it. There are psychical acts of very varying value which yet agree in possessing the characteristic of being unconscious. The unconscious comprises, on the one hand, acts which are merely latent, temporarily unconscious, but which differ in no other respect from conscious ones and, on the other hand, processes such as repressed ones, which if they were to become conscious would be bound to stand out in the crudest contrast to the rest of the conscious processes. It would put an end to all misunderstandings if, from now on, in describing the various kinds of psychical acts we were to disregard the question of whether they were conscious or unconscious, and were to classify and correlate them only according to their relation to instincts and aims, according to their composition and according to which of the hierarchy of psychical systems they belong to. This, however, is for various reasons impracticable, so that we cannot escape the ambiguity of using the words 'conscious' and 'unconscious' sometimes in a descriptive and sometimes in a systematic sense, in which latter they signify inclusion in particular systems and possession of certain characteristics. We might attempt to avoid confusion by giving the psychical systems which we have distinguished certain arbitrarily chosen names which have no reference to the attribute of being conscious. Only we should first have to specify what the grounds are on which we distinguish the systems, and in doing this we should not be able to evade the attribute of being conscious, seeing that it forms the point of departure for all our investigations.[1] Perhaps we may look for some assistance from the proposal to employ, at any rate in writing, the abbreviation *Cs.* for consciousness and *Ucs.* for what is unconscious, when we are using the two words in the systematic sense.[2]

Proceeding now to an account of the positive findings of

[1] [Freud recurs to this below on p. 192.]

[2] [Freud had already introduced these abbreviations in *The Interpretation of Dreams* (1900*a*), *Standard Ed.*, **5**, 540 ff.]

172

psycho-analysis, we may say that in general a psychical act goes through two phases as regards its state, between which is interposed a kind of testing (censorship). In the first phase the psychical act is unconscious and belongs to the system *Ucs.*; if, on testing, it is rejected by the censorship, it is not allowed to pass into the second phase; it is then said to be 'repressed' and must remain unconscious. If, however, it passes this testing, it enters the second phase and thenceforth belongs to the second system, which we will call the system *Cs.* But the fact that it belongs to that system does not yet unequivocally determine its relation to consciousness. It is not yet conscious, but it is certainly *capable of becoming conscious* (to use Breuer's expression)[1]—that is, it can now, given certain conditions, become an object of consciousness without any special resistance. In consideration of this capacity for becoming conscious we also call the system *Cs.* the 'preconscious'. If it should turn out that a certain censorship also plays a part in determining whether the preconscious becomes conscious, we shall discriminate more sharply between the systems *Pcs.* and *Cs.* [Cf. p. 191 f.]. For the present let it suffice us to bear in mind that the system *Pcs.* shares the characteristics of the system *Cs.* and that the rigorous censorship exercises its office at the point of transition from the *Ucs.* to the *Pcs.* (or *Cs.*).

By accepting the existence of these two (or three) psychical systems, psycho-analysis has departed a step further from the descriptive 'psychology of consciousness' and has raised new problems and acquired a new content. Up till now, it has differed from that psychology mainly by reason of its *dynamic* view of mental processes; now in addition it seems to take account of psychical *topography* as well, and to indicate in respect of any given mental act within what system or between what systems it takes place. On account of this attempt, too, it has been given the name of 'depth-psychology'.[2] We shall hear that it can be further enriched by taking yet another point of view into account. [Cf. p. 181.]

If we are to take the topography of mental acts seriously we must direct our interest to a doubt which arises at this point.

1 [See *Studies on Hysteria*, Breuer and Freud (1895), *Standard Ed.*, **2**, 225.]

2 [By Bleuler (1914). See the 'History of the Psycho-Analytic Movement' (1914*d*), above, p. 41.]

When a psychical act (let us confine ourselves here to one which is in the nature of an idea[1]) is transposed from the system *Ucs.* into the system *Cs.* (or *Pcs.*), are we to suppose that this transposition involves a fresh record—as it were, a second registration—of the idea in question, which may thus be situated as well in a fresh psychical locality, and alongside of which the original unconscious registration continues to exist?[2] Or are we rather to believe that the transposition consists in a change in the state of the idea, a change involving the same material and occurring in the same locality? This question may appear abstruse, but it must be raised if we wish to form a more definite conception of psychical topography, of the dimension of depth in the mind. It is a difficult one because it goes beyond pure psychology and touches on the relations of the mental apparatus to anatomy. We know that in the very roughest sense such relations exist. Research has given irrefutable proof that mental activity is bound up with the function of the brain as it is with no other organ. We are taken a step further—we do not know how much—by the discovery of the unequal importance of the different parts of the brain and their special relations to particular parts of the body and to particular mental activities. But every attempt to go on from there to discover a localization of mental processes, every endeavour to think of ideas as stored up in nerve-cells and of excitations as travelling along nerve-fibres, has miscarried completely.[3] The same fate would await any theory which attempted to recognize, let us say, the anatomical position of the system *Cs.*—conscious mental activity—as being in the cortex, and to localize the unconscious processes in the subcortical parts of the brain.[4] There is a hiatus here which at present cannot be filled, nor is it one of the tasks of psychology

[1] [The German word here is '*Vorstellung*', which covers the English terms 'idea', 'image' and 'presentation'.]

[2] [The conception of an idea being present in the mind in more than one 'registration' was first put forward by Freud in a letter to Fliess of December 6, 1896 (Freud, 1950*a*, Letter 52). It is used in connection with the theory of memory in Chapter VII (Section B) of *The Interpretation of Dreams* (1900*a*), *Standard Ed.*, **5**, 539; and it is alluded to again in Section F of the same chapter (ibid., 610) in an argument which foreshadows the present one.]

[3] [Freud had himself been much concerned with the question of the localization of cerebral functions in his work on aphasia (1891*b*).]

[4] [Freud had insisted on this as early as in his preface to his translation of Bernheim's *De la suggestion* (Freud, 1888–9).]

to fill it. Our psychical topography has *for the present* nothing to do with anatomy; it has reference not to anatomical localities, but to regions in the mental apparatus, wherever they may be situated in the body.

In this respect, then, our work is untrammelled and may proceed according to its own requirements. It will, however, be useful to remind ourselves that as things stand our hypotheses set out to be no more than graphic illustrations. The first of the two possibilities which we considered—namely, that the *Cs.* phase of an idea implies a fresh registration of it, which is situated in another place—is doubtless the cruder but also the more convenient. The second hypothesis—that of a merely *functional* change of state—is *a priori* more probable, but it is less plastic, less easy to manipulate. With the first, or topographical, hypothesis is bound up that of a topographical separation of the systems *Ucs.* and *Cs.* and also the possibility that an idea may exist simultaneously in two places in the mental apparatus—indeed, that if it is not inhibited by the censorship, it regularly advances from the one position to the other, possibly without losing its first location or registration.

This view may seem odd, but it can be supported by observations from psycho-analytic practice. If we communicate to a patient some idea which he has at one time repressed but which we have discovered in him, our telling him makes at first no change in his mental condition. Above all, it does not remove the repression nor undo its effects, as might perhaps be expected from the fact that the previously unconscious idea has now become conscious. On the contrary, all that we shall achieve at first will be a fresh rejection of the repressed idea. But now the patient has in actual fact the same idea in two forms in different places in his mental apparatus: first, he has the conscious memory of the auditory trace of the idea, conveyed in what we told him; and secondly, he also has—as we know for certain—the unconscious memory of his experience as it was in its earlier form.[1] Actually there is no lifting of the repression until the conscious idea, after the resistances have been overcome, has

[1] [The topographical picture of the distinction between conscious and unconscious ideas is presented in Freud's discussion of the case of 'Little Hans' (1909*b*), *Standard Ed.*, **10**, 120 f., and at greater length in the closing paragraphs of his technical paper 'On Beginning the Treatment' (1913*c*).]

entered into connection with the unconscious memory-trace. It is only through the making conscious of the latter itself that success is achieved. On superficial consideration this would seem to show that conscious and unconscious ideas are distinct registrations, topographically separated, of the same content. But a moment's reflection shows that the identity of the information given to the patient with his repressed memory is only apparent. To have heard something and to have experienced something are in their psychological nature two quite different things, even though the content of both is the same.

So for the moment we are not in a position to decide between the two possibilities that we have discussed. Perhaps later on we shall come upon factors which may turn the balance in favour of one or the other. Perhaps we shall make the discovery that our question was inadequately framed and that the difference between an unconscious and a conscious idea has to be defined in quite another way.[1]

[1] [This argument is taken up again on p. 201.]

III. Unconscious Emotions

We have limited the foregoing discussion to ideas; we may now raise a new question, the answer to which is bound to contribute to the elucidation of our theoretical views. We have said that there are conscious and unconscious ideas; but are there also unconscious instinctual impulses, emotions and feelings, or is it in this instance meaningless to form combinations of the kind?

I am in fact of the opinion that the antithesis of conscious and unconscious is not applicable to instincts. An instinct can never become an object of consciousness—only the idea that represents the instinct can. Even in the unconscious, moreover, an instinct cannot be represented otherwise than by an idea. If the instinct did not attach itself to an idea or manifest itself as an affective state, we could know nothing about it. When we nevertheless speak of an unconscious instinctual impulse or of a repressed instinctual impulse, the looseness of phraseology is a harmless one. We can only mean an instinctual impulse the ideational representative of which is unconscious, for nothing else comes into consideration.[1]

We should expect the answer to the question about unconscious feelings, emotions and affects to be just as easily given. It is surely of the essence of an emotion that we should be aware of it, i.e. that it should become known to consciousness. Thus the possibility of the attribute of unconsciousness would be completely excluded as far as emotions, feelings and affects are concerned. But in psycho-analytic practice we are accustomed to speak of unconscious love, hate, anger, etc., and find it impossible to avoid even the strange conjunction, 'unconscious consciousness of guilt',[2] or a paradoxical 'unconscious anxiety'. Is there more meaning in the use of these terms than there is in speaking of 'unconscious instincts'?

The two cases are in fact not on all fours. In the first place, it may happen that an affective or emotional impulse is perceived but misconstrued. Owing to the repression of its proper representative it has been forced to become connected with another

[1] [Cf. the Editor's Note to 'Instincts and their Vicissitudes', p. 111 ff. above.]

[2] [German '*Schuldbewusstsein*', a common equivalent for '*Schuldgefühl*', 'sense of guilt'.]

idea, and is now regarded by consciousness as the manifestation of that idea. If we restore the true connection, we call the original affective impulse an 'unconscious' one. Yet its affect was never unconscious; all that had happened was that its *idea* had undergone repression. In general, the use of the terms 'unconscious affect' and 'unconscious emotion' has reference to the vicissitudes undergone, in consequence of repression, by the quantitative factor in the instinctual impulse. We know that three such vicissitudes are possible:[1] either the affect remains, wholly or in part, as it is; or it is transformed into a qualitatively different quota of affect, above all into anxiety; or it is suppressed, i.e. it is prevented from developing at all. (These possibilities may perhaps be studied even more easily in the dream-work than in neuroses.[2]) We know, too, that to suppress the development of affect is the true aim of repression and that its work is incomplete if this aim is not achieved. In every instance where repression has succeeded in inhibiting the development of affects, we term those affects (which we restore when we undo the work of repression) 'unconscious'. Thus it cannot be denied that the use of the terms in question is consistent; but in comparison with unconscious ideas there is the important difference that unconscious ideas continue to exist after repression as actual structures in the system *Ucs.*, whereas all that corresponds in that system to unconscious affects is a potential beginning which is prevented from developing. Strictly speaking, then, and although no fault can be found with the linguistic usage, there are no unconscious affects as there are unconscious ideas. But there may very well be in the system *Ucs.* affective structures which, like others, become conscious. The whole difference arises from the fact that ideas are cathexes—basically of memory-traces—whilst affects and emotions correspond to processes of discharge, the final manifestations of which are perceived as feelings. In the present state of our knowledge of affects and emotions we cannot express this difference more clearly.[3]

It is of especial interest to us to have established the fact that repression can succeed in inhibiting an instinctual impulse from

[1] Cf. the preceding paper on 'Repression' [p. 153].

[2] [The main discussion of affects in *The Interpretation of Dreams* (1900*a*) will be found in Section H of Chapter VI, *Standard Ed.*, **5**, 460–87.]

[3] [This question is discussed again in Chapter II of *The Ego and the Id* (1923*b*).]

being turned into a manifestation of affect. This shows us that the system *Cs.* normally controls affectivity as well as access to motility; and it enhances the importance of repression, since it shows that repression results not only in withholding things from consciousness, but also in preventing the development of affect and the setting-off of muscular activity. Conversely, too, we may say that as long as the system *Cs.* controls affectivity and motility, the mental condition of the person in question is spoken of as normal. Nevertheless, there is an unmistakable difference in the relation of the controlling system to the two contiguous processes of discharge.[1] Whereas the control by the *Cs.* over voluntary motility is firmly rooted, regularly withstands the onslaught of neurosis and only breaks down in psychosis, control by the *Cs.* over the development of affects is less secure. Even within the limits of normal life we can recognize that a constant struggle for primacy over affectivity goes on between the two systems *Cs.* and *Ucs.*, that certain spheres of influence are marked off from one another and that intermixtures between the operative forces occur.

The importance of the system *Cs.* (*Pcs.*)[2] as regards access to the release of affect and to action enables us also to understand the part played by substitutive ideas in determining the form taken by illness. It is possible for the development of affect to proceed directly from the system *Ucs.*; in that case the affect always has the character of anxiety, for which all 'repressed' affects are exchanged. Often, however, the instinctual impulse has to wait until it has found a substitutive idea in the system *Cs.* The development of affect can then proceed from this conscious substitute, and the nature of that substitute determines the qualitative character of the affect. We have asserted [p. 152] that in repression a severance takes place between the affect and the idea to which it belongs, and that each then undergoes its separate vicissitudes. Descriptively, this is incontrovertible; in actuality, however, the affect does not as a rule arise till the break-through to a new representation in the system *Cs.* has been successfully achieved.

[1] Affectivity manifests itself essentially in motor (secretory and vasomotor) discharge resulting in an (internal) alteration of the subject's own body without reference to the external world; motility, in actions designed to effect changes in the external world.

[2] [In the 1915 edition only, '(*Pcs.*)' does not occur.]

IV. Topography and Dynamics of Repression

We have arrived at the conclusion that repression is essentially a process affecting ideas on the border between the systems *Ucs.* and *Pcs.* (*Cs.*), and we can now make a fresh attempt to describe the process in greater detail.

It must be a matter of a *withdrawal* of cathexis; but the question is, in which system does the withdrawal take place and to which system does the cathexis that is withdrawn belong? The repressed idea remains capable of action in the *Ucs.*, and it must therefore have retained its cathexis. What has been withdrawn must be something else. [Cf. p. 202, below.] Let us take the case of repression proper ('after-pressure') [p. 148], as it affects an idea which is preconscious or even actually conscious. Here repression can only consist in withdrawing from the idea the (pre)conscious cathexis which belongs to the system *Pcs.* The idea then either remains uncathected, or receives cathexis from the *Ucs.*, or retains the *Ucs.* cathexis which it already had. Thus there is a withdrawal of the preconscious cathexis, retention of the unconscious cathexis, or replacement of the preconscious cathexis by an unconscious one. We notice, moreover, that we have based these reflections (as it were, without meaning to) on the assumption that the transition from the system *Ucs.* to the system next to it is not effected through the making of a new registration but through a change in its state, an alteration in its cathexis. The functional hypothesis has here easily defeated the topographical one. [See above, pp. 174–5.]

But this process of withdrawal of libido[1] is not adequate to make another characteristic of repression comprehensible to us. It is not clear why the idea which has remained cathected or has received cathexis from the *Ucs.* should not, in virtue of its cathexis, renew the attempt to penetrate into the system *Pcs.* If it could do so, the withdrawal of libido from it would have to be repeated, and the same performance would go on endlessly; but the outcome would not be repression. So, too, when it comes to describing *primal* repression, the mechanism just discussed of withdrawal of preconscious cathexis would fail to meet the case;

[1] [For the use of 'libido' here see four paragraphs lower down.]

for here we are dealing with an unconscious idea which has as yet received *no* cathexis from the *Pcs.* and therefore cannot have that cathexis withdrawn from it.

What we require, therefore, is another process which maintains the repression in the first case [i.e. the case of after-pressure] and, in the second [i.e. that of primal repression], ensures its being established as well as continued. This other process can only be found in the assumption of an *anticathexis*, by means of which the system *Pcs.* protects itself from the pressure upon it of the unconscious idea. We shall see from clinical examples how such an anticathexis, operating in the system *Pcs.*, manifests itself. It is this which represents the permanent expenditure [of energy] of a primal repression, and which also guarantees the permanence of that repression. Anticathexis is the sole mechanism of primal repression; in the case of repression proper ('after-pressure') there is in addition withdrawal of the *Pcs.* cathexis. It is very possible that it is precisely the cathexis which is withdrawn from the idea that is used for anticathexis.

We see how we have gradually been led into adopting a third point of view in our account of psychical phenomena. Besides the dynamic and the topographical points of view [p. 173], we have adopted the *economic* one. This endeavours to follow out the vicissitudes of amounts of excitation and to arrive at least at some *relative* estimate of their magnitude.

It will not be unreasonable to give a special name to this whole way of regarding our subject-matter, for it is the consummation of psycho-analytic research. I propose that when we have succeeded in describing a psychical process in its dynamic, topographical and economic aspects, we should speak of it as a *metapsychological*[1] presentation. We must say at once that in the present state of our knowledge there are only a few points at which we shall succeed in this.

Let us make a tentative effort to give a metapsychological description of the process of repression in the three transference neuroses which are familiar to us. Here we may replace

[1] [Freud had first used this term some twenty years earlier in a letter to Fliess of February 13, 1896. (Freud, 1950*a*, Letter 41.) He had only used it once before in his *published* works: in the *Psychopathology of Everyday Life* (1901*b*), Chapter XII (C).]

'cathexis' by 'libido',[1] because, as we know, it is the vicissitudes of *sexual* impulses with which we shall be dealing.

In anxiety hysteria a first phase of the process is frequently overlooked, and may perhaps be in fact missed out; on careful observation, however, it can be clearly discerned. It consists in anxiety appearing without the subject knowing what he is afraid of. We must suppose that there was present in the *Ucs.* some love-impulse demanding to be transposed into the system *Pcs.*; but the cathexis directed to it from the latter system has drawn back from the impulse (as though in an attempt at flight) and the unconscious libidinal cathexis of the rejected idea has been discharged in the form of anxiety.

On the occasion of a repetition (if there should be one) of this process, a first step is taken in the direction of mastering the unwelcome development of anxiety.[2] The [*Pcs.*] cathexis that has taken flight attaches itself to a substitutive idea which, on the one hand, is connected by association with the rejected idea, and, on the other, has escaped repression by reason of its remoteness from that idea. This substitutive idea—a 'substitute by displacement' [p. 155]—permits the still uninhibitable development of anxiety to be rationalized. It now plays the part of an anticathexis for the system *Cs.* (*Pcs.*),[3] by securing it against an emergence in the *Cs.* of the repressed idea. On the other hand it is, or acts as if it were, the point of departure for the release of the anxiety-affect, which has now really become quite uninhibitable. Clinical observation shows, for instance, that a child suffering from an animal phobia experiences anxiety under two kinds of conditions: in the first place, when his repressed love-impulse becomes intensified, and, in the second, when he perceives the animal he is afraid of. The substitutive idea acts in the one instance as a point at which there is a passage across from the system *Ucs.* to the system *Cs.*, and, in the other instance, as a self-sufficing source for the release of anxiety. The extending dominance of the system *Cs.* usually manifests itself in the fact that the first of these two modes of excitation of the substitutive idea gives place more and more to the second. The child may perhaps end by behaving as though he had no predilection whatever towards his father but had

[1] [Freud had already done this four paragraphs earlier.]

[2] [This is the 'second phase' of the process.]

[3] [In the 1915 edition only '(*Pcs.*)' does not occur.]

become quite free from him, and as though his fear of the animal was a real fear—except that this fear of the animal, fed as such a fear is from an unconscious instinctual source, proves obdurate and exaggerated in the face of all influences brought to bear from the system *Cs.*, and thereby betrays its derivation from the system *Ucs.*—In the second phase of anxiety hysteria, therefore, the anticathexis from the system *Cs.* has led to substitute-formation.

Soon the same mechanism finds a fresh application. The process of repression, as we know, is not yet completed, and it finds a further aim in the task of inhibiting the development of the anxiety which arises from the substitute.[1] This is achieved by the whole of the associated environment of the substitutive idea being cathected with special intensity, so that it can display a high degree of sensibility to excitation. Excitation of any point in this outer structure must inevitably, on account of its connection with the substitutive idea, give rise to a slight development of anxiety; and this is now used as a signal to inhibit, by means of a fresh flight on the part of the [*Pcs.*] cathexis, the further progress of the development of anxiety.[2] The further away the sensitive and vigilant anticathexes are situated from the feared substitute, the more precisely can the mechanism function which is designed to isolate the substitutive idea and to protect it from fresh excitations. These precautions naturally only guard against excitations which approach the substitutive idea from outside, through perception; they never guard against instinctual excitation, which reaches the substitutive idea from the direction of its link with the repressed idea. Thus the precautions do not begin to operate till the substitute has satisfactorily taken over representation of the repressed, and they can never operate with complete reliability. With each increase of instinctual excitation the protecting rampart round the substitutive idea must be shifted a little further outwards. The whole construction, which is set up in an analogous way in the other neuroses, is termed a *phobia*. The flight from a conscious

[1] [The 'third phase'.]

[2] [The notion of a small release of unpleasure acting as a 'signal' to prevent a much larger release is already to be found in Freud's 1895 'Project' (1950*a*, Part II, Section 6) and in *The Interpretation of Dreams* (1900*a*), *Standard Ed.*, **5**, 602. The idea is, of course, developed much further in *Inhibitions, Symptoms and Anxiety* (1926*d*), e.g. in Chapter XI, Section A (*b*).]

cathexis of the substitutive idea is manifested in the avoidances, renunciations and prohibitions by which we recognize anxiety hysteria.

Surveying the whole process, we may say that the third phase repeats the work of the second on an ampler scale. The system *Cs.* now protects itself against the activation of the substitutive idea by an anticathexis of its environment, just as previously it had secured itself against the emergence of the repressed idea by a cathexis of the substitutive idea. In this way the formation of substitutes by displacement has been further continued. We must also add that the system *Cs.* had earlier only one small area at which the repressed instinctual impulse could break through, namely, the substitutive idea; but that ultimately this *enclave* of unconscious influence extends to the whole phobic outer structure. Further, we may lay stress on the interesting consideration that by means of the whole defensive mechanism thus set in action a projection outward of the instinctual danger has been achieved. The ego behaves as if the danger of a development of anxiety threatened it not from the direction of an instinctual impulse but from the direction of a perception, and it is thus enabled to react against this external danger with the attempts at flight represented by phobic avoidances. In this process repression is successful in one particular: the release of anxiety can to some extent be dammed up, but only at a heavy sacrifice of personal freedom. Attempts at flight from the demands of instinct are, however, in general useless, and, in spite of everything, the result of phobic flight remains unsatisfactory.

A great deal of what we have found in anxiety hysteria also holds good for the other two neuroses, so that we can confine our discussion to their points of difference and to the part played by anticathexis. In conversion hysteria the instinctual cathexis of the repressed idea is changed into the innervation of the symptom. How far and in what circumstances the unconscious idea is drained empty by this discharge into innervation, so that it can relinquish its pressure upon the system *Cs.*—these and similar questions had better be reserved for a special investigation of hysteria.[1] In conversion hysteria the part played by the

[1] [Probably a reference to the missing metapsychological paper on conversion hysteria. (See Editor's Introduction, p. 106.)—Freud had already touched on the question in *Studies on Hysteria* (1895*d*), *Standard Ed.*, **2**, 166–7.]

anticathexis proceeding from the system *Cs.* (*Pcs.*)[1] is clear and becomes manifest in the formation of the symptom. It is the anticathexis that decides upon what portion of the instinctual representative the whole cathexis of the latter is able to be concentrated. The portion thus selected to be a symptom fulfils the condition of expressing the wishful aim of the instinctual impulse no less than the defensive or punitive efforts of the system *Cs.*; thus it becomes hypercathected, and it is maintained from both directions like the substitutive idea in anxiety hysteria. From this circumstance we may conclude without hesitation that the amount of energy expended by the system *Cs.* on repression need not be so great as the cathectic energy of the symptom; for the strength of the repression is measured by the amount of anticathexis expended, whereas the symptom is supported not only by this anticathexis but also by the instinctual cathexis from the system *Ucs.* which is condensed in the symptom.

As regards obsessional neurosis, we need only add to the observations brought forward in the preceding paper [p. 156 f.] that it is here that the anticathexis from the system *Cs.* comes most noticeably into the foreground. It is this which, organized as a reaction-formation, brings about the first repression, and which is later the point at which the repressed idea breaks through. We may venture the supposition that it is because of the predominance of the anticathexis and the absence of discharge that the work of repression seems far less successful in anxiety hysteria and in obsessional neurosis than in conversion hysteria.

[1] [In the 1915 edition only, '(*Pcs.*)' does not occur.]

V. The Special Characteristics of the System *Ucs.*

The distinction we have made between the two psychical systems receives fresh significance when we observe that processes in the one system, the *Ucs.*, show characteristics which are not met with again in the system immediately above it.

The nucleus of the *Ucs.* consists of instinctual representatives which seek to discharge their cathexis; that is to say, it consists of wishful impulses. These instinctual impulses are co-ordinate with one another, exist side by side without being influenced by one another, and are exempt from mutual contradiction. When two wishful impulses whose aims must appear to us incompatible become simultaneously active, the two impulses do not diminish each other or cancel each other out, but combine to form an intermediate aim, a compromise.

There are in this system no negation, no doubt, no degrees of certainty: all this is only introduced by the work of the censorship between the *Ucs.* and the *Pcs.* Negation is a substitute, at a higher level, for repression.[1] In the *Ucs.* there are only contents, cathected with greater or lesser strength.

The cathectic intensities [in the *Ucs.*] are much more mobile. By the process of *displacement* one idea may surrender to another its whole quota of cathexis; by the process of *condensation* it may appropriate the whole cathexis of several other ideas. I have proposed to regard these two processes as distinguishing marks of the so-called *primary psychical process*. In the system *Pcs.* the *secondary process*[2] is dominant. When a primary process is allowed to take its course in connection with elements belonging to the system *Pcs.*, it appears 'comic' and excites laughter.[3]

[1] [This had already been asserted by Freud in Chapter VI of his book on jokes (1905*c*). Cf., however, Freud's later discussion of negation (1925*h*).]

[2] Cf. the discussion in Chapter VII of *The Interpretation of Dreams* (1900*a*) [Section E, *Standard Ed.*, **5**, 588 ff.], based on ideas developed by Breuer in *Studies on Hysteria* (Breuer and Freud, 1895). [A comment on Freud's attribution of these hypotheses to Breuer will be found in the Editor's Introduction to the latter work (*Standard Ed.*, **2**, xxvii) and in a footnote to the same volume (ibid., 194).]

[3] [Freud had expressed this idea in very similar words in Chapter VII (E) of *The Interpretation of Dreams* (1900*a*), *Standard Ed.*, **5**, 605. The point is dealt with more fully in his book on jokes (1905*c*), especially in the second and third Sections of Chapter VII.]

The processes of the system *Ucs.* are *timeless*; i.e. they are not ordered temporally, are not altered by the passage of time; they have no reference to time at all. Reference to time is bound up, once again, with the work of the system *Cs.*[1]

The *Ucs.* processes pay just as little regard to *reality*. They are subject to the pleasure principle; their fate depends only on how strong they are and on whether they fulfil the demands of the pleasure-unpleasure regulation.[2]

To sum up: *exemption from mutual contradiction*, *primary process* (mobility of cathexes), *timelessness*, and *replacement of external by psychical reality*—these are the characteristics which we may expect to find in processes belonging to the system *Ucs.*[3]

Unconscious processes only become cognizable by us under the conditions of dreaming and of neurosis—that is to say, when processes of the higher, *Pcs.*, system are set back to an earlier stage by being lowered (by regression). In themselves they cannot be cognized, indeed are even incapable of carrying on their existence; for the system *Ucs.* is at a very early moment overlaid by the *Pcs.* which has taken over access to consciousness and to motility. Discharge from the system *Ucs.* passes into somatic

[1] [In the 1915 edition only, this read '*Pcs.*'.—Mentions of the 'timelessness' of the unconscious will be found scattered throughout 'Freud', writings. The earliest is perhaps a sentence dating from 1897 (Freud, 1950*a*, Draft M) in which he declares that 'disregard of the characteristic of time is no doubt an essential distinction between activity in the preconscious and unconscious'. The point is indirectly alluded to in *The Interpretation of Dreams* (1900*a*), *Standard Ed.*, **5**, 577–8, but the first explicit published mention of it seems to have been in a footnote added in 1907 to *The Psychopathology of Everyday Life* (1901*b*), near the end of the last chapter. Another passing allusion occurs in a footnote to the paper on narcissism (above, p. 96). Freud returned to the question more than once in his later writings: particularly in *Beyond the Pleasure Principle* (1920*g*), *Standard Ed.*, **18**, 28, and in Lecture XXXI of the *New Introductory Lectures* (1933*a*). A discussion on the subject took place at a meeting of the Vienna Psycho-Analytical Society on November 8, 1911, and the published minutes (*Zbl. psychoan.*, **2**, 476–7) give a very short summary of some remarks made by Freud on the occasion.]

[2] [Cf. Section 8 of 'The Two Principles of Mental Functioning, (1911*b*). 'Reality-testing' is dealt with at some length in the next paper (p. 231 ff., below).]

[3] We are reserving for a different context the mention of another notable privilege of the *Ucs.* [This may refer to the relation of the *Ucs.* to words (p. 201 ff.); or possibly to one of the unpublished papers in the series.]

innervation that leads to development of affect; but even this path of discharge is, as we have seen [p. 178 f.], contested by the *Pcs.* By itself, the system *Ucs.* would not in normal conditions be able to bring about any expedient muscular acts, with the exception of those already organized as reflexes.

The full significance of the characteristics of the system *Ucs.* described above could only be appreciated by us if we were to contrast and compare them with those of the system *Pcs.* But this would take us so far afield that I propose that we should once more call a halt and not undertake the comparison of the two till we can do so in connection with our discussion of the higher system.[1] Only the most pressing points of all will be mentioned at this stage.

The processes of the system *Pcs.* display—no matter whether they are already conscious or only capable of becoming conscious—an inhibition of the tendency of cathected ideas towards discharge. When a process passes from one idea to another, the first idea retains a part of its cathexis and only a small portion undergoes displacement. Displacements and condensations such as happen in the primary process are excluded or very much restricted. This circumstance caused Breuer to assume the existence of two different states of cathectic energy in mental life: one in which the energy is tonically 'bound' and the other in which it is freely mobile and presses towards discharge.[2] In my opinion this distinction represents the deepest insight we have gained up to the present into the nature of nervous energy, and I do not see how we can avoid making it. A metapsychological presentation would most urgently call for further discussion at this point, though perhaps that would be too daring an undertaking as yet.

Further, it devolves upon the system *Pcs.* to make communication possible between the different ideational contents so that they can influence one another, to give them an order in time,[3] and to set up a censorship or several censorships; 'reality-testing' too, and the reality-principle, are in its province. Conscious memory, moreover, seems to depend wholly on the *Pcs.*[4]

[1] [A probable reference to the lost paper on consciousness.]

[2] [Cf. footnote 2, on p. 186.]

[3] [There is a hint at the mechanism by which the *Pcs.* effects this in the penultimate paragraph of Freud's paper on the 'Mystic Writing-Pad' (1925*a*).]

[4] [Cf. above, p. 96 *n.*—In the 1915 edition only, this read '*Cs.*'.]

This should be clearly distinguished from the memory-traces in which the experiences of the *Ucs.* are fixed, and probably corresponds to a special registration such as we proposed (but later rejected) to account for the relation of conscious to unconscious ideas [p. 174 ff.]. In this connection, also, we shall find means for putting an end to our oscillations in regard to the naming of the higher system—which we have hitherto spoken of indifferently, sometimes as the *Pcs.* and sometimes as the *Cs.*

Nor will it be out of place here to utter a warning against any over-hasty generalization of what we have brought to light concerning the distribution of the various mental functions between the two systems. We are describing the state of affairs as it appears in the adult human being, in whom the system *Ucs.* operates, strictly speaking, only as a preliminary stage of the higher organization. The question of what the content and connections of that system are during the development of the individual, and of what significance it possesses in animals—these are points on which no conclusion can be deduced from our description: they must be investigated independently.[1] Moreover, in human beings we must be prepared to find possible pathological conditions under which the two systems alter, or even exchange, both their content and their characteristics.

[1] [One of the very few remarks made by Freud on the metapsychology of animals will be found at the end of Chapter I of his *Outline of Psycho-Analysis* (1940*a*).]

VI. Communication between the Two Systems

It would nevertheless be wrong to imagine that the *Ucs.* remains at rest while the whole work of the mind is performed by the *Pcs.*—that the *Ucs.* is something finished with, a vestigial organ, a residuum from the process of development. It is wrong also to suppose that communication between the two systems is confined to the act of repression, with the *Pcs.* casting everything that seems disturbing to it into the abyss of the *Ucs.* On the contrary, the *Ucs.* is alive and capable of development and maintains a number of other relations with the *Pcs.*, amongst them that of co-operation. In brief, it must be said that the *Ucs.* is continued into what are known as derivatives,[1] that it is accessible to the impressions of life, that it constantly influences the *Pcs.*, and is even, for its part, subjected to influences from the *Pcs.*

Study of the derivatives of the *Ucs.* will completely disappoint our expectations of a schematically clear-cut distinction between the two psychical systems. This will no doubt give rise to dissatisfaction with our results and will probably be used to cast doubts on the value of the way in which we have divided up the psychical processes. Our answer is, however, that we have no other aim but that of translating into theory the results of observation, and we deny that there is any obligation on us to achieve at our first attempt a well-rounded theory which will commend itself by its simplicity. We shall defend the complications of our theory so long as we find that they meet the results of observation, and we shall not abandon our expectations of being led in the end by those very complications to the discovery of a state of affairs which, while simple in itself, can account for all the complications of reality.

Among the derivatives of the *Ucs.* instinctual impulses, of the sort we have described, there are some which unite in themselves characters of an opposite kind. On the one hand, they are highly organized, free from self-contradiction, have made use of every acquisition of the system *Cs.* and would hardly be distinguished in our judgement from the formations of that system On the other hand they are unconscious and are incapable of

[1] [See 'Repression', p. 149.]

becoming conscious. Thus *qualitatively* they belong to the system *Pcs.*, but *factually* to the *Ucs.* Their origin is what decides their fate. We may compare them with individuals of mixed race who, taken all round, resemble white men, but who betray their coloured descent by some striking feature or other, and on that account are excluded from society and enjoy none of the privileges of white people. Of such a nature are those phantasies of normal people as well as of neurotics which we have recognized as preliminary stages in the formation both of dreams and of symptoms and which, in spite of their high degree of organization, remain repressed and therefore cannot become conscious.[1] They draw near to consciousness and remain undisturbed so long as they do not have an intense cathexis, but as soon as they exceed a certain height of cathexis they are thrust back. Substitutive formations, too, are highly organized derivatives of the *Ucs.* of this kind; but these succeed in breaking through into consciousness, when circumstances are favourable —for example, if they happen to join forces with an anticathexis from the *Pcs.*

When, elsewhere,[2] we come to examine more closely the preconditions for becoming conscious, we shall be able to find a solution of some of the difficulties that arise at this juncture. Here it seems a good plan to look at things from the angle of consciousness, in contrast to our previous approach, which was upwards from the *Ucs.* To consciousness the whole sum of psychical processes presents itself as the realm of the preconscious. A very great part of this preconscious originates in the unconscious, has the character of its derivatives and is subjected to a censorship before it can become conscious. Another part of the *Pcs.* is capable of becoming conscious without any censorship. Here we come upon a contradiction of an earlier assumption. In discussing the subject of repression we were obliged to place the censorship which is decisive for becoming conscious between the systems *Ucs.* and *Pcs.* [p. 173]. Now it becomes probable that there is a censorship between the *Pcs.* and the *Cs.*[3] Nevertheless

[1] [This question is elaborated in a footnote added in 1920 to Section 5 of the third of Freud's *Three Essays* (1905*d*), *Standard Ed.*, **7**, 226 *n.*]

[2] [Another probable reference to the lost paper on consciousness.]

[3] [See p. 173. The point had already been raised by Freud in Chapter VII (F) of *The Interpretation of Dreams* (1900*a*), *Standard Ed.*, **5**, 615, and 617–18. It is discussed at greater length below, p. 193 f.]

we shall do well not to regard this complication as a difficulty, but to assume that to every transition from one system to that immediately above it (that is, every advance to a higher stage of psychical organization) there corresponds a new censorship. This, it may be remarked, does away with the assumption of a continuous laying down of new registrations [p. 174].

The reason for all these difficulties is to be found in the circumstance that the attribute of being conscious, which is the only characteristic of psychical processes that is directly presented to us, is in no way suited to serve as a criterion for the differentiation of systems. [Cf. p. 172 above.] Apart from the fact that the conscious is not always conscious but also at times latent, observation has shown that much that shares the characteristics of the system *Pcs.* does not become conscious; and we learn in addition that the act of becoming conscious is dependent on the attention of the *Pcs.* being turned in certain directions.[1] Hence consciousness stands in no simple relation either to the different systems or to repression. The truth is that it is not only the psychically repressed that remains alien to consciousness, but also some of the impulses which dominate our

[1] [Literally: 'we learn in addition that becoming conscious is restricted by certain directions of its attention.' The 'its' almost certainly refers to the *Pcs.* This rather obscure sentence would probably be clearer if we possessed the lost paper on consciousness. The gap here is particularly tantalizing, as it seems likely that the reference is to a discussion of the function of 'attention'—a subject on which Freud's later writings throw very little light. There are two or three passages in *The Interpretation of Dreams* (1900*a*) which seem relevant in this connection: 'The excitatory processes occurring in [the preconscious] can enter consciousness without further impediment provided that certain other conditions are fulfilled: for instance . . . that the function which can only be described as "attention" is distributed in a particular way' (*Standard Ed.*, **5**, 541). 'Becoming conscious is connected with the application of a particular psychical function, that of attention' (ibid., 593). 'The system *Pcs.* not merely bars access to consciousness, it also . . . has at its disposal for distribution a mobile cathectic energy, a part of which is familiar to us in the form of attention' (ibid., 615). In contrast to the paucity of allusions to the subject in Freud's later writings, the 'Project' of 1895 treats of attention at great length and regards it as one of the principal forces at work in the mental apparatus (Freud, 1950*a*, especially Section 1 of Part III). He there (as well as in his paper on 'The Two Principles of Mental Functioning', 1911*b*) relates it in particular to the function of 'reality-testing'. See the Editor's Note to 'A Metapsychological Supplement to the Theory of Dreams' (below, p. 220), where the relation of attention to the system *Pcpt.* is considered.]

ego—something, therefore, that forms the strongest functional antithesis to the repressed. The more we seek to win our way to a metapsychological view of mental life, the more we must learn to emancipate ourselves from the importance of the symptom of 'being conscious'.[1]

So long as we still cling to this belief we see our generalizations regularly broken through by exceptions. On the one hand we find that derivatives of the *Ucs.*[2] become conscious as substitutive formations and symptoms—generally, it is true, after having undergone great distortion as compared with the unconscious, though often retaining many characteristics which call for repression. On the other hand, we find that many preconscious formations remain unconscious, though we should have expected that, from their nature, they might very well have become conscious. Probably in the latter case the stronger attraction of the *Ucs.* is asserting itself. We are led to look for the more important distinction as lying, not between the conscious and the preconscious, but between the preconscious and the unconscious. The *Ucs.* is turned back on the frontier of the *Pcs.* by the censorship, but derivatives of the *Ucs.* can circumvent this censorship, achieve a high degree of organization and reach a certain intensity of cathexis in the *Pcs.* When, however, this intensity is exceeded and they try to force themselves into consciousness, they are recognized as derivatives of the *Ucs.* and are repressed afresh at the new frontier of censorship, between the *Pcs.* and the *Cs.* Thus the first of these censorships is exercised against the *Ucs.* itself, and the second against its *Pcs.* derivatives. One might suppose that in the course of individual development the censorship had taken a step forward.

In psycho-analytic treatment the existence of the second censorship, located between the systems *Pcs.* and *Cs.*, is proved beyond question. We require the patient to form numerous derivatives of the *Ucs.*, we make him pledge himself to overcome the objections of the censorship to these preconscious formations becoming conscious, and by overthrowing *this* censorship, we

[1] [The complication discussed in this paragraph was reinforced by Freud at the end of Chapter I of *The Ego and the Id* (1923*b*), and in the following chapter he propounded his new structural picture of the mind, which so greatly simplified his whole description of its workings.]

[2] [All the German editions read '*Vbw*' (*Pcs.*). It seems probable that this is a misprint for '*Ubw*' (*Ucs.*).]

open up the way to abrogating the repression accomplished by the *earlier* one. To this let us add that the existence of the censorship between the *Pcs.* and the *Cs.* teaches us that becoming conscious is no mere act of perception, but is probably also a *hypercathexis*,[1] a further advance in the psychical organization.

Let us turn to the communications between the *Ucs.* and the other systems, less in order to establish anything new than in order to avoid omitting what is most prominent. At the roots of instinctual activity the systems communicate with one another most extensively. One portion of the processes which are there excited passes through the *Ucs.*, as through a preparatory stage, and reaches the highest psychical development in the *Cs.*; another portion is retained as *Ucs.* But the *Ucs.* is also affected by experiences originating from external perception. Normally all the paths from perception to the *Ucs.* remain open, and only those leading on from the *Ucs.* are subject to blocking by repression.

It is a very remarkable thing that the *Ucs.* of one human being can react upon that of another, without passing through the *Cs.* This deserves closer investigation, especially with a view to finding out whether preconscious activity can be excluded as playing a part in it; but, descriptively speaking, the fact is incontestable. [Cf. an example of this in Freud, 1913*i*.]

The content of the system *Pcs.* (or *Cs.*) is derived partly from instinctual life (through the medium of the *Ucs.*), and partly from perception. It is doubtful how far the processes of this system can exert a direct influence on the *Ucs.*; examination of pathological cases often reveals an almost incredible independence and lack of susceptibility to influence on the part of the *Ucs.* A complete divergence of their trends, a total severance of the two systems, is what above all characterizes a condition of illness. Nevertheless, psycho-analytic treatment is based upon an influencing of the *Ucs.* from the direction of the *Cs.*, and at any rate shows that this, though a laborious task, is not impossible. The derivatives of the *Ucs.* which act as intermediaries between the two systems open the way, as we have already said [pp. 193–4], towards accomplishing this. But we may safely assume that a spontaneously effected alteration in the *Ucs.* from the direction of the *Cs.* is a difficult and slow process.

Co-operation between a preconscious and an unconscious

[1] [Cf. below, p. 202.]

impulse, even when the latter is intensely repressed, may come about if there is a situation in which the unconscious impulse can act in the same sense as one of the dominant trends. The repression is removed in this instance, and the repressed activity is admitted as a reinforcement of the one intended by the ego. The unconscious becomes ego-syntonic in respect of this single conjunction without any change taking place in its repression apart from this. In this co-operation the influence of the *Ucs.* is unmistakable: the reinforced tendencies reveal themselves as being nevertheless different from the normal; they make specially perfect functioning possible, and they manifest a resistance in the face of opposition which is similar to that offered, for instance, by obsessional symptoms.

The content of the *Ucs.* may be compared with an aboriginal population in the mind. If inherited mental formations exist in the human being—something analogous to instinct[1] in animals—these constitute the nucleus of the *Ucs.* Later there is added to them what is discarded during childhood development as unserviceable; and this need not differ in its nature from what is inherited. A sharp and final division between the content of the two systems does not, as a rule, take place till puberty.

[1] [The German word here is '*Instinkt*', not the usual '*Trieb*'. (See Editor's Note to 'Instincts and their Vicissitudes', p. 111 above.)—The question of the inheritance of mental formations was to be discussed by Freud soon afterwards in Lecture XXIII of his *Introductory Lectures* (1916–17) and in his 'Wolf Man' case history (1918*b*), *Standard Ed.*, **17**, 97.]

VII. Assessment of the Unconscious

What we have put together in the preceding discussions is probably as much as we can say about the *Ucs.* so long as we only draw upon our knowledge of dream-life and the transference neuroses. It is certainly not much, and at some points it gives an impression of obscurity and confusion; and above all it offers us no possibility of co-ordinating or subsuming the *Ucs.* into any context with which we are already familiar. It is only the analysis of one of the affections which we call narcissistic psychoneuroses that promises to furnish us with conceptions through which the enigmatic *Ucs.* will be brought more within our reach and, as it were, made tangible.

Since the publication of a work by Abraham (1908)—which that conscientious author has attributed to my instigation—we have tried to base our characterization of Kraepelin's 'dementia praecox' (Bleuler's 'schizophrenia') on its position with reference to the antithesis between ego and object. In the transference neuroses (anxiety hysteria, conversion hysteria and obsessional neurosis) there was nothing to give special prominence to this antithesis. We knew, indeed, that frustration in regard to the object brings on the outbreak of the neurosis and that the neurosis involves a renunciation of the real object; we knew too that the libido that is withdrawn from the real object reverts first to a phantasied object and then to one that had been repressed (introversion).[1] But in these disorders object-cathexis in general is retained with great energy, and more detailed examination of the process of repression has obliged us to assume that object-cathexis persists in the system *Ucs.* in spite of—or rather in consequence of—repression. [Cf. p. 149.] Indeed, the capacity for transference, of which we make use for therapeutic purposes in these affections, presupposes an unimpaired object-cathexis.

In the case of schizophrenia, on the other hand, we have been driven to the assumption that after the process of repression the libido that has been withdrawn does not seek a new object, but retreats into the ego; that is to say, that here the object-cathexes

[1] [The process is described in detail in Section (*a*) of Freud's paper on 'Types of Onset of Neurosis' (1912*c*).]

are given up and a primitive objectless condition of narcissism is re-established. The incapacity of these patients for transference (so far as the pathological process extends), their consequent inaccessibility to therapeutic efforts, their characteristic repudiation of the external world, the appearance of signs of a hypercathexis of their own ego, the final outcome in complete apathy—all these clinical features seem to agree excellently with the assumption that their object-cathexes have been given up. As regards the relation of the two psychical systems to each other, all observers have been struck by the fact that in schizophrenia a great deal is expressed as being conscious which in the transference neuroses can only be shown to be present in the *Ucs.* by psycho-analysis. But to begin with we were not able to establish any intelligible connection between the ego-object relation and the relationships of consciousness.

What we are seeking seems to present itself in the following unexpected way. In schizophrenics we observe—especially in the initial stages, which are so instructive—a number of changes in *speech*, some of which deserve to be regarded from a particular point of view. The patient often devotes peculiar care to his way of expressing himself, which becomes 'stilted' and 'precious'. The construction of his sentences undergoes a peculiar disorganization, making them so incomprehensible to us that his remarks seem nonsensical. Some reference to bodily organs or innervations is often given prominence in the content of these remarks. To this may be added the fact that in such symptoms of schizophrenia as are comparable with the substitutive formations of hysteria or obsessional neurosis, the relation between the substitute and the repressed material nevertheless displays peculiarities which would surprise us in these two forms of neurosis.

Dr. Victor Tausk of Vienna has placed at my disposal some observations that he has made in the initial stages of schizophrenia in a female patient, which are particularly valuable in that the patient was ready to explain her utterances herself.[1] I will take two of his examples to illustrate the view I wish to put forward, and I have no doubt that every observer could easily produce plenty of such material.

A patient of Tausk's, a girl who was brought to the clinic

[1] [A paper referring to the same patient was later published by Tausk (1919).]

after a quarrel with her lover, complained that *her eyes were not right, they were twisted.* This she herself explained by bringing forward a series of reproaches against her lover in coherent language. 'She could not understand him at all, he looked different every time; he was a hypocrite, an eye-twister,[1] he had twisted her eyes; now she had twisted eyes; they were not her eyes any more; now she saw the world with different eyes.'

The patient's comments on her unintelligible remark have the value of an analysis, for they contain the equivalent of the remark expressed in a generally comprehensible form. They throw light at the same time on the meaning and the genesis of schizophrenic word-formation. I agree with Tausk in stressing in this example the point that the patient's relation to a bodily organ (the eye) has arrogated to itself the representation of the whole content [of her thoughts]. Here the schizophrenic utterance exhibits a hypochondriac trait: it has become '*organ-speech*'.[2]

A second communication by the same patient was as follows: 'She was standing in church. Suddenly she felt a jerk; she had to *change her position, as though somebody was putting her into a position, as though she was being put in a certain position.*'

Now came the analysis of this through a fresh series of reproaches against her lover. 'He was common, he had made her common, too, though she was naturally refined. He had made her like himself by making her think that he was superior to her; now she had become like him, because she thought she would be better if she were like him. He had *given a false impression of his position*; now she was just like him' (by identification), 'he had *put her in a false position*'.

The physical movement of 'changing her position', Tausk remarks, depicted the words 'putting her in a false position' and her identification with her lover. I would call attention once more to the fact that the whole train of thought is dominated by the element which has for its content a bodily innervation (or, rather, the sensation of it). Furthermore, a hysterical woman would, in the first example, have *in fact* convulsively twisted her eyes, and, in the second, have given actual

[1] [The German '*Augenverdreher*' has the figurative meaning of 'deceiver'.]

[2] [Cf. Freud's discussion of hypochondria in his paper on narcissism (1914*c*), above, p. 83 ff.]

jerks, instead of having the *impulse* to do so or the *sensation* of doing so: and in neither example would she have any accompanying conscious thoughts, nor would she have been able to express any such thoughts afterwards.

These two observations, then, argue in favour of what we have called hypochondriacal speech or 'organ-speech'. But, what seems to us more important, they also point to something else, of which we have innumerable instances (for example, in the cases collected in Bleuler's monograph [1911]) and which may be reduced to a definite formula. In schizophrenia *words* are subjected to the same process as that which makes the dream-images out of latent dream-thoughts—to what we have called the primary psychical process. They undergo condensation, and by means of displacement transfer their cathexes to one another in their entirety. The process may go so far that a single word, if it is specially suitable on account of its numerous connections, takes over the representation of a whole train of thought.[1] The works of Bleuler, Jung and their pupils offer a quantity of material which particularly supports this assertion.[2]

Before we draw any conclusion from impressions such as these, let us consider further the distinctions between the formation of substitutes in schizophrenia on the one hand, and in hysteria and obsessional neurosis on the other—subtle distinctions which nevertheless make a strange impression. A patient whom I have at present under observation has allowed himself to be withdrawn from all the interests of life on account of a bad condition of the skin of his face. He declares that he has blackheads and deep holes in his face which everyone notices. Analysis shows that he is playing out his castration complex upon his skin. At first he worked at these blackheads remorselessly; and it gave him great satisfaction to squeeze them out, because, as he said, something spurted out when he did so. Then he began to think that a deep cavity appeared wherever he had got rid of a blackhead, and he reproached himself most vehemently with having ruined his skin for ever by 'constantly

[1] [*The Interpretation of Dreams* (1900*a*), *Standard Ed.*, **5**, 595.]

[2] The dream-work, too, occasionally treats words like things, and so creates very similar 'schizophrenic' utterances or neologisms. [See *The Interpretation of Dreams* (1900*a*), *Standard Ed.*, **4**, 295 ff. A distinction between what happens in dreams and in schizophrenia is drawn, however, in 'A Metapsychological Supplement to the Theory of Dreams', p. 229 below.]

fiddling about with his hand'. Pressing out the content of the blackheads is clearly to him a substitute for masturbation. The cavity which then appears owing to his fault is the female genital, i.e. the fulfilment of the threat of castration (or the phantasy representing that threat) provoked by his masturbating. This substitutive formation has, in spite of its hypochondriacal character, considerable resemblance to a hysterical conversion; and yet we have a feeling that something different must be going on here, that a substitutive formation such as this cannot be attributed to hysteria, even before we can say in what the difference consists. A tiny little cavity such as a pore of the skin would hardly be used by a hysteric as a symbol for the vagina, which he is otherwise ready to compare with every imaginable object that encloses a hollow space. Besides, we should expect the multiplicity of these little cavities to prevent him from using them as a substitute for the female genital. The same applies to the case of a young patient reported by Tausk some years ago to the Vienna Psycho-Analytical Society. This patient behaved in other respects exactly as though he were suffering from an obsessional neurosis; he took hours to wash and dress, and so on. It was noticeable, however, that he was able to give the meaning of his inhibitions without any resistance. In putting on his stockings, for instance, he was disturbed by the idea that he must pull apart the stitches in the knitting, i.e. the holes, and to him every hole was a symbol of the female genital aperture. This again is a thing which we cannot attribute to an obsessional neurotic. Reitler observed a patient of the latter sort, who also suffered from having to take a long time over putting on his stockings; this man, after overcoming his resistances, found as the explanation that his foot symbolized a penis, that putting on the stocking stood for a masturbatory act, and that he had to keep on pulling the stocking on and off, partly in order to complete the picture of masturbation, and partly in order to undo that act.

If we ask ourselves what it is that gives the character of strangeness to the substitutive formation and the symptom in schizophrenia, we eventually come to realize that it is the predominance of what has to do with words over what has to do with things. As far as the thing goes, there is only a very slight similarity between squeezing out a blackhead and an emission from the penis, and still less similarity between the innumerable shallow pores of the skin and the vagina; but in the former case there is, in both instances, a 'spurting out', while in the latter the cynical saying, 'a hole is a hole', is true verbally. What has dictated the substitution is not the resemblance between the things denoted but the sameness of the words used to express them. Where the two—word and thing—do not coincide, the formation of substitutes in schizophrenia deviates from that in the transference neuroses.

If now we put this finding alongside the hypothesis that in schizophrenia object-cathexes are given up, we shall be obliged to modify the hypothesis by adding that the cathexis of the *word*-presentations of objects is retained. What we have permissibly called the conscious presentation[1] of the object can now be split up into the presentation of the *word* and the presentation of the *thing*; the latter consists in the cathexis, if not of the direct memory-images of the thing, at least of remoter memory-traces derived from these. We now seem to know all at once what the difference is between a conscious and an unconscious presentation [see p. 176]. The two are not, as we supposed, different registrations of the same content in different psychical localities, nor yet different functional states of cathexis in the same locality; but the conscious presentation comprises the presentation of the thing plus the presentation of the word belonging to it, while the unconscious presentation is the presentation of the thing alone. The system *Ucs.* contains the thing-cathexes of the objects, the first and true object-cathexes; the system *Pcs.* comes

[1] ['*Vorstellung*.' This word has as a rule been translated above by 'idea'. (See footnote 1, p. 174.) From this point till the end of the paper, '*Vorstellung*' is uniformly translated by 'presentation'—'*Wortvorstellung*' 'presentation of the word' or 'word-presentation'; '*Sachvorstellung*' 'presentation of the thing' or 'thing-presentation'. These words were formerly translated by the somewhat misleading 'verbal idea' and 'concrete idea'. In 'Mourning and Melancholia' (below, p. 256) Freud replaced '*Sachvorstellung*' by the synonymous '*Dingvorstellung*'; and he had used this second version earlier, in *The Interpretation of Dreams* (1900*a*), *Standard Ed.*, **4**, 295–6, and near the beginning of Chapter IV of his book on jokes (1905*c*).—The distinction between 'word-presentations' and 'thing-presentations' was already in his mind when he wrote these earlier works, and it no doubt derives from his studies on the aphasias. The matter was discussed at some length in his monograph on the subject (1891*b*), though in somewhat different terminology. The relevant passage in that work has been translated below in Appendix C (p. 209).]

about by this thing-presentation being hypercathected through being linked with the word-presentations corresponding to it. It is these hypercathexes, we may suppose, that bring about a higher psychical organization and make it possible for the primary process to be succeeded by the secondary process which is dominant in the *Pcs.* Now, too, we are in a position to state precisely what it is that repression denies to the rejected presentation in the transference neuroses [p. 180]: what it denies to the presentation is translation into words which shall remain attached to the object. A presentation which is not put into words, or a psychical act which is not hypercathected, remains thereafter in the *Ucs.* in a state of repression.

I should like to point out at what an early date we already possessed the insight which to-day enables us to understand one of the most striking characteristics of schizophrenia. In the last few pages of *The Interpretation of Dreams*, which was published in 1900, the view was developed that thought-processes, i.e. those acts of cathexis which are comparatively remote from perception, are in themselves without quality and unconscious, and that they attain their capacity to become conscious only through being linked with the residues of perceptions of *words*.[1] But word-presentations, for their part too, are derived from sense-perceptions, in the same way as thing-presentations are; the question might therefore be raised why presentations of objects cannot become conscious through the medium of their *own* perceptual residues. Probably, however, thought proceeds in systems so far remote from the original perceptual residues that they have no longer retained anything of the qualities of those residues, and, in order to become conscious, need to be reinforced by new qualities. Moreover, by being linked with words, cathexes can be provided with quality even when they represent only *relations* between presentations of objects and are thus unable to derive any quality from perceptions. Such relations, which become comprehensible only through words, form a major part of our thought-processes. As we can see, being linked with word-

[1] [*The Interpretation of Dreams* (1900*a*), *Standard Ed.*, **5**, 617. See also ibid., 574. This hypothesis had in fact been put forward (though not published) by Freud even earlier, in his 'Project' of 1895 (1950*a*, towards the beginning of Section 1 of Part III). It had also been mentioned by him more recently, in his paper on 'The Two Principles of Mental Functioning' (1911*b*).]

presentations is not yet the same thing as becoming conscious, but only makes it possible to become so; it is therefore characteristic of the system *Pcs.* and of that system alone.[1] With these discussions, however, we have evidently departed from our subject proper and find ourselves plunged into problems concerning the preconscious and the conscious, which for good reasons we are reserving for separate treatment.[2]

As regards schizophrenia, which we only touch on here so far as seems indispensable for a general understanding of the *Ucs.*, a doubt must occur to us whether the process here termed repression has anything at all in common with the repression which takes place in the transference neuroses. The formula that repression is a process which occurs between the systems *Ucs.* and *Pcs.* (or *Cs.*), and results in keeping something at a distance from consciousness [p. 147], must in any event be modified, in order that it may also be able to include the case of dementia praecox and other narcissistic affections. But the ego's attempt at flight, which expresses itself in the withdrawal of the conscious cathexis, nevertheless remains a factor common [to the two classes of neurosis]. The most superficial reflection shows us how much more radically and profoundly this attempt at flight, this flight of the ego, is put into operation in the narcissistic neuroses.

If, in schizophrenia, this flight consists in withdrawal of instinctual cathexis from the points which represent the *unconscious* presentation of the object, it may seem strange that the part of the presentation of this object which belongs to the system *Pcs.*—namely, the word-presentations corresponding to it—should, on the contrary, receive a more intense cathexis. We might rather expect that the word-presentation, being the preconscious part, would have to sustain the first impact of repression and that it would be totally uncathectable after repression had proceeded as far as the unconscious thing-presentations. This, it is true, is difficult to understand. It turns out that the cathexis of the word-presentation is not part of the act of repression, but represents the first of the attempts at recovery or cure which so conspicuously dominate the clinical picture of

[1] [Freud took up this subject again at the beginning of Chapter II of *The Ego and the Id* (1923*b*).]

[2] [This seems likely to be another reference to the unpublished paper on consciousness. See, however, below, p. 232.]

schizophrenia.[1] These endeavours are directed towards regaining the lost object, and it may well be that to achieve this purpose they set off on a path that leads to the object *via* the verbal part of it, but then find themselves obliged to be content with words instead of things. It is a general truth that our mental activity moves in two opposite directions: either it starts from the instincts and passes through the system *Ucs.* to conscious thought-activity; or, beginning with an instigation from outside, it passes through the system *Cs.* and *Pcs.* till it reaches the *Ucs.* cathexes of the ego and objects. This second path must, in spite of the repression which has taken place, remain traversable, and it lies open to some extent to the endeavours made by the neurosis to regain its objects. When we think in abstractions there is a danger that we may neglect the relations of words to unconscious thing-presentations, and it must be confessed that the expression and content of our philosophizing then begins to acquire an unwelcome resemblance to the mode of operation of schizophrenics.[2] We may, on the other hand, attempt a characterization of the schizophrenic's mode of thought by saying that he treats concrete things as though they were abstract.

If we have made a true assessment of the nature of the *Ucs.* and have correctly defined the difference between an unconscious and a preconscious presentation, then our researches will inevitably bring us back from many other points to this same piece of insight.

[1] [See Part III of Freud's Schreber analysis (1911*c*).—A further schizophrenic attempt at recovery is mentioned below, p. 230.]

[2] [Freud had already made this point at the end of the second essay in *Totem and Taboo* (1912–13), *Standard Ed.*, **13**, 73.]

APPENDIX A

FREUD AND EWALD HERING

Among Freud's seniors in Vienna was the physiologist Ewald Hering (1834–1918), who, as we learn from Dr. Jones (1953, 244), offered the young man a post as his assistant at Prague in 1884. An episode some forty years later seems to suggest, as Ernst Kris (1956) pointed out, that Hering's influence may have contributed to Freud's views on the unconscious. (Cf. above p. 162.) In 1880 Samuel Butler published his *Unconscious Memory*. This included a translation of a lecture delivered by Hering in 1870, 'Über das Gedächtnis als eine allgemeine Funktion der organisierten Materie' ('On Memory as a Universal Function of Organized Matter'), with which Butler found himself in general agreement. A book with the title *The Unconscious*, by Israel Levine, was published in England in 1923; and a German translation of it by Anna Freud appeared in 1926. One section of it, however (Part I, Section 13), which deals with Samuel Butler, was translated by Freud himself. The author, Levine, though he mentioned Hering's lecture, was more concerned with Butler than with Hering, and in that connection (on page 34 of the German translation) Freud added a footnote as follows:—

'German readers, familiar with this lecture of Hering's and regarding it as a masterpiece, would not, of course, be inclined to bring into the foreground the considerations based on it by Butler. Moreover, some pertinent remarks are to be found in Hering which allow psychology the right to assume the existence of unconscious mental activity: "Who could hope to disentangle the fabric of our inner life with its thousandfold complexities, if we were willing to pursue its threads only so far as they traverse consciousness? . . . Chains such as these of unconscious material nerve-processes, which end in a link accompanied by a conscious perception, have been described as 'unconscious trains of ideas' and 'unconscious inferences'; and from the standpoint of psychology this can be justified. For the mind would often slip through the fingers of psychology, if psychology refused to keep a hold on the mind's unconscious states." [Hering, 1870, 11 and 13.]'

APPENDIX B

PSYCHO-PHYSICAL PARALLELISM

[It has been pointed out above (p. 163) that Freud's earlier views on the relation between the mind and the nervous system were greatly influenced by Hughlings-Jackson. This is particularly shown by the following passage extracted from his monograph on aphasia (1891*b*, 56–8). It is especially instructive to compare the last sentences on the subject of latent memories with Freud's later position. In order to preserve a uniform terminology, a new translation has been made.]

After this digression we return to the consideration of aphasia. We may recall that on the basis of Meynert's teachings the theory has grown up that the speech apparatus consists of distinct cortical centres in whose cells the word-presentations are contained, these centres being separated by a functionless cortical region, and linked together by white fibres (associative fasciculi). The question may at once be raised whether a hypothesis of this kind, which encloses presentations in nerve cells, can possibly be correct and permissible. I think not.

The tendency of earlier periods in medicine was to localize whole mental faculties, as they are defined by psychological nomenclature, in certain regions of the brain. By contrast, therefore, it was bound to seem a great advance when Wernicke declared that only the simplest psychical elements, the different sensory presentations, could legitimately be localized—localized at the central termination of the peripheral nerve which has received the impression. But shall we not be making the same mistake in principle, whether what we are trying to localize is a complicated concept, a whole mental activity, or a psychical element? Is it justifiable to take a nerve fibre, which for the whole length of its course has been a purely physiologcal structure and has been subject to purely physiological modifications, and to plunge its end into the sphere of the mind and to fit this end out with a presentation or a mnemic image? If 'will', 'intelligence', and so on, are recognized as being psychological technical terms to which very complicated states of affairs correspond in the physiological world, can we feel any more sure that a 'simple sensory presentation' is anything other than a technical term of the same kind?

It is probable that the chain of physiological events in the nervous system does not stand in a causal connection with the psychical events. The physiological events do not cease as soon as the psychical ones begin; on the contrary, the physiological chain continues. What happens is simply that, after a certain point of time, each (or some) of its links has a psychical phenomenon corresponding to it. Accordingly, the psychical is a process parallel to the physiological—'a dependent concomitant'.[1]

I know quite well that I cannot accuse the people whose views I am here disputing of having executed this jump and change in their scientific angle of approach [i.e. from the physiological to the psychological] without consideration. They obviously mean nothing else than that the physiological modification of the nerve fibres which accompanies sensory excitation produces another modification in the central nerve cell, and that this latter modification becomes the physiological correlate of the 'presentation'. Since they can say a great deal more about presentations than about the modifications, of which no physiological characterization whatever has yet been reached and which are unknown, they make use of the elliptical statement that the presentation is localized in the nerve cell. This way of putting matters, however, at once leads to a confusion between the two things, which need have no resemblance to each other. In psychology a simple presentation is something elementary for us, which we can sharply distinguish from its connections with other presentations. This leads us to suppose that the physiological correlate of the presentation—i.e. the modification that originates from the excited nerve fibre with its termination at the centre—is something simple too, which can be localized at a particular point. To draw a parallel of this kind is of course entirely unjustifiable; the characteristics of the modification must be established on their own account and independently of their psychological counterpart.[2]

[1] [In English in the original. The phrase is from Hughlings-Jackson.]

[2] Hughlings-Jackson has given the most emphatic warning against confusions of this kind between the physical and the psychical in the process of speech: 'In all our studies of diseases of the nervous system

What, then, is the physiological correlate of a simple presentation or of the same presentation when it recurs? Clearly nothing static, but something in the nature of a process. This process admits of localization. It starts from a particular point in the cortex and spreads from there over the whole cortex or along certain tracts. When this process is completed, it leaves a modification behind in the cortex that has been affected by it—the possibility of remember ng. It is highly doubtful whether there is anything psychical that corresponds to this modification either. Our consciousness shows nothing of a sort to justify, from the psychical point of view, the name of a 'latent mnemic image'. But whenever the same state of the cortex is provoked again, the psychical aspect comes into being once more as a mnemic image . . .

we must be on our guard against the fallacy that what are physical states in lower centres fine away into psychical states in higher centres; that, for example, vibrations of sensory nerves become sensations, or that somehow or another an idea produces a movement.' (1878, 306.)

APPENDIX C

WORDS AND THINGS

[The final section of Freud's paper on 'The Unconscious' seems to have roots in his early monograph on aphasia (1891*b*). It may be of interest, therefore, to reproduce here a passage from that work which, though not particularly easy to follow in itself, nevertheless throws light on the assumptions that underlay some of Freud's later views. The passage has the further incidental interest of presenting Freud in the very unusual position of talking in the technical language of the 'academic' psychology of the later nineteenth century. The passage here quoted follows after a train of destructive and constructive anatomical and physiological argument which has led Freud to a hypothetical scheme of neurological functioning which he describes as the 'speech apparatus'. It must be noted, however, that there is an important and perhaps confusing difference between the terminology Freud uses here and in 'The Unconscious'. What he here calls the 'object-presentation' is what in 'The Unconscious' he calls the 'thing-presentation'; while what in 'The Unconscious' he calls the 'object-presentation' denotes a complex made up of the combined 'thing-presentation' and 'word-presentation'—a complex which has no name given to it in the *Aphasia* passage. The translation has been made specially for this occasion, since, for terminological reasons, the published one was not entirely adapted to the present purpose. As in the last section of 'The Unconscious', we have here always used the word 'presentation' to render the German '*Vorstellung*', while 'image' stands for the German '*Bild*'. The passage runs from p. 74 to p. 81 of the original German edition.]

I now propose to consider what hypotheses are required to explain disturbances of speech on the basis of a speech apparatus constructed in this manner—in other words, what the study of disturbance of speech teaches us about the function of this apparatus. In doing so I shall keep the psychological and anatomical sides of the question as separate as possible.

From the point of view of psychology the unit of the function of speech is the 'word', a complex presentation, which proves to be a combination put together from auditory, visual and kinaesthetic elements. We owe our knowledge of this combination to pathology, which shows us that in organic lesions of the apparatus of speech a disintegration of speech takes place along the lines on which the combination is put together. We shall thus expect to find that the absence of one of these elements of the word-presentation will prove to be the most important indication for enabling us to arrive at a localization of the disease. Four components of the word-presentation are usually distinguished: the 'sound-image', the 'visual letter-image', the 'motor speech-image' and the 'motor writing-image'. This combination, however, turns out to be more complicated when one enters into the probable process of association that takes place in each of the various activities of speech:—

(1) We learn to *speak* by associating a 'sound-image of a word' with a 'sense of the innervation of a word'.[1] After we have spoken, we are also in possession of a 'motor speech-presentation' (centripetal sensations from the organs of speech); so that, in a motor respect, the 'word' is doubly determined for us. Of the two determining elements, the first—the innervatory word-presentation—seems to have the least value from a psychological point of view; indeed its appearance at all as a psychical factor may be disputed. In addition to this, after speaking, we receive a 'sound-image' of the spoken word. So long as we have not developed our power of speech very far, this second sound-image need not be the same as the first one, but only associated with it.[2] At this stage of speech-development—that of early childhood—we make use of a language constructed by ourselves. We behave in this like motor aphasics, for we associate a variety of extraneous verbal sounds with a single one produced by ourselves.

[1] ['It was once supposed that actively initiated movements involved a peculiar sort of sensation connected directly with the discharge of nervous impulses from the motor areas of the brain to the muscles. . . . The existence of this "innervation-sense", or sense of energy put forth, is now generally denied.' Stout (1938, 258). This last remark is confirmed by Freud a few lines lower down.]

[2] [The second sound-image is the sound-image of the word spoken by ourselves, and the first one is that of the word we are imitating (the sound-image mentioned at the beginning of the paragraph).]

(2) We learn to speak the language of other people by endeavouring to make the sound-image produced by ourselves as like as possible to the one which gave rise to our speech-innervation. We learn in this way to 'repeat'—to 'say after' another person. When we juxtapose words in connected speech, we hold back the innervation of the next word till the sound-image or the motor speech-presentation (or both) of the preceding word has reached us. The security of our speech is thus overdetermined,[1] and can easily stand the loss of one or other of the determining factors. On the other hand, a loss of the correction exercised by the second sound-image and by the motor speech-image explains some of the peculiarities of paraphasia, both physiological and pathological.

(3) We learn to *spell* by linking the visual images of the letters with new sound-images, which, for their part, must remind us of verbal sounds which we already know. We at once 'repeat' the sound-image that denotes the letter; so that letters, too, are seen to be determined by two sound-images which coincide, and two motor presentations which correspond to each other.

(4) We learn to *read* by linking up in accordance with certain rules the succession of innervatory and motor word-presentations which we receive when we speak separate letters, so that new motor word-presentations arise. As soon as we have spoken these new word-presentations aloud, we discover from their sound-images that the two motor images and sound-images which we have received in this way have long been familiar to us and are identical with the images used in speaking. We then associate the meaning which was attached to the primary verbal sounds with the speech-images which have been acquired by spelling. We now read with understanding. If what was spoken primarily was a dialect and not a literary language, the motor and sound-images of the words acquired through spelling have to be super-associated with the old images; thus we have to learn a new language—a task which is facilitated by the similarity between the dialect and the literary language.

It will be seen from this description of learning to read that it is a very complicated process, in which the course of the

[1] [In German '*überbestimmt*'. The synonymous term '*überdeterminiert*' is the one used so frequently in Freud's later writings to express the notion of multiple causation. Cf. *Standard Ed.*, **2**, 212 *n.*]

associations must repeatedly move backwards and forwards. We shall also be prepared to find that disturbances of reading in aphasia are bound to occur in a great variety of ways. The only thing that decisively indicates a lesion in the *visual* element of reading is a disturbance in the reading of *separate letters*. The *combination* of letters into a word takes place during transmission to the speech-tract and will thus be abolished in *motor* aphasia. An *understanding* of what is read is arrived at only through the medium of the sound-images produced by the words that have been spoken, or through the medium of the motor word-images that arose in speaking. It is therefore seen to be a function that is extinguished not only where there are motor lesions, but also where there are *acoustic* ones. Understanding what is read is further seen to be a function independent of the actual performance of reading. Anyone can discover from self-observation that there are several kinds of reading, in some of which we do without an understanding of what is read. When I am reading proofs with a view to paying special attention to the visual images of the letters and other typographical signs, the sense of what I read escapes me so completely that I have to read the proofs through again specially, if I want to correct the style. When, on the other hand, I am reading a book that interests me, a novel, for instance, I overlook all the misprints; and it may happen that the names of the characters in it leave only a confused impression on my mind—a recollection, perhaps, that they are long or short, or contain some unusual letter, such as an 'x' or a 'z'. When I have to read aloud, and have to pay particular attention to the sound-images of my words and the intervals between them, I am once more in danger of concerning myself too little with the meaning of the words; and as soon as I get tired I read in such a way that, though other people can still understand what I am reading, I myself no longer know what I have read. These are phenomena of divided attention, which arise precisely here because an understanding of what is read only comes about in such a very circuitous way. If the process of reading itself offers difficulties, there is no longer any question of understanding. This is made clear by analogy with our behaviour when we are learning to read; and we must be careful not to regard the absence of understanding as evidence of the interruption of a tract. Reading aloud is not to be regarded as a process in any way different from reading to oneself, apart from the fact that it helps to divert attention from the sensory part of the process of reading.

(5) We learn to *write* by reproducing the visual images of the letters by means of innervatory images of the hand, till the same or similar visual images appear. As a rule, the writing images are only similar to, and super-associated with, the reading images, since what we learn to read is *print* and what we learn to write is *hand-writing*. Writing proves to be a comparatively simple process and one that is not so easily disturbed as reading.

(6) It is to be assumed that later on, too, we carry out these different functions of speech along the same associative paths as those along which we learnt them. At this later stage, abbreviations and substitutions may occur, but it is not always easy to say what their nature is. Their importance is diminished by the consideration that in cases of organic lesion the apparatus of speech will probably be damaged to some extent as a whole and be compelled to return to the modes of association which are primary, well-established and lengthier. As regards reading, the 'visual word-image' undoubtedly makes its influence felt with practised readers, so that individual words (particularly proper names) can be read even without spelling them.

A word is thus a complex presentation consisting of the images enumerated above; or, to put it in another way, there corresponds to the word a complicated associative process into which the elements of visual, acoustic and kinaesthetic origin enumerated above enter together.

A word, however, acquires its *meaning* by being linked to an 'object-presentation',[1] at all events if we restrict ourselves to a consideration of substantives. The object-presentation itself is once again a complex of associations made up of the greatest variety of visual, acoustic, tactile, kinaesthetic and other presentations. Philosophy tells us that an object-presentation consists in nothing more than this—that the appearance of there being a 'thing' to whose various 'attributes' these sense-impressions bear witness is merely due to the fact that, in enumerating the sense-impressions which we have received from an object, we also assume the possibility of there being a large number of further impressions in the same chain of associations (J. S.

[1] [The 'thing-presentation' of the paper on 'The Unconscious' (p. 201 ff.).]

Mill).[1] The object-presentation is thus seen to be one which is not closed and almost one which cannot be closed, while the word-presentation is seen to be something closed, even though capable of extension.

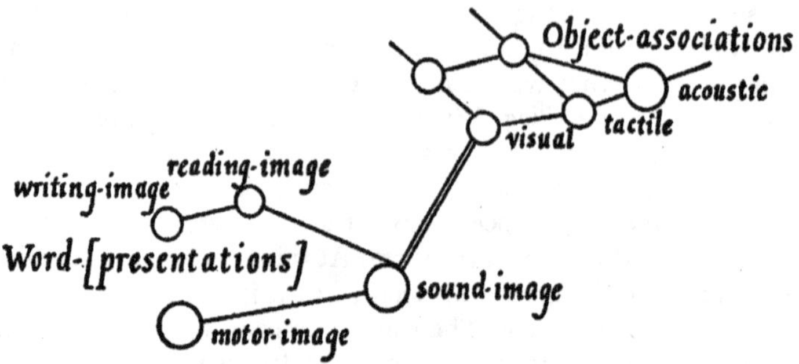

Psychological Diagram of a Word-Presentation

The word-presentation is shown as a closed complex of presentations, whereas the object-presentation is shown as an open one. The word-presentation is not linked to the object-presentation by *all* its constituent elements, but only by its sound-image. Among the object-associations, it is the visual ones which stand for the object, in the same kind of way as the sound-image stands for the word. The connections linking the sound-image of the word with object-associations other than the visual ones are not indicated.

The pathology of disorders of speech leads us to assert that *the word-presentation is linked at its sensory end (by its sound-images) with the object-presentation.* We thus arrive at the existence of two classes of disturbance of speech: (1) A first-order aphasia, *verbal aphasia,* in which only the associations between the separate elements of the word-presentation are disturbed; and (2) a second-order aphasia, *asymbolic aphasia,* in which the association between the word-presentation and the object-presentation is disturbed.

I use the term 'asymbolia' in a sense other than that in which it has been ordinarily used since Finkelnburg,[2] because the relation between word [-presentation] and object-presentation rather than that between object and object-presentation seems to me to deserve to be described as a 'symbolic' one. For dis-

[1] Cf. J. S. Mill, *A System of Logic* (1843), **1**, Book I, Chapter III, also *An Examination of Sir William Hamilton's Philosophy* (1865).

[2] Quoted by Spamer (1876).

turbances in the recognition of objects, which Finkelnburg classes as asymbolia, I should like to propose the term 'agnosia'. It is possible that 'agnostic' disturbances (which can only occur in cases of bilateral and extensive cortical lesions) may also entail a disturbance of speech, since all incitements to spontaneous speaking arise from the field of object-associations. I should call such disturbances of speech third-order aphasias or *agnostic aphasias*. Clinical observation has in fact brought to our knowledge a few cases which require to be viewed in this way. . . .

PART II

Discussion of "The unconscious"

1

Metapsychology and clinical practice: lessons from Freud's "The unconscious"

Peter Wegner[1]

Some observations on the genesis of the 1915 essay "The unconscious"

Freud's essay "The unconscious" was written as the third of twelve on psychoanalytic meta-theory planned in 1915. We know from the correspondence that the papers had to be written in a timescale of a few days or weeks. At the beginning of April 1915, Freud reported to Ferenczi that he had completed the second essay in the "synthetic series" (Falzeder & Brabant, 1996, p. 55, letter 542F, dated 8 April 1915), and by the end of April the third paper ("The unconscious") was also finished and lying in the "publisher's portfolio" at the *Zeitschrift* (Falzeder & Brabant, 1996, p. 58, letter 544F, dated 23 April 1915).

By 4 May 1915, two days before his sixtieth birthday, Freud wrote to Abraham,

> The work is now taking shape. I have five essays ready: that on *Instincts and their vicissitudes*, which may well be rather arid, but indispensable as an introduction, also finding its justification in those that follow, then *Repression, the Unconscious, Metapsychological supplement to the theory of dreams*, and *Mourning and melancholia*. The first four are to be published in the just started volume of the

> *Zeitschrift*, all the rest I am keeping for myself. If the war lasts long enough, I hope to get together about a dozen such papers and in quieter times to offer them to the ignorant world under the title: *Essays in Preparation of a Metapsychology*. I think that on the whole it will represent progress. (Falzeder, 2002, p. 309, letter 276f, dated 4 May 1915).

From the end of 1914, Freud seems to have been more closely occupied with this proposal, writing to Lou Andreas-Salomé, "I am working in private at certain matters which are wide in scope and also perhaps rich in content. After two months of inability to work my interest seems liberated again" (Pfeiffer, 1985, letter dated 25 November 1914). He also wrote to Abraham: "In addition I have begun a larger comprehensive work which has in passing produced the ψα solution of the problem of time and space" (Falzeder, 2002, letter 256F, dated 25 November 1914) and then, "The only thing that is going satisfyingly is my work, which does indeed lead from interval to interval to respectable novelties and conclusions. I recently succeeded in finding a characteristic of both systems, Cs. and Ucs . . ." (Falzeder, 2002, p. 291, letter 260F, dated 21 December 1914).

Until recently, only five of Freud's essays in the series had been published: "Instincts and their vicissitudes" (1915c), "Repression" (1915d), "The unconscious" (1915e), "A metapsychological supplement to the theory of dreams" (1917d) and "Mourning and melancholia" (1917e). The whereabouts of the other papers remained unclear. Freud probably wrote them all, but rejected or even destroyed some of them. It so happened that in 1983, in London, Ilse Grubrich-Simitis discovered one of the missing essays: "Übersicht über Übertragungsneurosen. Ein bisher unbekanntes Manuskript" (Overview of transference neuroses. A previously unknown manuscript). On the genesis of the metapsychological essays and their scientific contexts, see also Grubrich-Simitis in Freud, 1987.

The International Psychoanalytical Association had been founded only a few years earlier in 1910 (cf. Wegner, 2011) and Freud had already completed a substantial period of full-time psychoanalytic practice. In 1914, as well as some other important clinical papers (e.g., "Remembering, repeating and working-through" (1914g) and "Observations on transference love" (1915a)), he was able to publish the key work "On narcissism: an introduction (1914c). Freud wrote to Andreas-Salomé, "I would like to observe that my account of narcissism is in the first place what I shall one day describe as 'metapsychological', i.e., purely conditioned by 'topographical-dynamic' factors without relation to the conscious processes" (Pfeiffer, 1985, letter dated 31 January 1915).

While Freud was writing these papers, the political situation was growing increasingly tumultuous. On 23 July 1914, Austria–Hungary issued Serbia with an ultimatum that ultimately caused the First World War. The wartime conditions not only forced many psychoanalysts (including Abraham and Ferenczi) to restrict or temporarily close their practices, but also prevented many patients from continuing their analyses. Two of Freud's sons were conscripted and quickly embroiled in wartime activities. Early in 1915, Freud reported that wartime conditions had made it impossible for him to see more than two to three patients daily, and he wrote,

> My productivity probably has to do with the great improvement in my intestinal activity. Now, whether I owe this to a mechanical factor, the hardness of the war bread, or to a psychic one, my of necessity altered relationship to money, I will leave open to question. In any case the war has already cost me a loss of about 40,000 crowns. If I have bought health in compensation for it, I can only quote the cadger [*Schnorrer*] who tells the baron: "I consider nothing too expensive for my health". (Falzeder & Brabant, 1996, p. 55, letter 542F, dated 8 April 1915)

Freud not only had more time because of the cancelled treatment sessions, but he also incurred substantial financial losses. To Andreas-Salomé, he wrote, 'Fruit of the present time will probably take the form of a book consisting of twelve essays beginning with one on instincts and their vicissitudes ... The book is finished except for the necessary revision caused by the arranging and fitting in of the individual essays' (Pfeiffer, 1985, letter dated 30 July 1915).

In "The unconscious" (1915e), the focus here, "topographical or systematic viewpoint . . . is the central point that Freud had already touched on in his essay on the unconscious in 1912, in which he distinguished between the descriptive, the dynamic and the systematic unconscious" (Holder, 1992, p. 18). The unconscious is not identical with what is repressed in any systematic respect. The repressed is only one part of the unconscious. Other parts consist of the wishes and fantasies that are not obstructed from realisation into preconscious or conscious representations (cf. Holder, 1992, p. 19). Having already postulated a "censorship" between the unconscious and conscious systems in the seventh chapter of *The Interpretation of Dreams* (1900a), Freud then amplified this idea with a further "censorship" between the preconscious and conscious systems. The movements and restrictions of drive representatives, thoughts and affects between the conscious, preconscious, and unconscious systems are described from topographical perspectives. Finally, a highly complex structure of functioning is delineated between conscious and unconscious. The following example demonstrates the vast scale of Freud's intellectual achievement in theorising these connections:

> We now seem to know all at once what the difference is between a conscious and an unconscious presentation. The two are not, as we supposed, different registrations of the same content in different psychical localities, nor yet different functional states of cathexis in the same locality; but the conscious presentation comprises the presentation of the thing plus the presentation of the word belonging to it, while the unconscious presentation is the presentation of the thing alone. The system *Ucs.* contains the thing-cathexes of the objects, the first and true object-cathexes; the system *Pcs.* comes about by this thing-presentation being hypercathected through being linked with the word-presentations corresponding to it. It is these hypercathexes, we may suppose, that bring about a higher psychical organization and make it possible for the primary process to be succeeded by the secondary process which is dominant in the Pcs. Now, too, we are in a position to state precisely what it is that repression denies to the rejected presentation in the transference neuroses: what it denies to the presentation is translation into words which shall remain attached to the object. A presentation which is not put into words, or a psychical act which is not hypercathected, remains thereafter in the *Ucs.* in a state of repression. (Freud, 1915e, pp. 201–202)

Some observations on the development of a "metapsychology"

The arguments concerning whether or not a metapsychology is intrinsically justified or necessary have been the subject of fierce dispute over the past hundred years. Freud himself had no doubt that the "psychology of the unconscious" required a theoretical conceptualisation in order to oppose the common roots of "superstition" and the "mythological view of the world" with a scientifically based psychology that "leads behind consciousness" (Freud, 1901b, p. 258f). He first used the concept of metapsychology in a letter to Fliess (Masson, 1985, p. 301; cf. Loch, 1980, p. 1298). In "The unconscious", he then defined the necessary components of a meta-theory:

> I propose that when we have succeeded in describing a psychical process in its dynamic, topographical and economic aspects, we should speak of it as a metapsychological presentation. We must say at once that in the present state of our knowledge there are only a few points at which we shall succeed in this. (1915e, p. 181)

The topographical perspective finally paved the way to the "structural" one (cf. Freud, 1920g, 1923b). Later, Hartmann (1958) and Hartmann and Kris (1945) added the *genetic*, and Rapaport and Gill (1959) the *adaptive* perspectives as an amplification and necessary extension of a *metapsychology* (cf. Akhtar, 2009b, p. 171; Laplanche & Pontalis, 1973, p. 249; Loch, 1980, p. 1298). Rapaport and Gill thereby unwittingly referred to Edward Glover, who had long ago drawn the same conclusions:

> No mental event can be described in terms of instinct alone, of ego-structure alone, or of functional mechanism alone. Even together these three angles [*dynamic, structural and economic*, my italics] of approach are insufficient. Each event should be estimated also in terms of its *developmental genetic* [my italics] or regression significance, and in the last resort should be assessed in relation to environmental factors past and present. The list of these criteria, namely *the relation of the total ego to its environment*, is the most promising of all. It suggests that the most practical (*clinical*) criterion of weakness or strength should be in terms of *adaptation*. (Glover, 1943, p. 8)

The five perspectives provide an adequate description for the foundations of a psychoanalytic meta-theory and to some extent actualise an approach to Freud's legacy. These five are:

> the *dynamic* (forces), the *economic* (how these forces interact and conflict, which can be expressed as equilibrium of energy), the *structural* (the shaping and development of constant reaction

> forms in the personality), and the *genetic* (referring to specific successive maturational stages) and the *adaptive* (everything happens within a psychosocial environment)' (Loch, 1999, p. 25).

These perspectives together describe a *three-person-metapsychology*, in which the third person, in addition to the child–mother (ego–environment, conscious–unconscious, and analyst–analysand) symbolises not only the father, but also the group (conscious–preconscious–unconscious [body-] ego–id–superego, father–mother–child, analysand–analyst–environment). Development is intrinsically inconceivable without the premise of a triangular structure.

The destiny of the theoretical and clinical adoption of this fundamental Freudian approach has been assessed in extremely different ways. Over the past few decades, meta-theory has been differentiated by new individual findings, insights, simplifications, and amplifications, but almost all the endeavours conclude by suggesting that a continuation or integration is yet to come. We have only to consider the works of Melanie Klein and her successors, Bion, Hartmann, Winnicott, Kohut, Balint, and the French school, including the new approaches to psychosomatics, to realise that psychoanalytic knowledge is being differentiated and diversified in a way that makes any efforts at integration seem impossible. Earlier, Bergmann (1993) had tried at least to describe the form of more recent approaches in their tendencies by referring to "heretics, modifiers, and extenders" of Freud's meta-theory. The recently published, *The Unconscious. Further Reflections* (Calich & Hinz, 2007), aims to represent, comment on, and assess more contemporary trends. This volume also demonstrates the difficulties with which contemporary psychoanalysis now has to deal in seeking to approach a universally recognised metapsychology. Integration of the various approaches does not seem possible, for the time being. It is, therefore, no coincidence that psychoanalytic treatment technique has been main focus of psychoanalytic research for the past few decades (cf. Etchegoyen, 1991).

In German psychoanalysis, Loch has constantly striven to connect and integrate Freud's legacy with more recent metapsychological insights as well (cf. Eickhoff, 1995, p. 176). Loch's last major work, posthumously published in the *Jahrbuch der Psychoanalyse* in 1995, with which he "purposely concluded" his scientific work (Loch, 1995, p. 103, note by F.-W. Eickhoff), was intended as a lecture for the 39th International Psychoanalytical Association Congress in 1995 in San Francisco ("Psychic reality: its influence on the analyst and the patient today"). He succinctly emphasises *construction* as the actual psychoanalytic tool of treatment technique. In attempting to discover a criterion for differentiating between material and psychic reality, he takes into consideration time, the development of dreaming, defence mechanisms, perceiving, thinking, and actions in a series of amplifications, transcriptions (e.g., primary process and secondary process), and transformations (e.g., from the primary dual union to the three-person relationship). Loch finally reaches the conclusion that "psychic reality is conditioned by the denial of material reality and vice versa", for "material reality is concrete, while psychic reality is abstract" (2010[1995], p. 256). Furthermore, "*the psychic world, the inner, private* world through the perception of the external world" is constructed by *experiences, sensory perceptions* and *non-sensory ideas* (Loch, 2010[1995], pp. 275, 285). Accordingly, *external reality* is also a product of our *constructions*. As Freud stated, "If the analysis is carried out correctly, we produce in him an assured conviction of the truth of the construction which achieves the same therapeutic result as a recaptured memory" (1937d, pp. 265–266). The childhood experiences constructed or remembered in the psychoanalytic process can, with Freud, be regarded as right or wrong, but mainly as "compounded of truth and falsehood" (Freud, 1916–1917, p. 367, quoted by Eickhoff, 1995, p. 176). Eickhoff finally writes,

> Loch relativizes Freud's distinction [between *right* and *wrong*, my italics] in a different way, by—I think to his own surprise—denying the psychic nature of unconscious phenomena as timeless, since these have to be connected with temporal reference-points, and classifying them as external and localisable, adding that psychoanalytic therapy can succeed when interpretations are experienced as concrete, external reality: concretely experienced constructions lay a new foundation for the analysand's actions and thinking. From this viewpoint, the partners in the psychoanalytic dialogue construct their psychic reality in the interpretive process within the transference and countertransference dynamics—two aspects of the same phenomenon—in the here-and-now in the hope of achieving a better foundation for the inner mental state and for future action. (1995, p. 176).

However, what preconditions have to be fulfilled on the patient's part for him to be able to experience the psychoanalyst's interpretations and attitude as concrete, external reality? He needs to be able to feel and think about himself and experience himself as a person in time. He has to be able to recognise the other and himself as separate from each other. He must be able to distinguish concrete material reality from abstract psychic reality. If all these preconditions are fulfilled only to a limited extent, or partly submerged, the psychoanalytic work requires a great deal of patience because they will have to be recovered or newly created. The clinical illustration below illustrates that this was the case with Mrs E, although she tried to conceal this catastrophe from me. From no other patient have I learnt so much about what a disastrous experience it can be not to feel. The development and perception of a real feeling and its transformation into language meant a new form of existence for Mrs E and she reached this point only after a very long analysis.

Clinical illustration

Mrs E reported in the initial interviews (Wegner, 2012b) that she had had a "happy childhood" and that it was only during puberty that she had felt "so different from other people". She came to me because of her neurodermatitis. She had always felt "lonely" and felt a strong urge to form relationships on a "two-in-one" model, which meant completely adapting to the other person and leading a "life for two" (cf. McDougall, 1989), losing any sense of her own body, which violently rebelled against this.

Internally, she was not separated from a maternal–paternal object that could hardly be differentiated. She always experienced her sexuality as "difficult" and she could not tolerate her husband penetrating her. The rejection of sexual arousal ensued unconsciously through the skin treatments and later through many visits to doctors, to whom she presented her various bodily orifices. The analysis was dominated by actual physical illnesses that developed further and kept changing: neurodermatitis (which disappeared after three years of analysis), allergies, eating disorders, nausea, anxiety about bodily noises, ear and eye problems, blister inflammations, irritable bladder, anal thrombosis, and, finally, a hernia.

The psychological dimension of our work led to her feeling "completely open" and the anxiety that I could "reach into her" at any time. This defencelessness experienced in the transference represented the counterpart to her wish to be "two-in-one" with the other—an irresolvable inner conflict. It was only by establishing and understanding this transference conflict that any change became possible. However, she then felt as if she had been buried alive. She was frightened of going to sleep, and of death.

Mrs E then developed a compulsive obsessional system on an extraordinary scale. She transformed the shared flat into a fortress against invasive external dangers. Later, it seemed to her that she might dangerously contaminate others. The "exchange of bodily fluids" became an actual danger. She was afraid of contaminating my floor, my doorframe, or my hand and always "had" to ask me whether everything was all right with me. Finally, she managed to communicate the thought that she would also like me to "waste away", as she had done for so long.

The following session comes near the end of her analysis.

> *E*: I'm just thinking . . . well . . . I'm realising . . . that all the time I . . . hmm . . . that it's all about *contamination . . . transference of something . . . to somewhere* . . . that I'm getting so worried about it! All the same, I'm fairly unconcerned about actual dangers! As if they were two different things . . . that's actually really strange, isn't it? *Pause*.

> *E*: I'm just wondering why I'm actually so calm . . . hmm . . . it seems to me it's feeling . . . *in the eye of the storm*! There it's completely calm . . . *right in the middle* . . . which somehow would make sense because since yesterday I've been thinking . . . hmm . . . as we were talking yesterday about the article on *celibacy* . . . so the *exchange of bodily fluids* . . . isn't it the point at which various things come together . . . or separate . . . hmm . . . the *concrete* . . . and . . . the *symbolic* . . . the *dangerous* . . . and . . . the *wish*? *Pause*.

> *A*: Yes. Go on.

> *E*: Well, all the time I'm looking for the place where everything coincides. I know . . . there's still a missing connection. Yesterday when I left here and looked around me again . . . to see whether I had everything . . . whether I had a jacket there, an umbrella or

something else . . . then I noticed, or how should I put it . . . I wished *I could leave something here*. On the one hand, I'm afraid of forgetting something and, on the other hand, I feel the need to leave something here or I hope . . . something of mine will stay here.

A: Yes.

E: It's actually very simple . . . I must just *translate* what is *concrete* for me, but I can't make it out. *Pause*.

A: Categorise the present feeling correctly?

E: Yes, I think that's what I mean by my confusion. Then I'm confused and can't distinguish anything. I can't keep apart what's *concrete* and what's *not concrete*. *Silence*.

E: And that means, what's *real* and what's *not real*. *Pause*. If it's *not concrete*, it's *not real* either.

A: Only what's *concrete* is *real*!

E: Yes, exactly.

A: Because then you can't perceive your wish for something of yours to stay here with me . . . as if in my memory . . . because that's *not concrete*? And no feeling emerges because it's not concrete.

E: And no idea . . . how that could happen! But you recently said my persistent mistrust was hurtful and . . . I thought . . . but I wouldn't even know that! I already see the possibility . . . but it's not so easy because I can't imagine it! Of course I can theoretically have this idea or know something about it . . . but I can't *imagine it as felt*.

A: You can't feel it.

E: Exactly. I think, it's no wonder . . . no wonder if I can't feel it myself . . . when I find something hurtful. How then could I feel that something is hurtful to other people? When I can feel something I can suddenly imagine everything possible . . . but then it makes me *anxious* because then others may also feel something . . . that comes from me. I'm just thinking it's mad how all my behaviour or experience has totally changed. Before I mainly had problems when I got home . . . because of all the *contamination*

. . . and now I have more problems when I'm leaving the house or . . . say, going to see you. *Pause*. Before when my husband was away, I would start the great clean-up . . . disinfecting everything and so on . . . and now I get worried when he's coming home. *Long silence*.

A: The calm in the eye of the storm . . .

E: I meant the feeling . . . *of cowering in the middle of it*! So just *not running away*, despite the feeling of panic and disturbance. Sometimes I manage to have this feeling: *I'm cowering in the middle*! *Long silence*.

E: I've hardly said it . . . and it starts up again! No . . . *Pause* . . . something occurs to me . . .

. . . It's the indecent words that start up again . . . as with "f" [she means *fucking*]. I wanted to say something like . . . perhaps I just don't know what it means [she groans]. I say it quite simply . . . it feels as if I wished . . . I could take something away from here and something of mine could stay here. Hmm . . . after I somehow have a feeling that one thing might work . . . I hope it also works the other way round. But the question is why . . . is that so very dangerous? *Silence*.

A: Do you have an idea?

E: Hmm . . . perhaps it's just dangerous because I want it? Hmm . . . the theme of neediness. But do I really know what it means? *Silence*.

E: I don't believe I really know! *Pause*.

A: You don't have an idea . . . such as an idea about me, when you have these wishes?

E: Hmm . . . yes. *Silence*.

E: Yes . . . or . . . what you'll do with it! *Long silence*.

E: I think that's right. My idea is that for now it's going *into the void*.

A: You can't imagine your wish being received by me . . . without it being threatening or dangerous for me? *Silence*.

E: Or . . . whether you'll immediately want to get rid of it again . . .

A: That something of you can stay! Could it be that you can't imagine that the wish to receive something from me or leave something behind with me might be wonderful feelings that you could share with me and enjoy? An enriching experience that could make your life worthwhile and satisfying? *Long silence*.

E: Hmm . . . [coughing] . . . hmm . . . obviously that's a lovely idea [cries!!].

A: Sadness and happiness can both lead to tears . . . or being *moved* by something.

E: Hmm . . . that's actually what I wanted to say! That's right! I've noticed I'm crying right now. That's like a confirmation of what you've said . . .

A: I've moved you in a good way. Just as it moves me that you could receive this new thought. *Long silence*.

E: What's new . . . I think . . . is actually the *real* idea.

A: And if that's really imaginable, then it would be a completely different feeling from being alone? Then that's *not two-in-one* but *alone and as a pair*. *Long silence*.

E: The feeling of *being alone* is actually characterised by not being able to *get anywhere*. That everything that comes from me goes into the void . . . and isn't received. *Silence*.

A: And this feeling can also set in without actually being caused by the other person.

E: Logically. If you can have the idea . . . then . . . it can always work. *Long silence*.

E: Hmm . . . and then . . . then nothing more can happen to the idea either?

A: No! *Long silence*.

A: No . . . because this idea can now be felt, as a shared idea, shared with the other and not, for example, a hope or fantasy that is kept quiet. *Silence*.

E: That's the dependence on the other . . . that's also sometimes so unbearable.

A: Yes! We're coming to the end . . .

E: OK.

The analysis of Mrs E proceeded only after difficult, lengthy work on her psychosomatic symptoms, transforming the previously pervasive *pensée opératoire* to a capacity to express feelings verbally, and, finally, working through depressive feelings by developing a strong compulsive defence. At the same time, the patient always says that this also helps her "self-ego" to "defend itself". Nevertheless, she can recognise that this is only an intermediate step to Oedipal autonomy.

In our sessions during this time, the patient came nearer, in a narrow sense, to a transference neurosis state. Instinctual contents, aggressive as well as sexual, now were held in check only through powerful compulsive defences, but the pressure was such as to threaten to overcome the boundaries between the ucs, pcs, and cs. Mrs E had an additional problem, which was her confusion and incredulity over her inability to distinguish concrete reality and phantasy "reality" because, for her, only concrete (especially concrete bodily) reality could be remembered.

Freud designated as "inexpedient" (Freud, 1915e, pp. 167–168) this general objection to the existence and power of the unconscious "that is based on the equation—not, it is true, explicitly stated but taken as axiomatic—of what is conscious with what is mental". However, this is, of course, not a sufficient argument against a neurotic defence. For Mrs E, a sexual wish in the transference with regard to father/analyst is equated with a concrete sexual action, which, naturally, is strictly forbidden by her superego. In this session, in my opinion, her wish for mutual sexual transference from "something" to "somewhere" is put into words and, thereby, she comes to know the existence of unrecognised wishes as part of her psychic reality independent of her strict superego—that is, her voluntary control. In this context, another aspect makes her confusion more difficult, and that is the concrete sexual excitement experienced in the session connected with a sexual wish that, heretofore, was barely felt and had not yet been put into words. It is not only the storm of emotions that is threatening, but these are accompanied by "indecent" words that put her into panic and threaten the compulsive defences. At any rate, she can ask herself "why is this so dangerous?" The recognition of her dependency on others and the repressed wishes for dependency present a concrete existential threat because she would again be thrust into emptiness, that is, she would not be able to reach the Object by whom she would be rejected. The decisive progress in this session is that for a few moments the patient was able, within the transference–countertransference process, to be introduced to her wishes.

I wish to touch on only one of many related technical questions. Why, in this session, were the now apparent relationships not concretely interpreted? One might suppose that the patient's defences would have been threatened and her fears confirmed. This might actually be part of my unconscious motivation. I had learnt from her that, on the contrary, a too-concrete interpretation strengthened her defences and the above process would not have occurred. I tried to find a language sufficiently far from concrete so that the patient could develop her true understanding. There, I found myself in the territory of the uncertain! Which is the right word, what voice, what intonation? What brings the patient to a position to hear so that she can respond? What tone is acceptable so that she herself can find the connections without being forced into a "two-in-one" situation? This single session represents many sessions. The goal was for the patient to be able to find her own appropriate language for her feelings and thoughts and to access her own preconscious and unconscious. The recognition of the "here and now" psychic reality and, thereby, her actual wishes and feelings, is connected with the "hope of achieving a better internal feeling and her future interactions" (Eickhoff, 1995, p. 176).

A second question could arise about the latent but perceptible destructiveness of this patient. This aspect is not taken up in this session, but was before and afterwards. In this session, a destructiveness intervention would only have increased confusion, although in this patient's complex psychopathology the wish to destroy the primary object played an important role.

Some observations on clinical practice

On every level of national and international dialogue, psychoanalysts increasingly, in highly individual ways, each with a small number of clinical–theoretical concepts from the most diverse psychoanalytic schools and traditions, are carrying out their practical clinical work without feeling under any pressure to achieve any meta-theoretical classification. It seems that we work primarily in the so-called "here-

and-now" and are fully stretched by it, as one can see also in my clinical material.

Interestingly, at the same time, there is currently no evidence that it might still be possible to reach understanding about matters of treatment technique even when diverging school-based thinking plays a part. However, psychoanalytic technique seems to be something that can be formulated in such a systematically precise and refined way that differences can be brought out verbally, linguistically understood, and discussed.

It was Joseph Sandler who first sought to deploy this phenomenon as a source of advances in psychoanalysis. Accordingly, he envisaged new concepts that are both elastically formulated and able to be flexibly introduced into the canon of existing theories:

> Elastic concepts play a very important part in holding psychoanalytic theory together. As psychoanalysis is made up of formulations at varying levels of abstraction, and of part-theories which do not integrate well with one another, the existence of pliable, context-dependent concepts allows an overall framework of psychoanalytic theory to be assembled. Parts of this framework are rigorously spelled out, but can only articulate with similar part-theories if they are not tightly connected, if the concepts which form the joints are flexible. Above all, the value of such a loosely jointed theory is that it allows developments in psychoanalytic theory to take place without necessarily causing overt radical disruptions in the overall theoretical structure of psychoanalysis. The elastic and flexible concepts take up the strain of theoretical change, absorbing it while more organized newer theories or part-theories can develop. One of the best examples of this is Susan Isaacs' use of the concept of unconscious fantasy to absorb a view of fantasy which was radically different from Freud's. (Sandler, 1983, p. 36)

In fact, the concept of "unconscious fantasy" in many clinical domains has replaced the meta-theory of unconscious–preconscious–conscious or ego–id–superego and can relatively easily be applied in its place. Sandler sought to make equivalent advances by analysing domains of clinical practice that he termed "private" and mostly "unconsciously" guide different analysts in their technical behaviour.

> The psychoanalytic theories of technique and the related higher-level psychoanalytic psychologies have, of course, been explicitly formulated in different ways by different authors, but they represent what we might call the "public face" of psychoanalytic technique. The *private* aspect of the way we work with our patients—and I am speaking here of what can be regarded as *good* psychoanalytic work—may be significantly different from the more explicit *public* formulations. Moreover, the *private face* of our technical frame of reference is only partly available to consciousness. A large part consists of unconscious conceptual organizations which are based on what the newly-trained psychoanalyst has gained from his analysis, his teachers, his reading and his clinical experience. What he will consciously have in mind are psychoanalytic ideas of various sorts that are, for the most part, the *official* or *public* ones, in accord with the particular views of his own analyst. With time, however, the analyst will create, quite unconsciously, a large number of unconscious part-theories which can be called upon when necessary. I have pointed out elsewhere (Sandler, 1983) that the fact that they may contradict one another is no problem as long as they remain unconscious. Moreover, they are probably more useful and appropriate theories than the *official* and public ones, and when they can come together in a way that is plausible and acceptable to consciousness, a new theory may emerge which may represent a development in the more public domain of theory. (1992, p. 190).

These ideas were enthusiastically adopted, but, over time, it became clear that generating theories from "good practice" in this way proves highly complicated and often constitutes too great a challenge.

In reality, the practitioner's experience in the clinical situation (e.g., in an initial interview) resembles the young psychoanalyst's in the challenging encounter with diverging theoretical approaches: the investigative tool is the analyst alone, unaided by equipment, instruments, tests, and so on, and he is faced with the difficulty that "the object of investigation and the instrument of research . . . belong in the same category" (Loch, 1965, p. 21). The analyst thereby registers and processes signals in two directions, two vectors, as it were, in the psychodynamic field of the investigative situation: one vector is directed at conscious communications and their possible unconscious correlates, in which recognisable distortions of the patient's communications in the context of the here-and-now (such as countertransference aspects) are especially important. A second vector is directed at the processing activities (we might also say, the effects triggered by the signals) as they occur in the analyst, a dimension that I shall term "introspective" and that relates to (pre-)conscious internal processes and, to some extent, also to unconscious processes.

Even in the first few moments of an interview, the amount of data processed by the analyst increases to an infinite degree, especially since, along with the patient's information that is communicated and becomes perceptible, many reactive and verifying processes are added each time that are, to some extent, highly subjective. In other words, the psychoanalyst is dealing with a problem-solving situation that can be described as a complex system and in which he can continue to function skilfully as a therapist only by an artificial reduction or hierarchisation. Otherwise, the analyst system would collapse, which, in any case, often actually happens to some extent, and is of great diagnostic relevance on his part (cf. Wegner, 2012a, p. 231): for example, if an analyst, instead of following his patient's communications, starts to think on his own disturbing bodily sensations.

It seems to be an incontestable fact that the mass of the data to be processed in a psychoanalytic session in some conditions rapidly increases so to be infinite, just like the mass of partly contradictory psychoanalytic theories in the course of psychoanalytic history. But what problem-solving strategies can we deploy to reduce our data artificially, hierarchising them or understanding them as sets of processes? It seems to me that, in the vast majority of cases, we use a "natural" method, relying on chance or on our preconscious, leaving it to our so-called spontaneous countertransference reactions to process, structure, and formulate our interpretations, as well as their accompanying affects. This "natural" method is, of course, also incorporated and grounded in Freud's statement that the analyst "must turn his own unconscious like a receptive organ towards the transmitting unconscious of the patient" (Freud, 1912e, p. 115). On the other hand, what can and must still qualify as "art or skill" in clinical practice becomes questionable in conceptualising our meta-theoretical ideas. The combination of subjectivity, data, and organisation of data, as well as statements about realities, becomes disordered and we remain confused in uncertainty.

In any case, no hope has yet proved justified that further research will actually lead to simplification of our understanding of the interplay between internal and external reality or between psychic and material reality. We are realising that the conditions and functioning of the human psyche are even more complicated than we thought.

Concluding remarks

These considerations lead towards different conclusions that can be summarised here only in very broad terms. Either we deplore this situation as a significant deficiency and demand fundamental corrective measures, or we understand this fact as an acceptable element of current psychoanalytic knowledge. Adopting the first position would require systematically reducing the components of psychoanalytic theory while striving very hard to achieve a consensus about right and wrong meta-theoretical and clinical–technical concepts. I, personally, do not believe that this can succeed at present for fundamental reasons. For one thing, such an undertaking would entail the danger of additional splitting processes throughout the psychoanalytic movement. Adopting the second position would also require a strenuous effort because the concomitant *uncertainty* in the long term will place a burden on our entire training system and our internal and external understanding. In my personal view, however, we have no alternative to the latter position. As well as accepting new elastic theoretical and clinical concepts, this requires a great flexibility in theoretical thinking and behaviour, as well as the capacity to tolerate uncertainty in our work. However, this is something that can only succeed if our training specifically keeps this uncertainty open and makes it tolerable.

The need to recognise uncertainty is based on the fact that everything conscious belongs to an unconscious which we do not yet know and which will become accessible only when we "interpolate between them the unconscious acts which we have inferred" (Freud, 1915e, p. 167). Later work approaches in tendency with the discovery that a truth, or, rather, subjective truth, is not in itself the truth. Freud writes, "Like the physical, the psychical is not necessarily in reality what appears to us to be" (Freud, 1915e, p.171). Freud also stated, "it is a very remarkable thing that the Ucs. of one human being can react upon that of another, without passing through the Cs". And,

> . . . psycho-analytic treatment is based upon an influencing of the Ucs from the direction of the Cs., and at any rate shows that this, though a laborious task, is not impossible . . . [but] is a difficult and slow process. (p. 194).

There are the "various meanings of the unconscious" (Freud, 1915e, p. 172) that our own work complicates and, apart from that, we are confronted with the idea

> that the different latent mental processes inferred by us enjoy a high degree of mutual independence, as though they had no connection with one another, and knew nothing of one another. We must be prepared, if so, to assume the existence in us not only of a second consciousness, but of third, fourth, perhaps an unlimited number of states of consciousness, all unknown to us and to one another. (Freud 1915e, p. 170)

It is because of these facts, looked at from general meta-psychological construction, that our work at each point in time, and also at the end of psychoanalytic work with a particular patient, puts us in a "not yet" approach, also a future that we cannot know.

Another element that will clamour more for our attention in future is the currently increasing *fear of the psychoanalytic method* itself, evidenced, for example, in more and more psychoanalysts carrying out fewer and fewer high-frequency psychoanalyses, as indicated by various authors (Danckwardt, 2011a,b; Reith, 2011). Danckwardt goes one step further here in stating,

> Anxieties in the psychoanalytic situation are not only an expression of the analysand's pathology in the occurrence of transference and countertransference. They are an expression of anxieties that are evoked by the structure and processes of the psychoanalytic method. Such anxieties are contingent on the system and hence specific to the profession. The psychoanalytic method allows for a dialectical flood of words, sentences, sounds and images in order to render visible and perceptible the invisible psychic reality of the analysand. The psychoanalytic method entails anxieties of insecurity, of perceptual conflicts, of aporia, invasion, of the threat of being confused and of not being able to

> tolerate one's incompetence in the face of the real psychic structure of the analysand. These are anxieties about the loss of one's therapeutic omnipotence. In addition, there are anxieties about dependence of psychoanalytic insight on the current state and about the development of a psychoanalytic memory. (Danckwardt, 2011a, pp. 121–122)

These reflections I have put forward remain fragmentary and do not achieve what we actually wish for. How, in the state of theoretical uncertainty and provisionality, can we argue a way forward that will ensure the survival of psychoanalysis and continue to enable us to understand our patients well enough? How can we best prepare our training candidates for dealing with these uncertainties and making them part of their clinical practice without their recklessly yielding to complete arbitrariness? A difficult task—perhaps one that is always too difficult—but this is the very source of the motivation that is necessary to continue the quest.

Note

1. Translated by Sophie Leighton.

2

"The unconscious" in psychoanalysis and neuropsychology

Mark Solms

Most mental processes are unconscious

Freud states, "Our right to assume the existence of something mental that is unconscious and to employ that assumption for the purposes of our scientific work is disputed in many quarters" (p. 166).[1] This statement no longer holds true. In neuropsychology today, Freud's insistence that the mental unconscious is both necessary and legitimate is widely accepted.

However, the consensus was not won by the arguments that Freud set out in "The unconscious"; it derived from a different research tradition. Where Freud cited clinical psychopathological evidence (and the so-called psychopathology of everyday life), neuropsychological theorists independently postulated unconscious mental processes on the basis of clinical neuropathological evidence. Foremost were observations of "split-brain" cases in which psychological responses (e.g., blushing and giggling) were elicited in patients by stimuli flashed only to the isolated right hemisphere (e.g., pornographic images), of which the speaking left hemisphere was unaware (Galin, 1974). Also influential were reports of significant learning effects in amnesic cases, who, following bilateral mesial temporal lobectomy, had lost the ability to encode new conscious memories (Milner, Corkin, & Teuber 1968). Most striking were reports of "blindsight": cases of cortical blindness where the patients could localise visual stimuli of which they had no awareness (Weiskrantz, 1990). These examples provide evidence of unconscious processes that could only be described as mental: unconscious embarrassment, unconscious remembering, and unconscious seeing. The examples could easily be multiplied.

Experimental studies, such as Libet's (1985) demonstration that voluntary motor acts are initiated before a subject becomes aware of the decision to move (unconscious volition), have only strengthened the conviction. The general view today is just as Freud put it:

> that at any given moment consciousness includes only a small content, so that the greater part of what we call conscious knowledge must in any case be for very considerable periods of time in a state of latency, that is to say, of being psychically unconscious. (p. 167)

It is, likewise, now generally agreed that some mental processes are not merely "in a state of latency"; they are not "*capable of becoming conscious*" (p. 173). In other words, on the face of it, we all seem to agree that mental activity can be divided into three grades: what Freud called *Cs.*, *Pcs.*, and *Ucs.* (conscious, not currently conscious, not conscious).

However, at this point, neuropsychological notions of the unconscious begin to diverge from Freud's.

Unconscious processes are automatised cognition

It is true that Freud himself gradually came to recognise the inadequacy of his taxonomy, especially when he recognised that many ego processes, which deploy secondary processes and obey the reality principle, are dynamically unconscious (Freud, 1923b). But the existence of unconscious ego processes is not disputed. What is controversial is the very idea of *dynamically* unconscious processes, that is, of all the things that Freud theorised under the headings of "resistance", "censorship", and "repression". For Freud, these *mechanisms for the avoidance of unpleasure* were pivotal to his conception of the unconscious, giving rise as they do to the active exclusion of certain mental contents from awareness. With relatively rare exceptions (e.g., Ramachandran, 1994, Anderson et al., 2004), the unconscious of cognitive neuroscientists is theorised without any reference to such psychodynamic processes; in fact, it has no special relationship to affect at all. In contemporary neuropsychology, the unconscious is a repository of automatic and automatised information-processing capacities; it is a purely cognitive entity (see Bargh & Chartrand, 1999 for review). In cognitive neuroscience today, there is, in short, still no conception of the id.

Consequently, it makes no sense for cognitive neuroscientists to speak of the "special characteristics of the system unconscious", as Freud does (p. 187). Although some neuro*psychoanalysts* draw attention to clinical neuroscientific evidence and experimental findings that seem to confirm Freud's conception (e.g., Kaplan-Solms & Solms, 2000, Shevrin, Bond, Brakel, Hertel, & Williams, 1996), cognitive neuropsychologists characterise unconscious systems (e.g., their multiple memory systems) in very different terms. Also, they do not always speak of "conscious" *vs.* "unconscious" systems; they refer instead to "declarative" *vs.* "non-declarative" systems. This difference is not accidental.

Consciousness is endogenous

At this point it is important to draw attention to the fact, perhaps not widely recognised among psychoanalysts, that behavioural neuroscience is just as riven by competing "schools" as psychoanalysis is. Most pertinent for our purposes is the division between *cognitive* and *affective* neuroscientists. Affective neuroscientists bemoan the anthropocentrism of their cognitive colleagues, and their excessive focus on cortical processes. They argue that this scotomises the fundamental part played in mental life by phylogenetically ancient brainstem structures, and the instinctual and affective processes with which they are associated. The affective neuroscience tradition, which relies more on animal than human research, can be traced back to Darwin's *The Expression of Emotions in Man and Animals* (1872), and from Paul Maclean (1990) to the work of Jaak Panksepp (1998), who actually coined the term "affective neuroscience".

What I said about cognitive neuroscientists still having no conception of the id does not apply to affective neuroscientists. What Freud called the id is the principle object of study in affective neuroscience. Panksepp proclaims his research focus to be the "primary processes" of the mammalian brain, the raw instinctual affects. He argues that these are evolutionarily conserved in humans, where they play a fundamental but largely unrecognised role in behaviour. His findings in this respect are, therefore, of the utmost relevance to psychoanalysts (see Panksepp & Biven, 2012).

Unlike his cognitive colleagues, Panksepp would have little difficulty agreeing with this statement of Freud's:

> The content of the *Ucs.* may be compared with an aboriginal population in the mind. If inherited mental formations exist in the human being—something analogous to instinct in animals—these constitute the nucleus of the *Ucs.* Later there is added to them what is discarded during childhood development as unserviceable; and this need not differ in nature from what is inherited. (p. 195)

But there is one crucial respect in which Panksepp and colleagues *would* disagree with this statement, and this pulls the carpet right out from under us. They would not agree that the core content of what Freud calls the system *Ucs.*—that is, the deepest stratum of the mind—*is unconscious*. Panksepp, with Damasio (2010) and an increasing number of other scientists (e.g., Merker, 2009), would argue that the primitive brain structures that process that Freud called "instincts" (*Triebe* in German)—"the stimuli originating from within the organism and reaching the mind, as a measure of the demand made upon the mind for work in consequence of its connection with the body" (1915c, p. 122)—are the *very fount of consciousness* (see Solms & Panksepp, 2012). According to these scientists, consciousness derives from the activating core of the upper brainstem, a very ancient arousal mechanism.

We have known this for many years. A mere decade after the death of Freud, Moruzzi and Magoun (1949) first demonstrated that the state of being conscious, in the sense measured by EEG activation, is generated in a part of the brainstem then called the "reticular activating system". Total destruction of exteroceptive inputs had no impact on the endogenous consciousness-generating properties of the brainstem (e.g., sleep/waking). Moruzzi and Magoun's conclusions were confirmed by Penfield and Jasper (1954), whose extensive studies led them to the conclusion that *absence* seizures (paroxysmal obliterations of consciousness) could only be reliably triggered at an upper brainstem site. They were also impressed by the fact that removal of large parts of human cortex under local anaesthetic, even total hemispherectomy, had limited effects on consciousness. Cortical removal did not interrupt the presence of the sentient self, of *being* conscious, it merely deprived the patient of "certain forms of information" (Merker, 2009, p. 65). Lesions in the upper brainstem, by contrast, rapidly destroyed all consciousness, just as the induced seizures did. These observations demonstrated a point of fundamental importance: consciousness always comes from the upper brainstem. This contradicted an assumption of nineteenth-century behavioural neurology: that consciousness was derived from perception, and attached to the *cortex*. There appears to be no such thing as intrinsic cortical consciousness; the upper brainstem supplies it all.

Freud never questioned what is now called the "corticocentric fallacy". Despite occasional disclaimers to the effect that "our psychical topography has *for the present* nothing to do with anatomy" (p. 175), Freud repeatedly asserted that his system *Pcpt.-Cs.* was anatomically localisable and, moreover, that it was a cortical system. For example:

> What consciousness yields consists essentially of perceptions of excitations coming from the external world and of feelings of pleasure and unpleasure which can only arise from within the mental apparatus; it is therefore possible to assign to the system *Pcpt.-Cs.* a position in space. It must lie on the borderline between inside and outside; it must be turned towards the external world and must envelop the other psychical systems. It will be seen that there is nothing daringly new in these assumptions; *we have merely adopted the views on localization held by cerebral anatomy, which locates the 'seat' of consciousness in the cerebral cortex*—the outermost, enveloping layer of the central organ. Cerebral anatomy has no need to consider why, speaking anatomically, consciousness should be lodged on the surface of the brain instead of being safely housed somewhere in its inmost interior. (Freud, 1923b, p. 24, my italics)

The observations of Moruzzi and Magoun (1949) and Penfield and Jasper (1954) which overturned this classical assumption have stood the test of time, but greater anatomical precision has been added (see Merker, 2009, for review). Significantly, the periaquaductal grey, an intensely affective structure, appears to be a nodal point in the activating system. This is the smallest region of brain tissue in which damage leads to obliteration of consciousness. This underscores a major change in recent conceptions of the activating system: the deep structures that generate consciousness are not only responsible for the *level* (quantity) but also for a core *quality* of consciousness. The conscious states generated in the upper brainstem are inherently *affective*. This realisation is now revolutionising consciousness studies.

The classical conception is turned on its head. Consciousness is not generated in the cortex; it is generated in the brainstem. Moreover, consciousness is not inherently perceptual; it is inherently affective.

Basic (brainstem) consciousness consists in *states* rather than *objects* (cf. Mesulam, 2000). The upper brainstem structures that generate consciousness do not map our external senses; they map the internal state of the (visceral, autonomic) body. This mapping of the internal milieu generates not objects but, rather, the *subject* of perception. It generates the background state of *being* conscious. This is of paramount importance. We might picture this core quality of consciousness as the page upon which external perceptual objects are inscribed. The objects are accordingly perceived *by* an already sentient subject.

Affects are valenced states of the subject. These states are thought to represent the biological value of changing internal conditions (e.g., hunger, sexual arousal). When internal conditions favour survival and reproductive success, they feel "good", when not, they feel "bad". This is biological *value*, which is evidently what consciousness is *for*. It tells the subject how well it is doing. (At this level of the brain, consciousness is closely tied to homeostasis.) All of this is entirely consistent with Freud's conception of affect:

> The id, cut off from the external world, has a world of perception of its own. It detects with extraordinary acuteness certain changes in its interior, especially oscillations in the tension of its instinctual needs, and these changes become conscious as feelings

> in the pleasure–unpleasure series. It is hard to say, to be sure, by what means and with the help of what sensory terminal organs these perceptions come about. But it is an established fact that self-perceptions—coenaesthetic feelings and feelings of pleasure–unpleasure—govern the passage of events in the id with despotic force. The id obeys the inexorable pleasure principle. (Freud, 1940a[1938], p. 198)

Affect may, accordingly, be described as an interoceptive sensory modality, but that is not all it is. Affect is an intrinsic property of the brain. This property is also *expressed* in emotions, and emotions are, above all, peremptory forms of motor discharge. This reflects the fact that the changing internal conditions mentioned above are closely tied to changing external conditions. This is because, first, vital needs (represented as deviations from homeostatic set-points) can only be satisfied through interactions with the external world. Second, certain changes in external conditions have predictable implications for survival and reproductive success. Therefore, affects, although inherently subjective, are typically directed towards objects: "I feel like this *about* that" (cf. the philosophical concept of "aboutness"—intentionality). Damasio (1999) defines the relation "I feel like this about that" as the basic unit of consciousness, what he calls "core-consciousness".

In this view, consciousness derives from the deepest strata of the mind, it is inherently affective, and it is only secondarily "extended" (to use Damasio's term) upwards to the higher perceptual and cognitive mechanisms that Freud described as the systems *Pcpt.-Cs.* and *Pcs.* In other words, it is the *higher* systems that are unconscious "in themselves". They borrow consciousness via associative links from the lower system, not the other way round.

Despite this apparently fundamental contradiction of Freud's model, a moment's reflection reveals that it could not be otherwise. If the reality principle inhibits the pleasure principle, as it obviously must do, then where do the inexorable feelings of pleasure (and unpleasure) come from? Surely not from above. The pleasure principle is not a top-down control mechanism, quite the opposite. And how can one speak of *feelings* of pleasure and unpleasure without speaking of consciousness? The consciousness must come from below.

But this is not how Freud saw it:

> The process of something becoming conscious is above all linked with the perceptions which our sense organs receive from the external world. From the topographical point of view, therefore, it is a phenomenon which takes place in the outermost cortex of the ego. It is true that we also receive information from the inside of the body—the feelings, which actually exercise a more peremptory influence on our mental life than external perceptions; moreover, in certain circumstances the sense organs themselves transmit feelings, sensations of pain, in addition to the perceptions specific to them. Since, however, these sensations (as we call them in contrast to conscious perceptions) also emanate from the terminal organs *and since we regard all these as prolongations or offshoots of the cortical layer*, we are still able to maintain the assertion made above. The only distinction would be that, as regards the terminal organs of sensation and feeling, the body itself would take the place of the external world. (Freud, 1940a[1938], pp. 161–162, my italics)[2]

Affect is always conscious

On the other hand, Freud had no difficulty in recognising that affectivity is "more primordial, more elementary, than perceptions arising externally" (p. 22), in other words, that it is a more ancient form of consciousness than perception (see Freud, 1911b, p. 220). He also readily admitted that affects are consciously felt from the start; that *there is no such thing as unconscious affect*, analogous to unconscious ideas:

> It is surely of the essence of an emotion that we should be aware of it, i.e. that it should become known to consciousness. Thus the possibility of the attribute of unconsciousness would be completely excluded as far as emotions, feelings and affects are concerned. (p. 177)

Freud explained,

> The whole difference arises from the fact that ideas are cathexes —basically of memory-traces—whilst affects and emotions correspond to processes of discharge, the final manifestation of which are perceived as feelings. In the present state of our knowledge of affects and emotions we cannot express this difference more clearly. (p. 177)

In other words, affects are not stable *structures* that exist in the mind whether activated or not, they discharge *the processes of activation* themselves. Freud put this more clearly in his earliest metapsychological writings (1894a), when he still theorised the activation process as "quotas of affect . . . spread over the memory-traces of ideas somewhat as an electric charge is spread over the surface of a body" (p. 60). Later, however, he conceived of the activating process as *unconscious* "instinctual energy", only the *terminal* discharge of which was perceived as affect.

Strachey added a footnote to the last sentence of the quotation above (where Freud says that "in the present state of our knowledge of affects and emotions we cannot express this difference more clearly") referring the reader to the following passage in *The Ego and the Id*. This passage is of such basic importance that I must quote it in full, despite its length:

> Whereas the relation of *external* perceptions to the ego is quite perspicuous, that of *internal* perceptions to the ego requires special investigation. It gives rise once more to a doubt whether we are really right in referring the whole of consciousness to the single superficial system *Pcpt.-Cs*. Internal perceptions yield sensations of processes arising in the most diverse and certainly also the deepest strata of the mental apparatus. Very little is known about these sensations and feelings; those belonging to the pleasure–unpleasure series may still be regarded as the best examples of them. They are more primordial, more elementary, than perceptions arising externally and they can come about even when consciousness is clouded. I have elsewhere expressed my views about their greater economic significance and the metapsychological reasons for this. These sensations are multilocular, like external perceptions; they may come from different places simultaneously and may thus have different and even opposite qualities. Sensations of a pleasurable nature have not anything inherently impelling about them, whereas unpleasurable ones have in the highest degree. The latter impel towards change, towards discharge, and that is why we interpret unpleasure as implying a heightening and pleasure a lowering of energic cathexis. Let us call what becomes pleasure and unpleasure a quantitative and qualitative 'something' in the course of mental events; the question then is whether this 'something' can become conscious in the place where it is, or whether it must first be transmitted to the system *Pcpt*. Clinical experience decides for the

> latter. It shows us that this 'something' behaves like a repressed impulse. It can exert driving force without the ego noticing the compulsion. Not until there is resistance to the compulsion, a hold-up in the discharge reaction, does the 'something' at once become conscious as unpleasure. . . . It remains true, therefore, that sensations and feelings, too, only become conscious through reaching the system *Pcpt.*; if the way forward is barred, they do not come into being as sensations, although the 'something' that corresponds to them in the course of the excitation is the same as if they did. We then come to speak, in a condensed and not entirely correct manner, of 'unconscious feelings', keeping up an analogy with unconscious ideas which is not altogether justifiable. Actually the difference is that, whereas with *Ucs. ideas* connecting links must be created before they can be brought into *Cs.*, with *feelings*, which are themselves transmitted directly, this does not occur. In other words: the distinction between *Cs.* and *Pcs.* has no meaning where feelings are concerned; the *Pcs.* here drops out—and feelings are either conscious or unconscious. Even when they are attached to word-presentations, their becoming conscious is not due to that circumstance, but they become so directly. (Freud, 1923b, pp. 21–23)

Two points must be noted here. The first is that research in affective neuroscience strongly suggests that Freud's "something" *can* become conscious "in the place where it is" (in the upper brainstem and associated subcortical structures). There are multiple lines of evidence for this (see Merker, 2009 and Damasio, 2010 for reviews), but perhaps the most striking is the fact that children who are born without cortex (without any system *Pcpt.-Cs.*) display abundant evidence of affectivity.

These children are blind and deaf, etc.,[3] but they are not unconscious. They display normal sleep–waking cycles, and they suffer *absence* seizures in which their parents have no trouble recognising the lapses of consciousness and when the child is "back" again. Detailed clinical reports (Shewmon, Holmse, & Byrne, 1999) give further proof that the children not only qualify as "conscious" by the behavioural criteria of the Glasgow Coma Scale, they also show vivid emotional reactions:

> They express pleasure by smiling and laughter, and aversion by "fussing," arching of the back and crying (in many gradations), their faces being animated by these emotional states. A familiar

> adult can employ this responsiveness to build up play sequences predictably progressing from smiling, through giggling, to laughter and great excitement on the part of the child. (Merker, 2009, p. 79)

They also show associative emotional learning. They

> take behavioral initiatives within the severe limitations of their motor disabilities, in the form of instrumental behaviors such as making noise by kicking trinkets hanging in a special frame constructed for the purpose ("little room"), or activating favorite toys by switches, presumably based upon associative learning of the connection between actions and their effects. Such behaviors are accompanied by situationally appropriate signs of pleasure and excitement on the part of the child. (Merker, 2009, p. 79)

Although there is in these children significant degradation of the types of consciousness that are normally associated with adult cognition, there can be no doubt that they are conscious, both quantitatively and qualitatively. They are not only awake and alert, but also experience and express a full range of instinctual emotions. In short, subjective "being" is fully present. The fact that cortex is absent in these cases proves that core consciousness is both generated *and felt* subcortically—that instinctual energy can become conscious in the place where it is, without being transmitted to the system *Pcpt.-Cs*. This contradicts the theoretical assumptions of Freud, quoted above, to the effect that "feelings, too, only become conscious through reaching the system *Pcpt*". It appears that affects truly *are* conscious in themselves.

The only possible reason to doubt this is the fact that children without cortex cannot *tell* us what they feel (they cannot "declare" their feelings). This leads to a second point that needs to be made in relation to the lengthy quotation from *The Ego and the Id*, concerning the inherently conscious nature of affect.

Not all consciousness is declarative

In the closing sentences of the quotation, Freud says,

> Actually the difference is that, whereas with *Ucs. ideas* connecting links must be created before they can be brought into *Cs.*, with

> *feelings*, which are themselves transmitted directly, this does not occur. In other words: the distinction between *Cs*. and *Pcs*. has no meaning where feelings are concerned; the *Pcs*. here drops out—and feelings are either conscious or unconscious. Even when they are attached to word-presentations, their becoming conscious is not due to that circumstance, but they become so directly. (Freud, 1923b, p. 123)

In "The unconscious", Freud adds,

> The system *Ucs*. is at every moment overlaid by the *Pcs*. which has taken over access to motility. Discharge from the system *Ucs*. passes into somatic innervations that leads to the development of affect; but even this path of discharge is, as we have seen, contested by the *Pcs*. By itself, the system *Ucs*. would not in normal conditions be able to bring about any expedient muscular acts, with the exception of those already organized as reflexes. (pp. 187–188)

What is introduced here is a *developmental* point of view. Initially, the *Ucs*. has direct access to affectivity and motility, which are normally controlled by the *Cs*. (see p. 179), but this control is gradually "contested" and eventually "taken over" (p. 187) by the *Pcs*.

Freud concludes,

> We are describing the state of affairs as it appears in the adult human being, in whom the system *Ucs*. operates, strictly speaking, only as a preliminary stage of the higher [*Pcs*.] organization. The question of what the content and connections of that system are during the development of the individual, and of what significance it possesses in animals—these are points on which no conclusion can be deduced from our descriptions: they must be investigated independently. (p. 189)

This greatly clarifies the point at hand. The primordial plan of the mental apparatus (which pertains to many animals and young children) probably did not include the *Pcs*. organisation to which Freud attributes control of motility and consciousness (including, to a limited extent, affect).

The *Pcs*. organisation is bound up, more than anything else, with "word-presentations". Thus, we learn that, for Freud, consciousness in adult human beings is largely dependent upon *language*. Let us make Freud's position absolutely clear:

> We now seem to know all at once what the difference is between a conscious and an unconscious presentation. . . . The conscious presentation comprises the presentation of the thing plus the presentation of the word belonging to it, while the unconscious is the presentation of the thing alone. The system *Ucs.* contains the thing-cathexes of the objects, the first and true object-cathexes; the system *Pcs.* comes about by this thing-presentation being hypercathected through being linked with the word-presentations corresponding to it. It is these hypercathexes, we may suppose, that bring about a higher psychical organization and make it possible for the primary process to be succeeded by the secondary process which is dominant in the *Pcs*. . . . A presentation which is not put into words, or a psychical act which is not hypercathected, remains thereafter in the *Ucs.* in a state of repression. . . . Moreover, by being linked with words, cathexes can be provided with quality even when they represent only the *relations* between presentations of objects and are thus unable to derive any quality from perceptions. (pp. 210–212)

What this conception precludes is the distinction between what is nowadays called "primary" and "secondary" consciousness (Edelman, 1993). Freud's use of the word "consciousness" refers mainly to secondary consciousness, that is to say, *awareness of* consciousness as opposed to consciousness *itself*. Secondary consciousness is given various other names by different theorists, such as "reflective" consciousness, "access" consciousness, "declarative" consciousness, "autonoetic" consciousness, "extended" consciousness, "higher-order" thought, etc. Primary consciousness, by contrast, refers to the direct, *concrete stuff of sentience*. As we have seen, Freud was dimly aware of this distinction, but he did not think through the implications.

In light of contemporary knowledge, we can clarify: alongside the secondary (declarative, reflective) form of consciousness that Freud typically emphasised, two other (primary) forms of consciousness exist, which are *affective* consciousness and simple *perceptual* consciousness. These forms are not dependent on language.

As we have seen already, despite his topographic uncertainties, Freud recognised the primary nature of affective consciousness. He seems also to have indirectly recognised that simple perceptual consciousness is activated endogenously. Consider the following passage (which has several equivalents elsewhere in his writings):

> Cathectic innervations are sent out and withdrawn in rapid periodic impulses from within into the completely pervious system *Pcpt.-Cs*. So long as that system is cathected in this manner it receives perceptions (which are accompanied by consciousness) and passes the excitation onwards to the unconscious mnemic systems; but as soon as the [endogenous] cathexis is withdrawn, consciousness is extinguished and the functioning of the system comes to a standstill. It is as though the unconscious stretches out feelers, through the medium of the system *Pcpt.-Cs*., towards the external world and hastily withdraws them as soon as they have sampled the excitations coming from it. (Freud, 1925a, p. 231)

Please note that it is the unconscious that stretches out the feelers of perception "from within". However, the cathexes in question remain unconscious until they reach the cortical system *Pcpt.-Cs*. This reveals that even simple perceptual consciousness, in Freud's model, is ultimately endogenous. If we now add that he was *mistaken* in thinking that the cathectic "feelers" cannot generate consciousness until they reach the cortex, as we must, then we arrive at a different formulation—one that is more consistent with the findings of modern neuroscience: consciousness is *affective* until it reaches the cortex, at which point it becomes conscious *perception* ("I feel like this about that"). This gives rise to consciousness of objects, which might or might not then be *re-represented* in words (secondary consciousness).

The systems Cs. and Pcs. are unconscious in themselves

This formulation has substantial implications for Freudian metapsychology, some of which are addressed elsewhere (see Solms, 2013, for a start). Here, I would like to address only the most basic implication of the insight that the cognitive systems *Pcpt.-Cs*. and *Pcs*. are unconscious in themselves.

I begin by returning to an observation here cited twice already, which is that vision can occur unconsciously ("blindsight"). This implies that perception itself is an unconscious process, and poses the question: what does consciousness *add* to perception?

The answer is that consciousness adds *feeling* (Damasio, 1999, 2010), ultimately derived from the pleasure–unpleasure series. That is, consciousness adds *valence* to perception; it enables us to know:

"how do I feel about this; is this good or bad for me?". In terms of the scale of biological values that gave rise to consciousness in the first place, it enables us to decide: "does this situation enhance or reduce my chances of survival and reproductive success?" This is what consciousness adds to perception. It tells us what a particular situation *means*; and thereby tells us what to *do* about it—in the simplest terms: whether to approach or withdraw. Some such decisions are "unconditioned"; that is, the decision is made on an *instinctual* basis. This is what instinctual responses are for; they provide generic predictive models that spare us the dangers inherent in learning for ourselves.

Such situations are accounted for by the primitive mode of mental functioning that Freud called the "pleasure principle". However, a vast number of situations occur in life that cannot be predicted in advance. This is the purpose of *learning* from experience, and the whole mode of functioning that Freud called the "reality principle". The reality principle utilises "secondary process" inhibition (the mode of cognition that dominates in the *Pcs.*) to constrain the pleasure principle, and replaces it with the flexible solutions that only *thinking* can provide. The purpose of the reality principle, therefore, is to construct an individualised predictive model of the world.

Freud refers to thinking as "experimental action" (i.e., virtual or imaginary action). In contemporary neuropsychology, this is called "working memory". Working memory is conscious by definition. (Not all cognition is conscious; but here we are concerned only with conscious cognition.) The function of working memory is to "feel your way through" a problem. The feeling tells you how you are doing within the biological scale of values described above, which determines when you have hit upon a good solution (cf. Freud's concept of "signal affect").

Thinking is only necessary when problems arise. This requires the conscious "presence" of affect, that is, *attention* to the objects of perception and cognition. However, the whole purpose of the reality principle (of learning from experience) is to improve one's predictive model; that is, to minimise the chances of surprise—to *minimise the need for consciousness.* The classical model, therefore, is again turned on its head.

Freud's secondary process rests on the "binding" of "free" drive energies. Such binding (i.e., inhibition) creates a reserve of tonic activation that can be utilised for the function of thinking, just described, which Freud attributed to the *Pcs.* ego. In fact, Freud's earliest conception of the ego defined it as a network of "constantly cathected" neurons which exert collateral inhibitory effects on each other (Freud, 1895a). This prompted Carhart-Harris and Friston (2010) to equate Freud's ego "reservoir" with the "default mode network" of contemporary neuroscience. Be that as it may, Karl Friston's work is grounded in the same Helmholtzian energy concepts as Freud's (see Friston, 2010). His model (in terms of which prediction-error or "surprise"—equated with free energy—is minimised through the encoding of more accurate models of the world, resulting in better predictions) is entirely consistent with Freud's. His model reconceptualises Freud's reality principle in computational terms, with all of the advantages this entails for quantification and experimental modelling. According to this view, *free energy is untransformed affect*—energy released from the bound state, or blocked from the bound state, due to prediction errors.

It is of the outmost interest to note that in Friston's model, prediction error (mediated by surprise), which increases "incentive salience" (and, therefore, conscious attention) in perception and cognition, *is a bad thing* biologically speaking. The more veridical the brain's predictive model of the world, the less surprise, the less salience, the less attention, the more *automaticity*, the better. One is reminded of Freud's "Nirvana principle".

The very purpose of the reality principle, which first gave rise to secondary process cognition, is automaticity, which obviates the need for the subject to "feel its way" through unpredictable situations. This, in turn, suggests that the ideal of cognition is to forego conscious processing, and replace it with automatised processing—to shift from "episodic" to "procedural" modes of functioning (and, thereby, from cortical to subcortical modes). It appears that consciousness in cognition is a temporary measure: a compromise. But with reality being what it is—always uncertain and unpredictable, always full of surprises—there is little risk that we shall in our lifetimes actually reach the zombie-like state of Nirvana, which we now learn is what cognition aspires to. Affect is not so easily overcome.

Conclusion

This review of Freud's "The unconscious" in relation to contemporary neuropsychology suggests that his model is in need of significant revision, for at least three reasons: (1) the core of the system *Ucs.* (Freud's later id) is not unconscious, it is the fount of consciousness, which is primarily affective, (2) the systems *Pcpt.-Cs.* and *Pcs.* (Freud's later ego) are unconscious in themselves, and by inhibiting the *Ucs.* they aspire to remain so, but (3) they borrow consciousness as a compromise measure, and tolerate consciousness, in order to resolve uncertainties (to bind affect).

Notes

1. Unless otherwise indicated, all Freud citations are from "The unconscious" (1915e).

2. Freud's localisation of the system *Cs.* underwent many vicissitudes. Initially, he made no distinction between perceptual and affective consciousness (Freud, 1894a). Rather, he distinguished between *memory traces of perception* ("ideas") and the *energy that activates them*. This distinction coincided with the conventional assumptions of British empiricist philosophy, but Freud interestingly described the activating energy as "quotas of affect", which are "spread over the memory-traces of ideas somewhat as an electric charge is spread over the surface of a body" (Freud, 1894a, p. 60). Strachey (1962, p. 63) correctly described this as the "most fundamental of all [Freud's] hypotheses" but there is every reason to believe that Freud envisaged such activated memory traces of "ideas" as *cortical* processes. In his more elaborated (1895a) "Project" model, he explicitly attributed consciousness to a special system of cortical neurons (ω), which he located at the *motor* end of the forebrain. This location enabled consciousness to register discharge (or lack thereof) of the energy that accumulates inside the system of memory traces (now called the ψ system) from both endogenous and sensory sources. (Please note: from 1895 onward, Freud described mental energy as being *unconscious* in itself; it was no longer described as a "quota of affect".) Consciousness, which Freud now divided into two forms, arose from *the manner in which the energy excited the* ω *neurons*. It gave rise to *affective* consciousness when differences in the quantitative level of energy in the ψ system (caused by degrees of motor discharge) was registered in ω as pleasure–unpleasure, and it gave rise to *perceptual* consciousness when differences in qualitative aspects of exogenous energies (e.g., wavelength or frequency) derived from the different sense organs were transmitted, via perceptual (φ) neurons, through the memory traces of ideas (ψ), on to ω. In an 1896 revision of this "Project" model, Freud moved the ω neurons to a position between φ and ψ, and simultaneously acknowledged that

all energy in the mental apparatus was endogenously generated; energy did not literally enter the apparatus through the perceptual system. (Freud seemed to forget this later; e.g., 1920.) In *The Interpretation of Dreams* (1900a), however, Freud reverted to the "Project" arrangement, and again located the perceptual and consciousness systems at opposite ends of the mental apparatus. His indecision in this respect seems mainly to have derived from the fact that his perceptual (sensory) and consciousness (motor) systems formed an integrated functional unit, since motor discharge necessarily produces kinaesthetic (perceptual) information. Freud accordingly settled (in 1917) on a hybrid localisation of the perceptual and consciousness systems. In this final arrangement, φ (renamed "*Pcpt*" in 1900) and ω ("*Cs*") were combined into a single functional unit, the system "*Pcpt-Cs*". At this point Freud clarified that the *Pcpt-Cs* system is really a single system that is *excitable from two directions*: exogenous stimuli generate perceptual consciousness, endogenous stimuli generate affective consciousness. Freud also retreated from the notion that affective consciousness registers the quantitative "level" of excitation within the ψ system, and suggested instead that it—like perceptual consciousness—registers something qualitative such as wavelength (i.e., fluctuations in the level of energy within the *Pcs* system over a unit of time; see Freud 1920g). The main thing to notice in this brief history of Freud's localisation of consciousness is that it was, from first to last, conceptualised as a cortical process. (Although Freud did seem to have fleeting doubts about this at times; e.g., 1923b, p. 21.) See Solms (1997) for a first intimation that something was wrong with Freud's superficial localisation of the internal (affective) surface of the system *Pcpt-Cs*.

3. They lack perceptual *consciousness*. This does not mean they cannot process perceptual *information* via subcortical pathways. Consciousness is not a prerequisite for perception (cf. "blindsight").

3

Freud's "The unconscious": can this work be squared with a biological account?

Linda Brakel

"The unconscious", a relatively brief article written almost a century ago, has much packed into it, and much that is amazingly contemporary. Not only does Freud succinctly present his most seminal ideas about a contentful, meaningful unconscious, he does so in a fashion that (1) suggests the possibility of a link between the biology and psychology of the unconscious, (2) highlights the topographic, economic, dynamic, and structural aspects of his metapsychological framework, and (3) offers a subtle and effective philosophical argument against his detractors (and later ones) who assert that psychological processes and contents must be conscious, *by definition*.[1] Regarding this challenge to the very possibility of unconscious mentation, Freud (1915e, p. 167) says,

> . . . this [sort of] objection is based on the equation—not, it is true, explicitly stated but taken as axiomatic—of what is conscious with what is mental. This equation is either *petito principia* [Freud's italics] which begs the question whether everything that is psychical is also necessarily conscious; or else it is matter of convention, of nomenclature. In the latter case it is, of course, like any other convention, not open to refutation.

Freud is here arguing that those who would oppose the concept of a meaningful, representational unconscious must do so with more potent arguments than just ruling out unconscious mentation by definitional exclusion—that is, with the definitional stipulation that anything meaningfully mental or psychological is also and necessarily conscious.

John Searle, a renowned philosopher of mind, makes just such an argument by definition in his important 1992 work, *The Rediscovery of Mind*, asserting (p. 168), "Freud thinks that our unconscious mental states exist both as unconscious and as occurrent intrinsic intentional[2] states even when their ontology is that of the mental, even when they are unconscious". Searle then continues with the following question and a quick answer (p. 168): "Can he [Freud] make such a picture coherent? I [Searle] cannot find or invent a coherent interpretation of this theory".

Searle's problem with coherence hinges on what turns out to be his own restrictive understanding of "mental". Stating that he sees: (1) "true ascriptions of unconscious mental life as corresponding to an objective neurophysiological ontology, but described in terms of their capacity to cause conscious subjective mental phenomena" (p. 168), and (2) that mental phenomena simply are ". . . caused by neurophysiologic processes of the brain and are themselves features of the brain" (p. 1), Searle does not acknowledge that it is hard to fathom "how any version of a representational unconscious mental state [such as that held by Freud and psychoanalytic theorists] would fail to meet these criteria" (Brakel, 2009, p. 18). The puzzle can only be solved by realising that "*Searle essentially requires consciousness to be a necessary feature of the mental*. Thus if consciousness is an ontologic criterion for being mental, *by definition* nothing unconscious can be mental" (Brakel, 2009, p. 18).[3,4]

Freud demonstrates further philosophical acumen in "The unconscious" when he maintains that knowledge of the unconscious has the same status as knowledge regarding the minds of others (1915e, p. 169). We cannot really *know* that either is the case; and yet, assuming both that others have minds like ours, and that we all function owing to conscious *and unconscious* psychological processes, allows much that is observable to be readily explained and understood. In making this assumption, Freud is tacitly employing a philosophical tool known as "inference to the best explanation" (Lipton,

1991), which is frequently used by scientists (and other theorists) in evaluating the relative strength of various hypotheses. Interestingly, Freud follows this discussion by invoking Kant's (1781–1787) distinction—between that which we can apprehend, Kant's "things-as-they-appear", and that which we cannot apprehend but which underlies the things-as-they-appear, Kant's "things-in-themselves"—to warn us that, "Like the physical, the psychical is not necessarily in reality what it appears to us to be" (1915e, p. 171). In other words, Freud cautions us to remember that that which we perceive and/or believe regarding conscious mentation might or might not hold for unconscious mentation.

Continuing with his views on one of the most enduring problems in philosophy generally (and particularly in the philosophy of mind, metaphysics, and epistemology), Freud offers (albeit very briefly) in "The unconscious" a clear expression of his stance on the mind–body problem. Freud's position is one of great sophistication. Despite the differences between that which is present in consciousness and the unconscious (differences that I enumerate below), for Freud (1915e, p. 207, Appendix B) because both conscious and unconscious events and processes are psychological, they share "a dependent concomitant" relationship upon physiologic events in the nervous system.[5] It is the importance of this essentially biological view—particularly as it is in tension with other aspects of Freud's characterisation of the unconscious in "The unconscious—that I address in the body of this chapter.

The biological unconscious

From a biological standpoint, much of Freud's account of the workings of the unconscious in this 1915 article is actually totally unproblematic. To begin, Freud's claim that instinctual wishful impulses exist "side by side, without influencing one another" and are, thereby, "exempt from mutual contradiction" (1915e, p. 186) can easily be squared with much drive-organised behaviour seen in animals.[6] A hungry animal, driven to forage for food out in the open, but at the same time heeding the impulse to flee whenever out in the open so as to remain hidden from predators, exhibits both drive derived impulses strongly.

Equally apt for our animal model is Freud's further description of unconscious operations:

> When two wishful impulses whose aims appear to us incompatible become simultaneously active, the two impulses do not diminish each other or cancel each other out, but combine to form an intermediate aim, a compromise. (1915e, p. 186)

Thus, the forager forages quickly in short bursts, darting back for cover after each brief foray rather than remaining vulnerable, exposed out in the open over an extensive surface area and extended time period. While the amount of food and calories gained in this manner might not seem optimal, the compromise is necessary as the cost of being some predator's prey is of course highly prohibitive, resulting in almost certain death.

The primary process nature of unconscious mental operations that Freud next outlines (1915e, p. 186)—operations organized according to displacements, condensations, and the types of categorisations that follow from these primary process organisers—is likewise quite compatible with the very sort of animal behaviour that clearly shows selective (evolutionary) fitness. To return to our forager, for instance, certain singular visual features of various plants can veridically indicate nutrient richness and/or dangerous toxicity. Single perceptual features, including smell, taste, and texture, as well as the visual attributes of colour, shape, and size, are not only easily picked up by primary process thinkers, but, more significantly, can form the core of categorisations based on these primary process attributes. As I have stated in an earlier work (Brakel, 2010, p. 61),

> There are many types of a-rationally based primary process categories. These include categories formed associatively on the basis of superficial similarity, and those based on the similarity of [seemingly] inessential parts. Poets (and others) can use such a-rational categories for similes and metaphors. For example, Shakespeare can ask, "Shall I compare thee to a summer's day?"

I continue (p. 62),

> A-rational categories predicated on associative similarities also include family resemblance classifications of all sorts; categories formed owing to common functional roles of members; and categories arrived at because of a mood or feeling state being

> aroused. An instance of this last type can be seen in my friend Z ... [who] experiences a very distinct ... feeling of nostalgia whenever he views any Expressionist painting, smells a particular aroma (wood burning), or comes across a stray cat. Based upon the unique feelings any one (or some combination) of these seemingly disparate items occasion, they form for Z an a-rationally based primary process category.

And, returning to the issue most currently relevant,

> Further, birds (and other animals) can use a-rationally based categories for successful foraging. They tend to return to areas sharing some common small [from our human viewpoint] visual features associated with the best places to feed. Hummingbirds, for instance, choose fluted shapes of an orange-red shade. (Brakel, 2010, pp. 61–62)

(For more on primary process/a-rational categories, see Brakel, 2009, pp. 8, 16, 43–46.)

These primary process categories, as it turns out, are often capable of delivering more information and at greater speed than would assessments based on secondary process knowledge, such as familiarity with the exact locations of each of several specific species planted, and the particulars of the growth profile of each one of these plants. (For more on the possible evolutionary advantages of cognition organised according to the primary processes, see Brakel & Shevrin, 2003; and for a real life example of animal (pigeon) primary process categorisations, see Garlick, Gant, Brakel, & Blaisdell, 2011.)

* * *

That Freud himself was cognisant of the potential importance of his system Unconscious as a biologically relevant system is revealed in two passages in "The unconscious". The first is a bit tentative. Commenting on the system Unconscious, he says (1915e, p. 189),

> The question of what the content and connections of that system are during the development of the individual, and of what significance it possesses in animals—these are points on which no conclusion can be deduced from our description: they must be investigated independently.

Some six pages later, Freud (1915e, p. 195) seems much more assured, asserting

> The content of the *Ucs.* may be compared with an aboriginal population in the mind. If inherited mental formations exist in the human being—something analogous to instinct in animals—these constitute the nucleus of the *Ucs.*

And yet, as we proceed next to consider some of Freud's further comments in "The unconscious" about his system Unconscious, we will have to admit that there are serious problems arising for any notion of an essentially biological unconscious. I describe these comments and the conflict engendered in the next section.

The conflict

Freud's further characterisations of the unconscious in "The unconscious" directly conflict with any plausible biological account of such a system. Thus, continuing with his description of the fundamental unconscious operations, we find the following assertions (1915e, p. 187): "The processes of the system *Ucs.* are *timeless*, i.e. they are not ordered by the passage of time; they have no reference to time at all". Further, Freud puts forward that

> The *Ucs.* processes pay just as little regard to *reality*. They are subject to the pleasure principle; their fate depends only on how strong they are and on whether they fulfil the demands of the pleasure–unpleasure regulation. (1915e, p. 187)

The tension in Freud's thinking about the system Unconscious now becomes evident: although he seems to want this system of desires and wishes to be constituted by foundational and basic biological drives, his stated account of the unconscious forces us to confront the following difficult question: how can any biological system survive without regard to time and other aspects of reality? No biological organism would be capable of adapting to its environment without built-in registrations and adjustments due to considerations of time and reality. Even single-celled creatures must respond to reality by approaching environments with nutrients and avoiding those that are toxic. And just consider the exquisite precision in timing that a predator needs to catch its prey and that a prey animal needs to escape predation, each monitoring the predicted velocity, acceleration, and direction of the other.

Weighing empirical evidence

Pace Freud, unconscious processes, as it turns out, have been shown to be quite sensitive to both time and reality. Let me describe three research investigations, two addressing time and the third reality.

First, with respect to time, there are two probative studies on unconscious conditioning. The first is called "Further evidence for unconscious learning: preliminary support for the conditioning of facial EMG [electromyograms] to subliminal stimuli", by Bunce, Bernat, Wong, and Shevrin (1999), and the second is titled "Event-related brain correlates of associative learning without awareness", by Wong, Bernat, Snodgrass, and Shevrin (2004). Each of these two experiments involved the conditioning of responses to aversive stimuli, where successful conditioning was demonstrated by changes in a particular biological measure. In experiment one of this pair, the biological measure was the facial electromyograph (EMG), used to register muscle responses from specified muscles in the face. In experiment two, changes in brain waves called evoked-response potentials (ERPs), recorded at particular (well researched) scalp electrode sites, served as the measures of interest.

In both experiments, two sets of matched words (matched in terms of affective content) were presented to all of the participants. Initially, the word stimuli were all presented supraliminally, in other words in full conscious awareness, as the biological measures were recorded. In the next phase, the conditioning phase, both sets were presented subliminally, outside of awareness, but now half of the word items (making up the experimental set) were paired with aversive stimuli, while the other half of the words (constituting the control set) were not. What is so significant about these particular studies is that in the conditioning phase of both experiments, the experimental set stimuli to be conditioned were presented *subliminally, totally outside awareness*, followed by the delivery of the aversive stimulus *at a precise time interval* after the subliminal presentation. Thus, in the earlier (1999) study, after each subliminal presentation of a word stimulus from the experimental set, an aversive shock was delivered exactly 800 milliseconds later. In the second study (2004), a blast of white noise occurred exactly three seconds after subliminal presentation of each word item from the experimental stimulus set.

Next was the post-conditioning phase, in which the biological measures were re-examined, as the two sets of stimuli words (both experimental and control) were again all presented supraliminally. In both experiments, the differential biological reactions (EMGs in the first study and ERPs in the later one) to the experimental set and the control set of stimulus word items provided confirming evidence that aversive conditioning had indeed taken place, and, remarkably, with the items to be conditioned presented totally subliminally.

If participants' unconscious processes were not readily able to associate each of the subliminal stimulus words in the experimental sets with the aversive stimulus timed precisely to follow, aversive conditioning would not have been successfully achieved, and these results could not have been obtained. In short, then, these studies support the conclusion that unconscious processes can demonstrate extreme time sensitivity.

Turning next to the issue of the unconscious and reality, an experiment reported in 2001, "Subliminal visual oddball stimuli evoke a P300 component", by Bernat, Shevrin, and Snodgrass, provides simple and elegant evidence for the capacity of the unconscious to process and discriminate among important features of external reality. In this study, while brain waves—evoked-response potentials (ERPs)—were being measured at the several conventional scalp electrode sites, "The words LEFT and RIGHT were presented in a frequent-rare rate (80%–20%) [design], counterbalanced between subjects" (p. 159). (Thus, half of the participants received presentations of the word RIGHT 80% of the time, and LEFT 20% of the time; the other half of the participants were presented with the word LEFT 80% of the time, and RIGHT 20% of the time.) This is a typical "odd-ball" experimental set-up, in which the stimulus item delivered 80% of the time is the usual expected stimulus, whereas the item shown only 20% of the time is, thereby, the "odd-ball". Except there is one important difference: in the Bernat, Shevrin, and Snodgrass (2001) study, all of the "stimuli were presented at the objective detection threshold (. . . 1 msec presentations)" (p. 159). What this means is that all the presentations were totally subliminal, outside of any conscious awareness.

The results of this 2001 experiment were very similar to those obtained during standard supraliminal oddball experiments, where the subjects can consciously see all of the stimuli. This was the most important finding, and it was summarised as follows: ". . . a significantly larger amplitude [for the P300] component [of the ERPs] for rare vs. frequent stimulus presentations [was obtained] " (p. 159), showing that ". . .a P300 response can be evoked even when both rare and frequent stimuli are presented outside conscious awareness" (p. 169). Clearly, these totally subliminal presentations resulted in brain evidence that rare and frequent stimuli presentations can be distinguished, subliminally, and in the same manner as when presentations are supraliminal, illustrates that important aspects of external reality are, indeed, accurately apprehended by the unconscious.

Solutions (unfortunately not profound)

So how can this conflict about the unconscious, its potential biological relevance, and the clearly important biological factors of time and reality be resolved? What can we do with the tension in Freud's account of the unconscious in "The unconscious"? Is the unconscious insensitive to time and reality, or is the unconscious biologically adapted after all?

Taking up the issue of time first, let us see if we can arrive at some better understanding by looking more closely at Freud's (1915e, p. 187) views on the timelessness of the unconscious, examining the claims in his essay phrase by phrase. First, he states that the unconscious processes are not ordered temporally. Even assuming that this is true, and that the unconscious processes themselves are not structured in a time-orientated fashion, this in no way implies that some particular unconscious operations are incapable of *registering* stimuli and contents temporally, and in a sequential order, just as the unconscious conditioning studies by Wong and colleagues, in fact, convincingly demonstrate that they do. So, on this score, the tension can be relieved.

Next, Freud (again on p. 187) posits that the processes of the unconscious "are not altered by the passage of time". Actually, this statement, viewed from a biologic perspective, seems unproblematic. As long as a drive remains unsatisfied, it is biologically useful that it should not be altered. Put more strongly, an unfulfilled drive should, unless and until fulfilled, press ever more adamantly and peremptorily for satisfaction. Again, this part of the conflict evanesces.

But what about Freud's final comment in this series (p. 187) concerning time, claiming that the unconscious processes "have no reference to time at all"? To address this issue, let me tell the following real-life tale. It is a story that occurs more than occasionally. It is 2 p.m. Neither my dog Xenia nor I have eaten since breakfast. I am busy working and so I have been unaware (unconscious) of what I am assuming has been a growing unconscious desire/drive for food. Although she typically is not fed again until later in the day, Xenia probably wants food. (I am guessing this by the fact that her behaviour suggests that she usually wants food.) Perhaps, unlike the situation with me, Xenia has always been conscious of this desire. In any case, at 2.15 p.m. I do become conscious of my desire and my hunger. I think: "It is 2:15 pm and I haven't had anything to eat since breakfast at 10 a.m." Xenia's primary process-only drive for food lacks this secondary process time stamp. She is presumably *thinking* (in primary process fashion) something like "get food". Although she and I are both hungry, neither of us eats at 2.15 p.m. It is not time for her second feeding, and I return to some compelling work, again forgetting my hunger, rendering my desire to eat unconscious once more. And yet I can assume that both of us are still hungry, with the desire/wish/impulse for food growing stronger as time goes by. For me, my hunger and desire to eat grow in intensity even though I am again unconscious of this state of affairs. This assumption is borne out by my thought at 4 p.m: "Wow! It is now 4 p.m. and I still haven't had anything to eat since breakfast! I'm really hungry now!", whereas Xenia is now behaving as though she might *think* "GET FOOD!" For both of us, then, the pressure of the increasing drive intensity is registered, consciously and in a primary process fashion for Xenia, and unconsciously and in a primary process way for me, the increased drive intensity itself serving as a type of biological–psychological chronometer, indexing the passage of time. Obviously important, this sort of time registration indicator functions to change behaviour in order to address the increasing drive pressure. Thus, happy ending to the much-told tale: I eventually eat and never fail to feed my dog. Moreover, another aspect of the tension in Freud's account can move toward resolution.

Alluding to the registration and indexing of drive pressure and to the relative strength of various desires/wishes, brings us directly to the next and final topic—reality. Again quoting Freud (1915e) on p. 187,

> The *Ucs.* processes pay just as little regard to *reality*. They are subject to the pleasure principle; their fate depends only on how strong they are and on whether they fulfil the demands of the pleasure–unpleasure regulation.

But does this actually pose any problem from a biological standpoint? Indeed, it seems that a more troubling question biologically would be: should a desire/drive be regulated by something other than its satisfaction or lack thereof? If so, what would that regulator be? If I am hungry and have no food, shouldn't I still want food and with an increasingly pressing urgency?

So, again, what seemed so problematic perhaps is not!

* * *

And yet (even for me) there is still something unsatisfying and unfinished in my phrase-by-phrase attempt to allow Freud's characterisation of the system unconscious to be fully consistent with a biological system. Let me try the following, more global, but equally simple, non-profound solution.

One way to resolve both the problem with time and that with reality might be to posit another sort of time awareness and a different type of reality, both mediated, not by biological imperatives, but by socio-cultural norms. Reducing things to basic cases for the purpose of illustration: if I am hungry and it is nowhere near any sort of mealtime, my desire/drive for food clashes with social reality. If I have the urge to urinate and there are no toilets available, likewise, my desire is in conflict with cultural norms. Suppose I want to scream in anger, or sing out in joy in the midst of taking medical boards, or with my last analytic patient. And so on . . . In these examples, my drives and desires, both conscious and unconscious, can be simultaneously biologically-based, thoroughly grounded in biological time and reality, but also totally heedless of *social* reality, including its many *temporal* expectations.

Now, of course, things get more complicated when biological drives are simultaneously psychologically important, and socioculturally influenced. This is obviously true for my simple (and, I will admit, artificial) examples of hunger, food, and eating, as well as those concerning elimination and emotional expression. Further, one can expect that the complexities will increase exponentially when dealing with desires/drives/wishes that are, even on the face of it, predominantly psychological. Take, for instance, wishes for unavailable pre-Oedipal gratifications and/or for unacceptable and forbidden Oedipal objects. And yet, if we can think of psychologically relevant time and psychologically relevant reality (and here I mean to include psychic reality) in both a basic and fundamental biological way and in a complex socio-cultural manner, perhaps Freud's desire to link the unconscious to basic biological underpinnings can gain some real traction. For then it can truly be the case that the unconscious is best described as *both* biologically sensitive to time and reality *and* impervious to the many societal demands of reality and time.

Note that I am not claiming that Freud, in his classic 1915 "The unconscious", *really* intended this dual view both of time and reality. Rather, I put forward this suggestion for two reasons. First, to offer Freud a resolution he might have appreciated to a problem that was not directly stated. Second, and perhaps more significantly, because I, like Freud before me, consider psychoanalysis in its full psychological essence to be a theory and discipline that is essentially biologically based.

Notes

1. For a modern view that all that is mental/psychological must be conscious, see John Searle's (1992) *The Rediscovery of Mind*. And for contemporary arguments opposing Searle's claims, see my review of Searle's book (Brakel, 1994) and *Philosophy, Psychoanalysis, and the A-Rational Mind*, Chapter Two (Brakel, 2009). A very brief account of Brakel *vs.* Searle on this matter is taken up just below.
2. For Searle (1992, pp. 156–157), an intentional state is one that is "about something", hence intentionality implies "aboutness".
3. Searle has a similar restrictive view regarding primary process mediated associative mentation. As I point out (Brakel, 2009, pp. 18–19): Searle

> makes a distinction between rule-following processes, which [for him] are mental (and intentional), and associations such as those via resemblance (and presumably via the other primary process/associative

principles . . .), 'which need not have any mental content at all in addition to that of relata'. (Searle, p. 240)

4. Note that Galen Strawson (1994), another respected philosopher of mind, defends a position on the mental even more extreme than Searle's. For Strawson (p. 168), what is mental must not only be contentful, but experienced *now*.

5. Here is the relevant quotation from p. 207 in full:

> It is probable that the chain of physiologic events in the nervous system does not stand in a [simple one to one] causal connection with the psychical events. The physiologic events do not cease as soon as the psychical ones begin; on the contrary, the physiological chain continues. What happens is simply that, after a certain point of time, each (or some) of its links has a psychical phenomenon corresponding to it. Accordingly, the psychical is a process parallel to the physiological—a "dependent concomitant".

Strachey then reports that the phrase "dependent concomitant" is from Hughlings-Jackson and was written in English in Freud's original text. Note, too, that the text in square brackets above is my addition.

6. In prior work, I have taken the position that wishful impulses are, in fact, derived from biological drives.

4

A Hindu reading of Freud's "The unconscious"

Madhusudana Rao Vallabhaneni

In this contribution, I will compare and contrast Freud's model of the unconscious (1915e) with that of Hindu philosophy. Western readers, except those few who are familiar with Sanskrit and Hinduism, might find reading the latter passages challenging. Because of this anticipated challenge, I have chosen to iterate them frequently and provide nominal equivalents in English, whenever possible. The models presented here have overlaps as well as divergences, and my aim is not to uphold one over the other. Freud's view is clinical and psychoanalytic. Hindu philosophers' view is meditative and metaphysical. Hindu concepts presented here are philosophical and spiritual, but not religious. Freudian concepts are psychological and clinical, but not metaphysical or spiritual.

Freud was a mortalist. For him, the body was the substratum for the mind and the mind existed only in the context of birth and death of the body, not before and not after. Thus, the origin, development, and evolution of mind occur in the psychosomatic complex, a view consistent with Freud's (1925d) background as a neuroanatomist and neurologist. It is well known that Freud made an ambitious but unsuccessful attempt to formulate a neurologically based psychology in the 1880s (Freud, 1954). Freud continued to believe that in the future there will be a neurological explanation of mental phenomena. The current explosion in the discoveries in the field of physiology, neurology, and the applied aspects of the same in neuro-psychoanalysis (Kaplan-Solms & Solms, 2000) bears witness to Freud's foresight.

Hindu philosophers, in contrast, approach the study of human experience from a *transcendental perspective*, which is anchored in spiritualism. According to the Hindu philosophers, there are four entities involved in human experience: the body, the mind, the intellect, and *atman* (the supreme consciousness). In this view, the mind is only a part of the human being, and human experience transcends body and mind. The supreme consciousness of *atman* is the supraordinate container of the human experience. Clearly, this is a spiritual view. And the tension between this perspective and that of Freud's is readily evident. Before delving deeply into this tension, however, it is necessary to lay out the fundamentals of the two paradigms.

Preamble I: Hinduism

There are differing views of the transcendental experience. One of the popular and prominent schools is that of the *advaita* (Monism). Shankaracharya (788–820 AD), popularly known as Shankara, was the chief proponent of this school. The other prominent school is *triee vada*, the theory of three eternal principles based on Vedic concepts. Dayananda Saraswathi (1824–1883 AD) was the chief proponent of this school. Swami Nikhilananda (2002), a prominent *advaita* scholar, explains that

> ultimate reality is transcendental. It is not perceived by the senses or comprehended by the mind. It is a matter of indubitable experience for the inmost consciousness of man. It is directly and immediately experienced without the instrumentality of the senses and the mind, and does not depend for its proof upon any external authority. The perception of the external world is neither direct nor immediate, but is dependent upon the senses and the mind and is always coloured by them. On the other hand, the experience of Reality is both immediate and direct,[1] and becomes possible only when the senses and the mind, through the practice of rigid spiritual discipline, have been made absolutely calm. It is the consciousness in man that experiences the Consciousness, the two being, in reality, identical. (p. 17)

According to Shankara, the human experience (being) through the body and mind is only transitory and temporary, and, hence, unreal. Supreme self (*Brahman*) is the only reality and is not subject to change, except when operating through the equipment of the body and mind as embodied self (*jeevatma*). Nothing else exists but the absolute reality (*Brahman*), of which *jeevatma* is the embodied state. This is reflected in the Sanskrit aphorism "*ekah brahma dvitiya nasti neh na naasti kincham*" ("there is only one reality; there is no second. Not at all. Not in the least") (*Brahma Sutras*, English translation by Swami Vireswarananda, 2001).

In contrast, Dayananda held the view that there are three eternal principles, whose coming together forms the human being: the *prakriti* (primordial matter, the cause of the universe), *jeevatma* (embodied self), and *paramatma* (supreme self). These three principles are all real and eternal, with their specific properties and defined relatedness. In Dayananda's view, *prakriti* provides the necessary form for the body and mind, through which the individual self needs to manifest in order to experience relatedness. *Paramatma*, whose knowledge pervades *prakriti* and *jeevatma*, makes *Janma* (embodiment) possible. *Paramatma* by itself does not engage in embodiment. There is only one *Paramatma*, one *prakriti*, but an infinite number of *jeevatmas*, all real and eternal, corresponding to all the individuals in the universe. Thus, the *jeevatma* (individual self) and *paramatma* (supreme self) are transcendental in the sense that both continue beyond a given embodiment. *Jeevatma* is subject to the limitations of experience owing to the limitations of embodiment. *Paramatma* is not limited, because it is the substratum of the entire phenomenal world (Swami Dayananda Saraswati, 1975). The multiplicity in the world is real.

A beautiful metaphor presented in the following *mantra* (stanza) of *Mundakopanishad*, elegantly describes the relationship between *prakriti*, *jeevatma*, and *Paramatma*.

Dvau suparnaa sayujaa sakhaayaa
samaanam vriksham parishasvajaate
tayoranyah pippalam swadvattyanashnannanyo
abhichaakashiti.

Mundakopanishad—
Discourses by Swami Chinmayananda, 1977,
Chapter 3, Section 1, *mantra* I

> Two birds, (*jeevatma* and *Paramatma*) bound one to the other in close friendship, perch on the same tree (*prakriti*). One of them (*jeevatma*) eats the fruits of the tree with relish, while the other (*Paramatma*) looks on without eating (in detachment).

These two schools of Hindu philosophers agree on one common theme—that the embodied self, bound to the equipment it occupies, transcends into another body, subject to certain conditions. This concept of reincarnation is referred to as *samsara*, which will be elaborated later. The two schools differ, however, in their conceptualisations of the nature of consciousness in the individuals and its relationship to the ultimate reality. The followers of *advaita* (monism) believe that there is only one experiencing agency, *atman*, and when it transcends the cycle of embodiments into a different state of awareness, it attains the state of *Brahman* (liberated self), a state not conditioned by the limitations of the body, but instead marked by pure consciousness. In the liberated state of *Brahman*, *jeevatma* (the individual self) realises that its true nature is pure consciousness. Hence, for followers of *advaita*, only one reality exists—reality of the *Brahman* (the liberated state of self). In contrast, the followers of *triee vada* (Swami Dayananda and others) believe that there are two experiencing agencies: *jeevatma* (individual self), with limited knowledge and limited consciousness owing to embodiment and its specific nature, and *paramatma* (supreme self), with infinite knowledge and pure consciousness which is the source of all experience, because it is all-pervasive and eternal. In this view, *jeevatma* is the substratum of mind and intellect and *paramatma* is the substratum of *prakriti* (primordial matter) and *jeevatmas* (individual selves). According to *triee vada*, when *jeevatma* transcends the limitations of embodiment, it attains a blissful relatedness to *Paramatma*.

The transcendental nature of the experience described by Hindu philosophers is twofold. The first aspect of transcendence is *jeevatma* transcending the limitations of a given embodiment. Followers of *advaita* believe that *jeevatma* transcends into a different state, *Brahman*. Followers of *triee vada* believe that *jeevatma* transcends into a different state of relatedness to *Brahman*. Both schools refer to this transcendence as *nirvana* (*liberation* from limitations). The second aspect of transcendence is from one embodiment into another embodiment, a process referred to as reincarnation, the cycle of birth and rebirth. *Samsara* (the experience of the phenomenal world in the embodied state) comes to an end with *nirvana*. Thus, for the Hindu philosopher, there are two consciousnesses: that of *paramatma* (supreme self) and that of *jeevatma* (the embodied self).

Preamble II: Freud

Freud revolutionised our understanding of the mind. It has become a generally accepted fact that in the mind nothing happens by chance. It is well established, as Brenner (1973) noted,

> that when a thought, a feeling, an accidental forgetting, a dream, or a pathological symptom seems to be unrelated to what went on before in the mind, it is because its causal connection is with some unconscious mental process rather than with a conscious one. If the unconscious cause or causes can be discovered, then all apparent discrepancies disappear and the causal chain or sequence becomes clear. (p. 4)

Justifying the concept of the unconscious, Freud (1915e) wrote,

> our most personal daily experience acquaints us with the ideas that come into our head we do not know from where, and with intellectual conclusions arrived at we do not know how. All these conscious acts remain disconnected and unintelligible if we insist upon claiming that every mental act that occurs in us must also necessarily be experienced by us through consciousness; on the other hand, they fall into demonstrable connections if we interpolate between them the unconscious acts which we have inferred. A gain in meaning is a perfectly justifiable ground for going beyond the limits of direct experience. When, in addition, it turns out that the assumption of there being an unconscious enables us to construct a successful procedure by which we can exert an effective influence upon the course of conscious processes, this success will have given us an incontrovertible proof of the existence of what we have assumed. (p. 166)

The successful procedure referred to here is, of course, psychoanalysis. Freud rejects the idea that what is conscious is the totality of the mental. He considered the conventional equation of the psychical with the conscious as "totally inexpedient".

Freud (1900a, 1915e), in his topographical model of mind, differentiated between three systems of mind, which he called conscious, preconscious, and unconscious. The psychic elements and processes that could become conscious by an effort of attention he called preconscious, and those that were actively barred from consciousness he called unconscious. He called conscious the state of awareness at a given moment. To avoid confusion in using the terms conscious, preconscious, and unconscious sometimes in a descriptive, sometimes in a dynamic, and sometimes in a systematic sense, Freud employed abbreviations, *Ucs.*, *Pcs.*, *Cs.*, for representing the unconscious, preconscious, and conscious, respectively, in a systematic sense.

According to Freud (1915e), a psychical act goes through two phases with regard to its state and a censorship operates between these phases. The censorship between the conscious and preconscious is more permeable than between preconscious and unconscious. To begin with, a psychical act is unconscious and belongs to the system *Ucs.* If it is prevented by censorship from gaining entry into the second phase, it is said to be repressed and remains unconscious. If it escapes censorship, it enters the second phase, gaining entry into the system *Pcs.*, in which the psychical act is available to conscious awareness in the *Cs.* only if deliberate attention is focused upon it. For an unconscious psychical element in the *Ucs.* to become conscious in the *Cs.*, repression must be overcome, and deliberate attention must be focused upon it. We will know the unconscious only when it undergoes transformation into something conscious. For this to occur, certain resistances must be overcome. Freud (1915e) noted that

> the *Ucs.* is alive and capable of development and maintains a number of other relations with the *Pcs.*, amongst them that of co-operation. In brief, it must be said that the *Ucs.* is continued into what are known as derivatives, that it is accessible to the impressions of life, that it constantly influences the *Pcs.*, and is even, for its part, subjected to influences from the *Pcs.* (p. 190)

Freud was able to show convincingly that the unconscious elements in the *Ucs.* are similar in precision and complexity to those in the *Cs.*, and exert significant influence on mental functioning. The *Cs.* is only a small part of the mind, like the proverbial tip of the iceberg.

Freud (1923b) later formulated a new tripartite model of mind, comprising the id, the ego, and the superego. Id refers to psychic representatives of the drives, the ego consists of those functions that have to do with the relationship to the environment, and the superego comprises the moral aspects of our mind as well as our aspirations. The drives are assumed to be present from birth, but the ego and the superego both develop later. The id comprises the entire psychic apparatus at birth and the ego and superego were originally part of the id, and differentiated sufficiently in the course of growth to warrant their being considered as separate functional entities. The id refers to wishes, repressed memories, and fantasies through which libidinal and aggressive drives seek expression and satisfaction. It is ruled by the pleasure principle and is only interested in discharging tensions. It

> contains everything that is inherited, that is present at birth, that is laid down in the constitution—above all, therefore, the instincts, which originate from the somatic organization and which find a first psychical expression here (In the id) in forms unknown to us. (Freud, 1940a[1938], p. 145)

Id forms a large part of the *Ucs.* and is more or less controlled by the conscious part of the ego and superego.

Freud (1923b) described ego as "the coherent organization of the mental processes" (p. 17), which "tries to mediate between the world and the id to make the id pliable to the world" (p. 56) and governed by the reality principle. The conscious part of the ego is responsible for integration of perceptual data and for decision making. The unconscious aspect of the ego comprises defense mechanisms, such as repression, which counteract the powerful drives of the id. Freud held the view that the "ego is first and foremost a body-ego" (p. 26) arising from bodily excitations and sensations. He viewed the character of the ego as "a precipitate of abandoned object cathexis containing "the history of those objects' choices" (p. 29). Freud suggested that with its qualities of reason, adaptation, and sense of reality, anxiety, and defence mechanisms, the ego is able to gain a limited mastery of the unconscious instinctual forces that affect it" (p. 26).

Freud (1923b) employed the term superego to refer to moral conscience and ego ideal, which dictate what one should not do and what one ought to do and strive for, respectively. Being more sensitive to the strivings of the id, the superego is more immediately connected with the *Ucs*. than the ego. The superego is the heir of the Oedipus complex.[2] Successful negotiations through the Oedipal phase results in the child renouncing the possessive sexual longings for the parent of the opposite sex and the hostility towards the same-sex parent by strengthening the identification with the latter and enhancing affectionate functioning towards both parents.

As I (Vallabhaneni, 2005) observed before, Strachey (1961, pp. 7–8) had noted that in some of Freud's works the term "ego" seems to correspond to the notion of "self". Other psychoanalysts (Bettleheim, 1982, and Ornston, 1982), too, pointed out that in Strachey's translation of the German phrase "*das Ich*" into English as "ego", the meaning suggestive of "self-experience" seems to have been lost. I believe that

> Freud's self is a psychological concept referring to the totality of id, ego and superego. This totality is equivalent to psychological selfhood and thus captures the meaning of Freud's das Ich that many have been lost in Strachey's translation. Hence there is also at work in his thinking a more comprehensive notion of self as the unity of psyche and soma in the individual. Ultimately psychic life owes its existence to the living human body. Freud's notion of self eschews any form of psychic or spiritual determinism. For Freud, the only psychic reality is made of the mental activity of human beings. (Vallabhaneni, 2005, p. 363)

I am aware that the concepts of structural theory and notion of self in Freud's thinking followed his paper on "The unconscious" (Freud 1915e). I hope that this detour will help us to set the stage for comparison of Freud's views on unconscious phenomena with those of the Hindu philosophers in understanding human being (human experience), which is the ultimate goal for both psychoanalysis and philosophy.

Bhagavad Gita (circa 500 BC)

According to the Hindu philosopher, every human experience involves an experience within, the proverbial I, who is the subject and the knower of the field referred to as *kshethragna*. As one relates to different personas, one assumes an appropriate relative persona and a role, such as father, son, husband, friend, etc. This is also true in relation to objects, situations, and events. In the course of these infinite experiences, some questions arise for the curious investigator: "Who is this I? Who is the experiencer? And what is the nature of the fundamental I within? Is it the subject that perceives the object or another object of perception?" Logic dictates that the knower of the object must be different from the object itself. The truth of this fundamental I, the subject, the experiencer, is the subject of enquiry of all Hindu scriptures. This was what Krishna, the great seer and philosopher, taught Arjuna, his friend and disciple, in the battlefield of *Mahabharata*, when Arjuna became despondent and paralysed, unable to carry out his duty (*dharma*) to fight in the battle. Their *dialogue* forms the literary scaffold of the *Bhagavad Gita*, a book contained within the great Hindu epic, *Mahabharata*.

The greatest hero of the time, Arjuna, came under the influence of his suppressed and repressed emotions in the battlefield as he faced the enemy army, which included his close relatives who were father surrogates, his teachers, his friends, and other, more distant relatives. Arjuna, the middle of the five Pandava brothers, was made to live twelve years in the forest and one year incognito amid the unjust tyranny of his Kaurava cousins. Bound by the righteous policy "peace at all costs", of his eldest brother Yudhisthira, Arjuna could not give vent to his anger and frustrations. After long and strenuous struggles, when the Pandava brothers reached their native kingdom, their tyrant cousin Duryodhana, the eldest of the Kauravas, denied their right to half of the kingdom and also to all terms of conciliation. Hence, the epic battle of *Mahabharata* (5000 BC) ensued. On the first day of battle, Arjuna asked Krishna, the seer, philosopher, and friend, who was also his charioteer, to drive the chariot between the two forces to review the enemy lines. Looking at the larger and better equipped enemy army, commanded by well-known warriors of the time, who were, as above, his father surrogates, teachers, friends, and distant relatives, Arjuna could not bring himself to kill them to win. His subjective mind failed to control his objective mind because of the suppressed and repressed forces released in the crisis. Arjuna, the greatest hero of the time, suddenly became a despondent, bewildered neurotic, refusing to fight. The discussion ensues between Krishna and Arjuna, wherein Krishna addressed Arjuna's neurosis and enlightened him regarding the supreme reality of human being, thereby dispelling his neurosis (*agnana*). This exchange was recorded as the *Bhagavad Gita*; its resemblance to psychotherapeutic discourse has been noted by Reddy (2001, 2005). A particular view of mind and its problems is clearly present here.

Swami Chinmayananda (2002), a great teacher and philosopher, in the introduction to his commentary on *The Holy Bhagavad Gita*, stated that the mind

> may be considered as constituted of two distinct sides—one facing the world of stimuli that reach it from the objects of the world and the other facing the 'with-in' which reacts to the stimuli received. The outer mind facing the object is called the Objective Mind—in Sanskrit we call it the *manas* and the Inner mind is called the Subjective Mind—in Sanskrit, the *buddhi*. The individual is whole and healthy in whom the objective and subjective mind work in unison and in the moments of doubt the Objective Mind readily comes under the disciplining influence of the Subjective Mind. But unfortunately, except for a rare few, the majority of us have minds that are split. This split between the subjective and objective aspects of our mind is mainly created by the layers of egoistic desires in the individual. The greater the distance between these two aspects of mind, the greater the inner confusion in the individual . . . (p. 2, original italics)

Swami Chinmayananda went on to state that an individual experiences the world through the five organs of perception in the waking state, which include ears, skin, eyes, tongue, and nose. The stimuli that are received through these sense organs are passed on to the subjective mind through the intervening layer of impressions of past desires and past actions, referred to in Sanskrit as *vasanas*. These *vasanas* find expression in the external world through the five organs of action (effectors) referred to in Sanskrit as *karmendrias*, which include the vocal cords, legs, hands, genital organs, and anus. The stimuli received through the sense organs (*gnanendrias*) are processed in the "inner organ" of the mind, *antahkarana*; referred to by different names such as *manas*, *buddhi*, *ahankara*, or *chitta*, according to its respective functions. It is called *manas* from its considering the pros and cons of a thing, *buddhi* from its property of determining the truth of objects, *ahankara*, the ego, from its identification with the body as individual self, and *chitta* from its function of remembering things it is interested in (Swami Madhavananda's commentary on

Vivekachudamani, 2000, p. 134). It must be noted that these are only functional descriptions of *antahkarana*, and not different entities in themselves.

There is a continuous build-up of new impressions in the subjective mind, adding to the already existing ones, which influence and colour the impulses arising from the fresh stimuli from the objects. Similarly, the actions upon the objects in the external world also generate new impressions in the subjective mind. As a result of this build-up of the *vasanas*, an impregnable wall forms between the individual self and the supreme self. This wall renders the subjective mind dull and opaque. As a result, the awareness in the individual self (*jeevatma*) of its relationship with the supreme self (*Paramatma*) becomes dull and even unconscious. In summary, the *vasanas* are the main reservoir of unconscious states in the metaphorical structure of mind in Hindu philosophy.

Vasanas create desires in the mind, desires produce thoughts in the intellect, and thoughts manifest in the form of actions. Thus, the human being is determined by *vasanas*. *Vasanas* are generated by the contact of the individual self, *ahankara* (the ego), with the world of objects in the past and in the present. The stronger the *vasanas*, the more the individual (*jeevatma*) is subject to unconscious urges; the more one is controlled by one's urges, the greater are the "Bhagavad Gitations" in the mind. *Vasanas* kindle more desires, and more desires kindle more *vasanas*. The conditions of the body, mind, and intellect must be transcended in order for the self to regain (realise) its true nature and its relationship with the absolute reality. In other words, the reservoir of *vasanas* is to be cleared (exhausted) and, for this, one's desires, thoughts, and actions need to be corrected. This correction is possible only through the mental and spiritual aspects of the practice of yoga, aided by the study of philosophy. Only by the practice of actions without egoistic desires (*nishkama karma*), one achieves a purgation of already existing *vasanas*, and such actions also prevent further build-up of *vasanas*, which is an essential prerequisite for *yoga*. Through *yoga* only, the individual self realises its true nature and "comes to being" in relationship with the ultimate reality. "Selfless activity (*nishkama karma*) performed in a spirit of egoless adoration and reverence to the divine ideal (Supreme Self) would ultimately result in inner purification" (Swami Chinmayananda, 2002, p. 6).

Swami Chinmayananda points out that an experience is not possible without three fundamental factors (i) the experiencer, (ii) the object to experience and, (iii) the relationship between the two, the experiencing. When the subject identifies with the intellect, he becomes the thinker, experiencing the world of thoughts and ideas. When identified with the mind, he becomes the feeler, experiencing the world of emotions and feelings, and when identified with the body, he becomes the perceiver, experiencing the world of objects, thus acting out different roles as thinker, feeler and perceiver.

The physical body, including the five organs of perception and the five organs of action and their functions, are common to all humans. Also, the consciousness (*Om*), which is the core of man's composite personality, is one and the same in all human beings. The variable factor in man is the mind and intellectual equipment, which is the reservoir of *vasanas*. Animals also possess a mind, but man alone has the capacity to discriminate and analyse his feelings and thoughts as and when they arise. He also can allow his actions to be guided and directed by his power of discrimination (*viveka*) instead of being driven and carried away by momentary impulses and feelings. This faculty of discrimination, *viveka*, is the function of the intellect. This schema of the overall human being is represented in the following diagram:

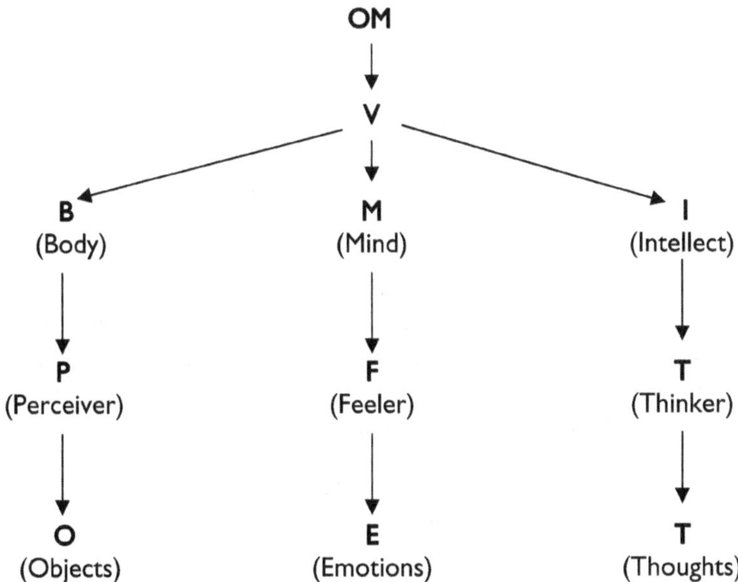

In the above diagram, *Om,* the symbol for the supreme consciousness, viewed through the veil of *vasanas*, expresses itself through the instruments of body (B), mind (M), and intellect (I), that is, the embodied self (*jeevatma*), and is as perceiver (P), feeler (F), and thinker (T). All these are the functional manifestations of *jeevatma,* in order to experience the object (O), emotion (E), and the thought (T). In the Hindu models of mind presented above, a great significance is accorded to the latent memory impressions of present and past (*vasanas*).

The specific properties of the supreme reality (*Om*), the knower of the human experience, and the process of knowing (knowledge) of the field of experience (body, mind, intellect, and the object world) are described in the following exchange between Krishna and Arjuna in the *Bhagavad Gita.*[3]

Arjuna asks Krishna:

> "*Prakritim purusham chaiva kshetram khetragnameva cha*
> *etad veditum icchaami gnanam gneyam cha kesava*"
>
> (*Bhagavad Gita*, XIII-1)

Translation: O'Krishna! I desire to learn about the primordial nature, the individual and supreme consciousness; the field of experience and activity; the knower of the field; and the knowledge and the object of knowledge.

Krishna replies:

> "*Maha Bhutan ahankaro buddhir avyaktam eva cha*
> *Indriyani dasaikam cha pancha chendriya gocharaha*"
>
> (*Bhagavad Gita*, XIII-6)

Translation: O'Arjuna! The field of experience and activity includes the five great elements of earth, water, air, fire, and ether. It also includes the ego, the intellect, and the lingering impressions of past actions. The ten senses together with the mind and the five objects of the senses including sound, sight, smell, touch, and taste constitute the field of activity and experience.

> "*Iccha dveshaha sukham dukham sanghatas chetana dhrutihi*
> *etah kshetram samasena savikaram udahatam*"
>
> (*Bhagavad Gita*, XIII-7)

Translation: The field of experience and activity also includes the body and the faculties of perception, desire and disdain, pleasure and pain, intelligence and forbearance, together with the alterations and derivatives of all these.

Krishna continues:

> "*Gneyam Yat tat pravakshami yaj gnatva mrutam asnute*
> *Anadi mat-param Brahma na sat tan nasad uchyate*"
>
> (*Bhagavad Gita*, XIII-13)

Translation: O'Arjuna! Now I will explain to you the Supreme Reality which must be known and by knowing which one achieves immortality. Being a state of pure consciousness, it has neither a beginning nor an end. It is neither a cause nor an effect. It is described as the Brahman or the ultimate truth.

> "*Sarvendriya gunabhasam Sarvendriya vivarjitam*
> *Asaktam sarva-bhruc chaiva nirgunam guna-bhoktrucha*"
>
> (*Bhagavad Gita*, XIII-15)

Translation: That consciousness, that is, of Atman, manifests through the functions of all the bodily senses and yet is devoid of materiality. It is unattached and yet forms the substrate, mind, and intellect. It is free from material qualities and yet it is the experiencer of the same.

> "*Bahir antaras cha Bhutanam acharam charam eva cha*
> *Sukshmatvat tad avigneyam durastham chanthike cha tat*"
>
> (*Bhagavad Gita*, XIII-16)

Translation: Being all pervasive, the Supreme Consciousness is present within and without all animate and inanimate beings. It is both stationary and moving, very near and yet far away. Being very subtle, it is nearly incomprehensible.

> "*Avibhktam cha bhuteshu vibhaktamiva cha sthitam*
> *Bhuta-bhartru cha taggneyam grasishnu prabhavishnu cha*"
>
> (*Bhagavad Gita*, XIII-17)

Translation: The Supreme Reality is undivided and yet appears to be divided among various beings. It is to be recognised as the substratum of the living beings and the creator and the destroyer of the object world.

> "*Jyotishm api taj jyotis tamasaha param uchyate*
> *Gnanam gneyam gnana-gamyam hrudi sarvasya vishtitam*"
>
> (*Bhagavad Gita*, XIII-18)

Translation: The Brahman is described as the illuminator of all that is beyond the darkness of ignorance. It is the knowledge and the object of knowledge, present in hearts of all. This state of Supreme Consciousness is attained only by the direct knowledge of the self.

Juxtaposing Freud and Hinduism

In an attempt to decipher the convergences and divergences between Freud's and Hinduism's view of the unconscious, I will divide my comments into the following six categories: (i) desire, (ii) timelessness, (iii) motivation, (iv) libido and aggression, (v) word and thing presentations, and (vi) psychophysical parallelism.

Desire

According to Freud (1915e) the nucleus of the unconscious consists of wishful impulses. He writes, "Unconscious processes pay just as little regard to reality. They are subject to the pleasure principle, their fate depends only on whether they fulfil the demands of the pleasure–unpleasure principle regulation" (p. 186). Describing the contents of the system *Ucs.*, Freud wrote (1915e),

> To sum up the characteristics of the system *Ucs.*: exemption from material contradiction, primary process (mobility of cathexis), timelessness, and replacement of external by psychical reality—these are the characteristics which we may expect to find in processes belonging to the system *Ucs* . . . Unconscious process only becomes cognizable by us under the conditions of dreaming and neuroses, that is to say when processes of the higher, *Pcs.* system are set back to an earlier stage by being lowered (by regression). (p. 187)

Ucs. also includes compromise formation, no negation, and no degrees of certainty. Freud considered latent memories as an "unquestionable" residuum of a psychical process. He rejected the idea that what is conscious is the totality of the mental. Referring to the latent states of mental life, Freud (1915e) noted,

> As far as their physical characteristics are concerned, they are totally inaccessible to us. No physiological concept or chemical process can give us any notion of their nature. On the other hand, we know for certain that they have abundant points of contact with conscious mental processes . . . the only respect in which they differ from conscious ones is precisely in the absence of consciousness. (p. 168)

Study of parapraxes, neurotic symptoms, and dreams bear indisputable proof of the psychical character of the latent mental acts. Freud (1915e) rejected the existence of a second consciousness in us, but argued in favour of the existence of psychical acts that lack consciousness. Freud (1915e) stated

> in psychoanalysis there is no choice but to assert that mental processes are in themselves unconscious, and to liken the perception of them by means of consciousness to the perception of the external world by means of the sense organs. (p. 171)

Perception of the *Ucs.* and the external world is never complete.

The unconscious in the Hindu model of the mind regards *Vasanas* (latent impressions of past actions) as providing the basis for the concept of reincarnation—the cycle of birth and rebirth in Hindu thought. As in Freud, there is no physiological or chemical explanation for the notion of the nature of *vasanas*. *Vasanas* are recognised only by their derivatives. And, similar to Freud's *Ucs.*, there are the concepts of timelessness and wish-dominance in *vasanas*, and these are also evident in the concept of reincarnation. Swami Chinmayananda (2002) writes,

> correct philosophical thinking guides man's intellect to the apprehension of continuity from the past—through the present —to the endless future. The spirit remaining the same, it gets seemingly conditioned by different body-equipments and comes to live through its self-ordained environments. (p. 66)

In *Bhagavad Gita*, Krishna says to Arjuna:

> *"Na jayate mriyate va kadachin nayam bhutva bhavitha va na bhuyaha*
> *Ajo nityaha saswatoyam purano na hanyate hanyamane sareere"*
>
> (*Bhagavad Gita*, II-20)

Translation: *Atman* is never born and never dies. It does not ever come into being nor does it ever cease to exist. It is eternal, changeless, and timeless. It does not die when the body dies.

Swami Chinmayananda (2002) comments, "This stanza labours to deny in the self, all the symptoms of mutability that are recognized and experienced by the body" (p. 80). These changes in the body, including birth, existence, growth, decay, disease, and death are common to all individuals.

Krishna continues:

> "*Vasamsi jeernani yadha vihaya navani gruhnathi naroparani*
> *Tadha sareerani vihaya jeernany anyani samyathi navani dehi*"
>
> (*Bhagavad Gita*, II-22)

Translation: Just as a man gives up his worn-out garments in favour of the new ones, the embodied soul gives up the worn-out body and enters a new one.

At the time of death, *vasanas* are carried over into the subtle body (*sookshma sareera*) which includes the three organs of action (hands, legs, and vocal organs), five organs of perception (eyes, ears, skin, nose, and tongue), five vital forces (*Pranas*); the mind (*manas*), the intellect (*buddhi*)m the ego (*ahankara*), the inflated sense of I, and the memory *(chitta*), that recollects the past experiences.

Timelessness

Vasanas, creating new *vasanas*, lead to a continuous cycle of birth and rebirth. This pattern implies a certain psychic determinism in the reincarnation concept. Swami Chinmayananda (2002), points out

> that which determines one man's personality as distinctly different from others, it is very well known, is the texture of the thoughts entertained by him. The texture of his thoughts is, again, in its turn, determined by the pattern of thinking (*vasanas*), which his mind has gained from its own past. (p. 221)

These predetermined "channels of thinking" created by one's own earlier ways of thinking (*vasanas*), determine the forms of the bodies taken in future and the circumstances around the birth in the world of objects.

Unlike in Freud, this determinism is spiritual, transcending birth, death, and time. Implicit in the concept of reincarnation is the idea of continuity, timelessness, and wish-fulfilment. *Atman* assumes the body (birth), only to fulfil the wishes in the reservoir of *vasanas*. Properties of eternity of *atman*, *paramatma*, and *prakriti* also point to timelessness. According to Freud, timelessness is one of the features of *Ucs*. In his model, there is no notion of reincarnation, but in the *Ucs* there is also no awareness of birth or death. Freud (1915e) maintains, "Reference to time is bound up once again with the work of the system *Cs*." (p. 187).

It is worth emphasising that, in Hindu thought, there are two types of determinism: psychic determinism (paralleling Freud) caused by the *vasanas* regarding the choice of action and thought, and spiritual determinism (not present in Freud's model) caused by *atman* in its effort to realise its true nature, that is, to be that of *Brahman*, as in *advaita* or in *jeevatma*'s efforts to attain communion with *paramatma*, as in *triee vada*.

Both the Hindu and Freudian models deny the presence of negation in the unconscious. However, Freud posits tolerance of contradiction in the *Ucs*., whereas in Hindu thought, contradiction is recognised at the level of *vasanas*, but not at the level of *atman* or *paramatma*, because the *vasanas* relate to the phenomenal world, and the *atman* and *paramatma* are transcendental. Freud (1915e) noted

> the nucleus of the Unconscious consists of instinctual representations (drives) which seek to discharge their catharsis, that is to say, it consists of wishful impulses. These instinctual impulses co-ordinate with one another, and are exempt from mutual contradictions. (p. 186)

Id is the reservoir of the instincts (drives) and forms the bulk of the unconscious.

Freud maintained that instinctual forces energise and impel the mind. Freud employed the word *drive* to denote a state of central excitation or tension in response to stimulation, not including the motor response, as in the case of "an instinct" in lower animals. The activity impelled by drives leads to either a cessation of excitation or tension or gratification. Hartmann (1948) pointed out that in humans the drive or the instinctual tension will be modified by experience and reflection, instead of being predetermined, as in the case with the instincts of lower animals.

Motivation

Freud also assumed that there is a psychic energy that is a part of the drives. This is only a psychological hypothesis that he employed to facilitate understanding of the mental life and not to be confused with the concept of physical energy. Further, Freud postulated a hypothetical measurement of the quantum of psychic energy invested in a mental representation of a person or a thing and called it *cathexis*. Brenner (1973) noted,

> Cathexis is purely a mental phenomenon. It is a Psychological, not a Physical concept . . . what are cathected of course, are various memories, thoughts and fantasies of the object which comprise what we call its mental or psychic representatives. The greater the cathexis, the more important the object is, psychologically speaking and vice versa. (p. 18)

Freud (1915e) initially proposed two instincts: sexual and self-preservative. Later, he (1920g) abandoned this duality and proposed two different instincts: those of life and death. The former gave rise to the erotic component of the mental apparatus and the latter to its destructive component. Freud maintained that sexual and aggressive drives participate in all instinctual manifestations, and are "regularly fused", though not necessarily in equal amounts. Like psychic energy and cathexis, these drives are only hypotheses and operational concepts. Freud employed the term "libido" to indicate the psychic energy associated with the sexual drive. Aggressive drive has no such name and is simply referred to as "aggressive drive" or "aggression". Brenner (1973) noted,

> In his original formulation, Freud attempted to relate the psychological theory of the drives to more fundamental biological concepts and proposed that the drives be called life and death drives respectively. These drives would correspond approximately to the processes of anabolism and catabolism and would have much more than psychological significance. They would be instinctual characteristics of all living matter—instincts of protoplasm itself as it were. (p. 21)

The concept of death drive is accepted by some analysts and not by others. Although Freud first defined a drive as a stimulus of mind which came from the body (Freud, 1905d) "in the case of aggressive drive the evidence for somatic basis is not at all clear" (Brenner, 1973, p. 22).

According to Hindu philosophers, *vasanas* impel the human mind and *gunas* impel *vasanas*. The influences under which the thoughts function in the mind and intellect are referred to as *gunas*. Thus, *gunas* are the driving force of the unconscious. There are three *gunas*: *rajas* (passion), *tamas* (inertia), and *satva* (tranquillity). *Guna* in Sanskrit means a rope. *Gunas* are the influences with which *atman* is metaphorically tied to the field (the body, mind, intellect, and the object world). The *gunas* are born of *Prakrit* (matter). Being products of the field, they generate a feeling of attachment, and both cause and are caused by *vasanas* that impel *atman* to go through the cycle of birth and rebirth.

Gunas are psychological in nature, in contrast to the drives, which are biological in origin. The *gunas* have no separate existence as attributes inherent in a substance. The *gunas* do not exist in a separate state in the individual. They are always in a fused state with each other in different proportions of each. An individual mind experiences and behaves according to the mood generated by the predominating *gunas* at any particular moment of observation. *Atman*, though indestructible and changeless, because of its identification and attachment to the field (body, mind, intellect, and object world) feels the changes in the field as its own. This illusion is maintained in the individual by the play of the *gunas*. *Gunas* cannot be defined directly, but are identified by the types of emotions that are aroused in, and distinct behaviours displayed by, an individual.

Libido and aggression

Fulfilment of sensuous and aesthetic desires is referred to as *kama* in Sanskrit. It includes both erotic and non-erotic desires if some thing or a person obstructs the fulfilment of a desire, *krodha* (the emotion of anger) results. Thus, *kama* (desire) under certain circumstances, gains expression as *krodha*. These emotions are the expressions of *rajas* (passion).

Krishna, in the *Bhagavad Gita*, cautions Arjuna against giving in to *rajas*:

> "*Kama esha, krodha esha, rajo-guna-samudbhavah,*
> *Mahashano maha-papma viddhy enam iha vairinam*"
>
> (*Bhagavad Gita*, III-37)

Translation: O'Arjuna! It is the desire arising from all consuming and sinful passion that turns into anger. Know this to be the greatest enemy in the world and know that one must control such passions and desires.

Here we see some similarities and real differences between Freud's thinking and that of the Hindu philosopher. Freud's conceptualisation of drives is anchored in the soma (body). Hindu philosophers' thinking about *gunas* and *kamas* is anchored in the psychology of emotions. The concept of fusion is common to drives in Freud and *gunas* in Hindu philosophy. The concept of "*kama*" is similar to the concept of "libido" in Freud. Aggression is closely associated with the concept of *kama* in Hindu thought. *Krodha* is a derivative of *kama*, which is "undifferentiated desire". *Gunas* are similar to drives in Freud, but different in that they are qualities and, hence, are of psychological nature. For Freud, the objective is mature instinctual satisfaction, whereas for the Hindu philosopher the objective is that of controlling, mastering, and transcending *gunas* and *kama*.

In Freud, the system *Ucs.* is governed by the pleasure principle, and external reality is replaced by psychic reality, which is illusory. The fate of the unconscious processes depends upon how strong they are and upon whether they fulfil the demands of the regulation of pleasure–unpleasure. Similar to Freud, in Hindu thinking the experience of reality is an illusion caused by *ahankara* (psychic reality), which results from *atman's* identification with mind, body, and intellect. This leads to *avidya* (microcosmic ignorance of the embodied self). This needs to be corrected in order to achieve self-realisation.

In Freud's formulation, drives impel the mental apparatus. In the Hindu philosophers' model of mind *Prana* (the vital breath) sustains life in the physical body. *Prana* is the primal energy or force, of which other physical forces are manifestations. In books of yoga, *Prana* is described as having five modifications, according to its five different functions. These are: (1) *Prana* (the vital energy that controls the breath), (2) *apana* (the vital energy that carries downward unassimilated food and drink), (3) *samana* (the vital energy that carries nutrition all over the body), (4) *vyana* (the vital energy that pervades entire body), and (5) *udana* (the vital energy by which the contents of the stomach are ejected through the mouth) (Swami Nikhilananda, 2002, p. 139).

Freud's concept of instincts includes dynamic, topographical, and economic points of view and attempts "to follow out the vicissitudes of amounts of excitation and to arrive at least at some relative estimate of their magnitude" (Freud 1915e, p. 181). This, I think, is the result of the influence of the linear sciences of biology and physics of his time. We do not find concepts similar to the economic point of view in Hindu philosophy. The structural hypothesis is a later formulation, which incorporated but did not replace the topographical view, which continues to contribute considerably to the understanding of clinical situations. According to the Hindu philosophers' view, *ahankara* (identification with the body) is the deepest *vasana* in an individual. This metaphorical location is analogous to the concepts in Freud's topographical view of the *Ucs*. In addition, the expression of *vasanas* in the birth and rebirth cycle implies a dynamic point of view.

Anxiety is common to both the Hindu philosopher and Freud. Mastering the agitation caused by emotions in the unconscious of *vasanas* through the practice of yoga is the goal for the Hindu philosopher, whereas for Freud, making the conflicts concerning these instincts conscious and dealing with them is the goal of psychoanalysis. According to him, successfully repressed affects exist as actual structures in the unconscious. Freud (1915e) noted,

> it is possible for the development of affect to proceed directly from the system *Ucs*., in that case the affect always has the character of anxiety, for which all repressed affects are exchanged. Often however, the instinctual impulse has to wait until it has formed a substitutive idea in the system *Cs*. The development of affect can proceed from this conscious substitute, and the nature of that substitute determines the qualitative character of the affect. (p. 179)

This is unique to Freud's thinking and there is no parallel concept noted in the Hindu philosophical thought.

Word and thing presentations

Repression leads to repetition compulsion of the unconscious psychic elements, which find expressions in the *Cs*. by finding substitutes. Freud (1915e) described the difference between the conscious and unconscious presentations:

> The two are not, as we supposed, different registrations of the same content in different Psychical localities, nor yet different functional states of cathexis in the same locality; but the conscious presentation comprises the presentation of thing plus the presentation of the word belonging to it, while the unconscious presentation is the presentation of the thing alone. The system *Ucs.* contains the thing—cathexis of the object, the first and true object cathexis, the system *Pcs.* comes about by this thing presentation being hypercathected through being linked with the word presentations linked to it. It is these hypercathexes, we may suppose, that bring about a higher Psychical organization and make it possible for the primary process to be succeeded by the secondary process which is dominant in *Pcs.* (p. 201)

A psychical act that is not attached to the word representation remains in the *Ucs.* in a state of repression.

We find a similar, though not identical, idea in Hindu philosophical thought. *Brahman*, the ultimate reality, is represented by the symbol "Om", which is composed of three Sanskrit letters "AOM". *Om* is the sacred name given to *paramatma* in all the four *vedas*, "This one name comprises many other names given to paramatma like *Virat, Agni, Viswa* . . ." etc. (Swami Dayananda, 1975, p. ii). *Om* is a sacred syllable for Hindus, representing *Brahman*: the impersonal absolute, omnipotent, omnipresent, ineffable, and incomprehensible ultimate reality. *Om* is also called *Pranava*. It is believed to be the basic sound of the word, containing all other sounds. Hindus believe that if it is repeated with correct intonation it can resonate through the body and activate the experience of consciousness sustaining the body and the object world. On the one hand, *Om* projects the mind beyond what is immediate and ineffable. On the other hand, it makes the ineffable more tangible. The day-to-day life of Hindus resonates with the sounds of *Om*, as every activity and prayer is started with chanting *Om*. *Om* provides word representation to the ineffable.

In Freud, word representation is necessary for the thing representation in the unconscious to become conscious, but for the Hindu philosopher, meditation on *OM* is very helpful in experiencing the ineffable, the absolute truth and the Brahman. In Freud, the thing belongs to the unconscious, which needs to find attachment to the word representation to experience the phenomenal world, but to the Hindu philosopher, the experience of *OM*, the thing is transcendental and spiritual, which is the ultimate goal of life.

For both the Hindu philosopher and Freud, the mind and intellect (the psychosomatic complex) is the seat of perception and action (reaction). The stimulus for desire—the instinct—arises from input from the object, through the five organs of perception, and forms the drive, a mental representation (the impression of latent memories, *vasanas*) that again is expressed in its pursuit of satisfaction from the object. Without the stimuli from the object world, there is no present experience or activation of previous memory impressions, both for Freud and the Hindu philosopher.

Psychophysical parallelism

Until the end of his life, Freud hoped that neuroscience would develop a method to explain the complex nature of the human mind. During his time, neuroscience had not advanced enough to provide such explanations. Freud successfully resisted giving in to "unsolvable difficulties of psycho-physical parallelism" (Freud, 1915e) and continued to develop psychoanalytic concepts and theories, awaiting discoveries that would establish physiological explanations for psychological states and processes. He wrote, "after we have completed our psychoanalytic work, we shall have to find a point of contact with Biology" (Freud, 1915e, p. 175). With the advent of neurophysiology (Alexander Romanovich Luria, 1902–1977), doors have been opened to identify neurological organisation of mental functions "without contradicting the fundamental assumptions of psychoanalysis". These advancements have enabled psychoanalysts (Kaplan-Solms & Solms, 2000) to identify the anatomical and physiological basis for psychological concepts. Solms (1998) recommended

> that we chart the neurological organization of the deepest strata of the mind, using a psychoanalytic version of syndrome analysis by studying the deep structure of mental changes that can be discerned in neurological patients with a psychoanalytic relationship.

Freud's efforts and dreams continue. It is to be hoped that we will find more answers soon.

The origins of Hindu philosophical thought go back to ancient times and there is no adequate frame to integrate modern scientific advances with Hindu philosophy. The metaphysical thinking of the

Hindu philosopher does not correspond to the scientific thought of the modern western world. It may be noted that there are scientific, post-Freudian models of unconscious phenomena which are much more compatible with scientific thinking, but these are not encompassed by the focus of this chapter.

Summary and conclusions

In my attempt to compare and contrast Freud's views on the unconscious with those of the Hindu philosophers, I noticed some striking similarities and differences, which I presented above in detail. I believe that the similarities are due to the common goal of these two disciplines, which is to understand the human being and human behaviour. The differences, I believe, are due to the methodology employed in this pursuit of understanding human being. At this point of our enquiry, it is worth recalling some of the ideas we started with.

- Freud's views are clinical and psychoanalytic, and are grounded in philosophical materialism. The body is the substratum for the mind and the experience of the phenomenal world ceases after the death of the individual. The inevitability of death is something to come to terms with. For Freud, the only reality is the reality of unconscious, that is, the psychic reality. The Hindu philosophers' views are grounded in the metaphysical and spiritual, as opposed to the materialism in Freudian theories. *Atman* and *paramatman* are spiritual concepts. *Atman* is the substratum of the body, mind, intellect, and the object world. *Paramatman* is the substratum for the *atman* and the phenomenal world in which *jeevatmas* operate. True reality is experienced only when *jeevatma* transcends into the state of *Brahman*, which is the ultimate reality in the Hindu philosophers' thinking. This reality is incomprehensible to *ahanakara*, the congregate of body, mind, intellect, and the object world. The notion of transcendental reality is not present in Freud's view, according to which, experience of the phenomenal world ceases with death.
- Freud was able to establish incontrovertible evidence for the presence of the unconscious in his clinical work and successfully

convey his understandings through his theoretical formulations. The Hindu philosophers' methodology is highly subjective, and, hence, not available for objective validation as in Freud. Also, the theoretical formulation and the language Hindu philosophers used to convey their concepts, avoiding reification of the ineffable, are difficult to understand.

- The characteristics of *Ucs.* described by Freud are applicable only to the experience in the phenomenal world and are quite similar to those described by the Hindu philosophers. The mind, in Hindu thought, is only one part of the metaphorical system that captures the human experience. *Atman* sustains the body, mind, intellect, and the object world, whereas *paramatman* sustains *atman* and body, mind, intellect, and the object world complex. *Atman* and *Brahmnan* are spiritual concepts. As such, there is a spiritual determinism operating which determines the nature of the human experience. This notion of transcendence is difficult to comprehend and accept without tangible evidence.
- Fulfilling the demands of mature instincts is Freud's goal, whereas controlling the demands of instincts and transcending *gunas* is the goal for the Hindu philosopher. For Freud, there is only one consciousness in the body–mind complex. For the Hindu philosopher, there are two forms of consciousness for *atman*: one is the embodied state and the other is the liberated state. *Ucs.* in Freud is impelled by drives, psychic energy, and cathexis, whereas the unconscious in the Hindu philosophers' conceptualisation, which is the congregate of *vasanas* and *ahankara* (ego), is impelled by *gunas* and *prana*. *Prana* is the supraordinate spiritual energy. There is no unconsciousness for either *atman* or *paramatman*. The consciousness of *jeevatma* is limited due to embodiment and the consciousness of *paramatma* is unlimited, as it is never embodied.
- In Freud's unconscious, there is no notion of death. In the conceptualisation of the Hindu philosopher, death is a transitory experience in the cycle of birth, death, and rebirth; none the less the prospect of death of the body causes anxiety in all. Freud put forth the concept of "death drive", which is anchored in the biology of the body. In Hindu thought, death is subject to spiritual determinism and is the result of *atman* passing on to another body. *Atman* goes through the cycle of birth, death, and rebirth in order

to clear the *vasanas* to reach the goal of self-realisation. There is also a denial of death implied in the Hindu concept of reincarnation. There is no death for *atman* or *paramatman*. They are eternal and changeless. The concepts of negation, contradiction, pleasure principle, drives, cathexis, energy, and primary process are similar in Hindu thought and Frued's formulation, but they apply only to the experience of the phenomenal world. These features are not present in *Brahman*, as it is pure consciousness.

- The Hindu philosophers' thinking is aspirational and not constricted by observations of the experience in the phenomenal world. They focus on pursuing the ultimate reality, which, to them, is transcendental. Their objective is attainment of self-realisation. Freud's thinking is explanatory, descriptive, and grounded in science. For Freud, there is no reality other than the psychic reality. His objective is recognising and understanding the unconscious in order to gain instinct mastery, self-integration, self-fulfilment, autonomy, and acceptance of loss, pain, and the inevitability of death.

Grotstein (2001) was right when he wrote,

> religion and psychoanalysis are parallel disciplines that have been examining the same myths and realities from different vertices. They converge in philosophy. Religion, particularly in its spiritual dimension, is more psychoanalytic than it ever suspected and conversely psychoanalysis is more spiritual than . . . it has yet recognized. (p. 325)

Psychoanalysis is very helpful in understanding the unconscious, but falls short in providing satisfactory understanding of the spiritual dimension of the human experience. So far, the common explanation offered by psychoanalysts has been that spiritualism is defensive and spiritual practices and experiences are regressive because of the "unconscious at work". Just as the unconscious does not cease to exist simply because one does not acknowledge it, the urge to know the answer to the proverbial Hindu philosophers' question "who am I" will not stop arising. Recent explosion of interest in spirituality among psychoanalysts (Coltart, 1992; Grotstein, 2001; Rubin, 1996) and an increase in the number of university programmes teaching and researching mediation across the Western world is reflective of an urge for understanding and gaining control of the mind from an alternate perspective.

Freud's discovery of the unconscious opened the floodgates to the understanding of the mind. He (1927c) acknowledged that the explanations of meditative and religious experiences as regressive do not negate their validity. I believe that the time is ripe for us to push the boundaries of psychoanalysis to gain understanding of these alternative formulations of mind and human being like those of the Hindu philosophers. Such efforts can only enrich our knowledge of the mind.

Notes

1. The resemblance of this enunciation to Bion's (1970) concept of "O" is striking. Bion used this term to denote that ultimate truth of the moment, or for the "thing-in-itself", which is immeasurable. In explicating this notion, Akhtar (2009a) states that

> this truth is out there waiting to be found by a receptive mind that has emptied itself of preconception, memory, and desire. Acquired knowledge can prepare the platform from which the leap of faith is taken, but it is leaving knowledge and experience behind that constitutes a step towards "O". (p. 192)

Akhtar proposes that Bion's "O" is a truncated form of Om, the Sanskrit word for the omnipresent Creator. He goes on to state that

> this is likely in light of the fact that Bion grew up until the age of eight in India, where he was taken care of by a Hindu maid who took him to many Hindu temples and exposed him to the chants of the word 'Om'. (p. 192)

2. Six decades later, Blos (1985) would clarify that the superego is the heir of the positive Oedipus complex and the ego ideal that of the negative Oedipus complex.

3. A word of caution must be entered as far as the translations of Sanskrit verses are concerned. These translations are mine, and although I am fluent in Sanskrit, it is not my mother tongue. This complicates the process of translation, which, in the case of poetry, is already riddled with difficulties. Dependent, to a considerable degree, upon the prosodic elements of language, poetry travels poorly across cultures. Akhtar (1999) has noted that while great prose has been written in a later adopted language (e.g., by Eugene Ionesco, Samuel Beckett, Vladimir Nabokov, and Salman Rushdie), there is no record of great poetry in a language other than one's mother tongue. Mindful of the difficulties in the path of translating the poetic passages of *Bhagavad Gita*, I have taken the "safer" path of rendering them in prose.

5

The repressed maternal in Freud's topography of mind

Kenneth Wright

Introduction

Although the idea of an unconscious mental life did not begin with Freud but was part of the intellectual background of his time (Ellenberger, 1970), the concept he inherited was purely descriptive, and referenced the fact that consciousness embraced only a small part of knowledge and memory at any particular moment, everything outside this point of consciousness being unconscious. It was not until Freud had worked clinically with hysterical patients, first with Charcot and later with Breuer (Freud (with Breuer), 1895d), that the concept of a *dynamic* unconscious began to take shape; as the evidence accumulated that hysterical symptoms were constructed from *unconscious* memories of traumatic events, the idea that psychic material could be *repressed*, and *actively maintained* in an unconscious state, became increasingly compelling. Freud soon realised he had stumbled on a powerful explanatory tool and began to apply it to other psychological phenomena. Jokes, parapraxes, slips of the tongue, and neurotic symptoms were, in turn, illuminated by its heuristic searchlight, and before long he had used it to unravel the mystery of dreams. By the time he had finished writing *The Interpretation of Dreams* (1900a), a work he regarded as his *magnum opus*, he had forged a more or less coherent theory of the dynamic unconscious and delineated what he saw as its major systemic features (system Ucs.).

In his metapsychological paper, "The unconscious" (Freud, 1915e), written fifteen years later, Freud takes stock of his theoretical achievements.[1] I stress the word "theoretical" because the work is a very abstract piece of writing and Freud himself was concerned on this account. While in *Studies on Hysteria*, he worries "that [his] case histories . . . read like short stories and . . . lack the serious stamp of science" (Freud (with Breuer), 1895d, p. 160), in "The unconscious" his doubts are of an opposite kind—he fears that the argument might be too abstract. He thinks that it "gives the impression of obscurity and confusion" (Freud, 1915e, p. 196), and is mindful of the danger that "when we think in abstractions . . . we may neglect the relation of words to unconscious thing-presentations, and . . . our philosophizing then begins to acquire an unwelcome resemblance to the mode of operation of schizophrenics" (Freud, 1915e, p. 204).

Although he is speaking with tongue in cheek, his anxiety about over-abstraction might still be justified. The text does not readily evoke imaginable realities and in spite of the assertion that his theory "meet[s] the results of observation: (Freud, 1915e, p. 190), it is hard to lay hold of the "thing-presentations" that correspond to the words he uses. While "word-presentation" and "thing-presentation" evoke at least a shadow of the experiential, other terms, such as "cathexis" and "anti-cathexis", seem curiously disembodied. At best, they evoke a mechanical structure of forces and counter-forces which is not well suited to the representation of living processes.

Freud blames these difficulties on the complexities of mental structure, but a more personal anxiety might have influenced his style. Psychoanalysis has always been vulnerable to criticism from the scientific community, and if Freud felt that his scientific reputation was at stake, the need to present his ideas in a "scientific" language would have been intense. The scientific requirement of "objectivity" is at variance with "story-like" origins, and it might be for this reason that Freud recast his clinical ideas in such an experience-distant form.[2] From this perspective, the topographical model emerges as a compromise formation; in a superficial reading, it appears as disembodied and depersonalised, but barely concealed behind its "scientific" language form, is a more lively set of ideas that refuse to be suppressed.[3]

Mechanism *vs.* agency

If one steps back from the dry terminology of Freud's paper and listens to the feel of the writing, there is a moment near the end of the final section when his somewhat tortuous struggle with disembodied ideas gives way to a quickened and lighter rhythm. The altered mood might not mark a *eureka* experience—in fact, he is *re*discovering something he has always known. Nevertheless, the writing conveys a renewed sense of life and a feeling of getting back on track:

> *We now seem to know all at once* what the difference is between a conscious and an unconscious presentation. The two are not, as we supposed, different registrations of the same content in different psychic localities, nor yet different functional states of cathexis in the same locality; but the conscious presentation comprises the presentation of the thing *plus* the presentation of the word belonging to it, while the unconscious presentation is the presentation of the thing alone. The system Ucs. contains the thing-cathexes of the objects, *the first and true object-cathexes*; the system Pcs. comes about through this thing-presentation being hypercathected *through being linked with the word presentation corresponding to it*. (Freud, 1915e, 201–202, my italics)

The mechanistic terms are still in place, but, in spite of this, something seems to have come together; Freud has rediscovered the importance of linking words with the "body" of experience, "*the first and true object-cathexes*". The system Pcs., overlapping with what he later calls the "ego", "comes about *through this thing-presentation . . . being linked with the word-presentation corresponding to it*". In re-establishing a link with the living base of his thinking, Freud has reintegrated something within himself, and having previously rid himself of the "body" of his ideas in the interests of "science", he can now re-envisage it in a moment of understanding.

This renewed grasp of his topic includes a clearer view of repression, a concept central to his theory of the dynamic unconscious as the realm of banished thing-presentations:

> Now too we are in a position to state precisely what it is that repression *denies* to the *rejected* presentation in the transference neuroses: what it denies to the presentation is *translation into words*

> *which shall remain attached to the object.* A presentation which is not put into words, or a psychical act which is not hypercathected, remains thereafter in a state of repression. (Freud, 1915e, p. 202, my italics)

I discuss later the possibility that Freud is *repressing* the thing-presentations of his own ideas, but the way the "mechanism" works is made clear. While recognition is given to an unconscious "idea" by putting it into words, repression "denies" the "translation into words" that would give it a place in the scheme of things.

In explaining the mechanism of repression, Freud continues to use his scientific terminology of *cathexis* and *anticathexis*, *withdrawal of cathexis*, *excitation*, and *after-pressure*, but a more personal, *agent-centred* account keeps showing through: the unconscious content (thing-presentation) is *prevented* from becoming conscious through the *activity* of the *censorship*. In words of this kind, a more subjective theme pushes into the scientific account: the thing-presentation is *denied access* to the word-presentation, and *turned away* from the *translation into words* that would allow it to become conscious (known). In his paper "Repression", Freud tells us that "*the essence of repression lies simply in turning something away, and keeping it at a distance, from the conscious*" (Freud, 1915d, p. 147), an insight important enough to italicise, but this means that, in repression, there must be a censoring *agent* who *does* the "turning away", and in unimpeded consciousness, a "*translator*" providing the words, and *making them available* to the unconscious thing-presentations. In this more subjective language, Freud's relational understanding lives on; and by refusing to be strait-jacketed by his "scientific" ("schizophrenic") language, it will eventually find a fuller, though always constrained, expression in his structural theory of *ego*, *superego*, and *id* (Freud, 1923b).

A relational perspective

With some poetic licence, it could be said that *word presentation*, *thing presentation*, the *censorship* (or *censor*) and the not quite explicit *translator* (of images into words), emerge as the principal *dramatis personae* in Freud's latent topography of the mind. *Conscious* and *unconscious* are not psychic agents in this sense, but qualities of psychic contents; *consciousness*, and, perhaps, also the *system Pcs.*, do have executive power in some degree (Freud 1915e, p. 165, editor's note) and, thus, qualify to be part of the intrapsychic cast. Such considerations are interesting for the light they throw on Freud's intellectual and emotional struggles, which I discuss later, but they also provide entry to a more relational perspective on unconscious–conscious transformations. A relational perspective is more in tune with contemporary psychoanalysis than Freud's mechanistic account, and in what follows I attempt to construct an image of the unconscious–conscious interface from within this frame of reference.[4]

I will start with Freud's newly appreciated insight[5] that "becoming conscious" involves *linking* word-presentations with thing-presentations. This stark formula could best be described as atomic: "atom" A (the thing-presentation) combines with "atom" B (the corresponding word-presentation), to make a new entity A-B (a unit, or "molecule" of consciousness).[6] Neat as it is, this formula does not do justice to the richness of the intrapsychic event as experienced in the clinical situation; this could perhaps be more fully rendered as *giving verbal form to a non-verbal apprehension*. The term "verbal *form*" introduces the idea of "shape" into the equation, while the idea of a "non-verbal *apprehension*" retrieves the idea of an agent who "senses" the "thing-presentation". This expanded view introduces an aesthetic dimension into the process—there is a now a living "subject" actively searching for verbal "forms" that will match the intuited "shapes" of his thing-presentations.

The idea of shape is important to my argument. The possibility of *words* having shape was first put forward by Werner and Kaplan (1963) in their discussion of language development, and in a different frame of reference, the "shape" of *experience* is central to a theory of art which I discuss in more detail below (Langer, 1942, 1953). I make use of both sets of ideas in developing a relational approach to consciousness, but first I consider the work of Werner and Kaplan.[7]

These authors presented evidence from the drawings of young children showing that they frequently experienced words in a physiognomic way. They found that each word had its own particular "shape", as though the child's experience of an object had somehow inscribed itself into the structure of the corresponding word. This kind of observation is compatible with theories of language acquisition which emphasise the interpenetration of words and experience in early development (e.g., Bruner, 1983; Loewald, 1978),[8] for if, as such theories suggest, the word is first experienced as an integral part of the object or situation in which it is heard, it is not difficult to see that the "shape", or impress, of that experience could remain with the word as it acquired symbolic function.[9] Moreover, it is easy to imagine that phrases, and even sentences, could be "shaped" in a similar way, and we know from Stern's (1985) work on maternal attunement that the mother actually moulds her response (including her words) to the perceived "shape" of the infant's experience.[10]

From this perspective, language is not simply an objective system of signs that comes from the external world of the father; it is also a more plastic medium, taking root in the infant's maternal world, and gradually moulded to the contours of lived and remembered experience. To think of it in this way enlarges the conception of a "word-presentation" and suggests an alternative model of the way words and experience could interact. In Freud's more objective "paternal" model, a word-presentation (as conventional symbol) abuts experience from the outside, forging a simple link with the schema (thing-presentation), thus giving it a name and a place in consciousness. In a more subjective "maternal" reading, the subject *searches* for a word with the right "shape" (as in Werner and Kaplan) and *matches* this to the "shape" of the thing-presentation (an experiential "shape"). The first account is mechanical and conventionally semantic, the second "aesthetic" and based on a sense of structural and sensory affinity.

This aesthetic dimension of becoming conscious can be elaborated by reference to Langer's theory of art (Langer, 1942, 1953), which describes how the "shape" of experience is represented in the art object.[11] Langer argues that while words in their objective usage (*discursive symbols*) have *conventional* referents, there being no *formal* similarity between a word and that which it represents, aesthetic symbols are *presentational*, and *display* their "meaning", or vital import, through their form. In other words, an aesthetic (*presentational*) symbol reveals its "meaning" by analogically replicating an experiential form in its actual structure;[12] this enables the experiential form to be recognised in the aesthetic symbol, facilitating greater awareness, or consciousness, of what the experience is *like*.[13]

In what follows, I use Langer's distinction between *discursive* and *presentational* symbols to explore events at the conscious–unconscious interface. I argue that while traditional descriptions of analysis emphasise the "paternal" *discursive* use of language (its capacity to describe and explain phenomena), the actual practice of analysis is frequently closer to a *presentational* "maternal" mode. In this regard, I will show how Langer's image of the *aesthetic* process can be mapped on to the *analytic* process, thereby facilitating discussion of events at the analytic interface—the interface between conscious and unconscious.

The aesthetic interface

In Langer's account of artistic creation, aesthetic transformation of the self is brought about by the artist making a semblance of something felt. This is something in the artist's unconscious world of thing-presentations that he feels a need to express. He can "sense" this "something", but often cannot say in advance of his work exactly what it is. In this sense, the artistic process is a means of giving form to this intuited "something" and making it manifest in his work. Directed by his inner "sense" of what he is "holding" in his mind, he proceeds by trial and error—this feels right, that does not. In every decision he is guided by this sense of "fit", the degree of "resonance" between the form he is making and what he is trying to express. It is seldom a linear process; there are many false starts and abortive pieces of work, but gradually a form takes shape, and one day he *knows* he has "got it right". He says to himself, "*That* is it! *That* is what I've been looking for!"

In these terms, the project of art is a means of realising (giving form to) an inner structure. It involves an often extended process of intuitive matching: of the forms the artist is making, to the dimly sensed part of himself he is trying to express. In order to engage in such activity, he needs a space that is set apart from ordinary action, into which he can bring elements of his emotional life. It must feel safe enough for such exposure to be possible, and free enough to allow these unknown parts of himself to engage in dialogue with the forms he is making. In Winnicott's (1953) terms, this is a *transitional* space, in which inner and outer are free to intermingle, and the mental is not clearly differentiated from its external embodiment.

If we map this account of the aesthetic interface on to the analytic interface of the consulting room, we can see that the artist's work is similar in many respects to analysis, at least in its more aesthetic form.

Here, too, there are uncharted, dimly sensed feelings (unconscious, unrepresented), and a work (the work of analysis) unfolding within a sequestered space. Here, too, there is a search for forms, and an ongoing, and largely intuitive, sensing of whether they fit the unconscious feeling-structures (thing-presentations) which are the object of attention. Here, too, there are false starts and abortive pieces of work, and sometimes, too, experiences of emerging self-realisation, of somehow being on the right track: "Yes, *that's* how it is! *That* feels right!" And finally, there is the "product" of analysis, the transformed mental structure in both analyst and patient. This is the counterpart of the work of art and results from the complex interweaving of words and experience that go to make up the analytic dialogue.

The analytic interface

Analysis, however, is different from art; not only are there two people involved in the process, but the analytic medium is language, which, as we have seen, can be used in two radically different ways. Stemming from this difference are two divergent approaches to analysis: one, which I call intuitive and "maternal", the other cognitive and "paternal". In my description, I emphasised the first and downplayed the second, but psychoanalysis as a discipline has evolved between these poles, and each individual analysis is played out in their field of influence.[14] At one pole there is a "separate" analyst, giving verbal insight through interpretation; at the other, a "symbiotic" (Searles, 1973) or "maternally preoccupied" analyst (Winnicott, 1956), holding, containing, and mirroring, and providing an atmosphere conducive to growth (Wright, 1991). Freud's paper "The unconscious" (1915e) reflects the cognitive pole, contemporary psychoanalysis the intuitive, but neither exists in pure form, and practice moves between them, with key psychoanalytic figures often identified with one pole to the exclusion of the other. Historically speaking, the cognitive pole has been comprehensively discussed; the intuitive pole is harder to define, and a language adequate to describe it has proved elusive.

Langer's theory of the artistic process goes some way towards meeting this deficit, for in elaborating the concept of *presentational symbolism*, she has staked out a new symbolic territory in which forms and images take the place of words in the mediation of knowledge. The technique of interpretation evolved within an essentially cognitive view of consciousness—a paternal domain—and depends, in Langer's terms, on describing the structure of experience *in discursive language* (naming) and offering *explanations* for it ("you feel this way because . . ."). By contrast, in the more "maternal" *presentational* mode, words are used to *conjure up experience*, the aim being *to capture its lived qualities* rather than to name it and talk *about* it.

This "maternal" use of language has been well documented by Ogden (1997), who observed that a great deal of psychoanalysis can be thought of as a conversation in which patient and analyst are attempting to describe what the patient's life and experience are *like*. In the manner of art, it has to create *semblances* of life, and discover forms for feelings and experiences yet to be realised. "Semblances" are not just forms *of* words, but *images* formed *by* words, and over time, the conversation moves through successive *images*, towards an *imagined structure* that evokes, and convincingly *portrays*, the patient's *sense* of his own experience.[15] In Ogden's words, this way of working involves creating

> a *metaphorical* language adequate to the creation of sounds and meanings that reflect what it feels like to think, feel, and physically experience (in short to be alive as a human being to the extent that one is capable) at a given moment. (Ogden, 1997, p. 3, my italics)

Ogden, thus, highlights the crucial elements of the process: creating a *metaphorical* (i.e., image-based) language, and one that is *adequate* to the task of creating multi-modal image structures. The *adequacy* of the language depends on both its metaphorical aptness, and the degree to which it captures the nuances of experience; it also depends on the sounds of the words—on prosody, tone of voice, the feel of the words in the mouth—and the way these relate to the "feel" of what they are trying to grasp. Such complexity is a long way from Freud's original conception of "telling" the patient what his symptom means (a "paternal" view of analysis), and, although by the time he wrote "The unconscious", he had learned that "telling" was not enough (Freud, 1915e, p. 175), he gave little explanation of why this might be so. Apart from dealing with the patient's "resistance", he gave little advice as to how the "telling" could be made more effective.

Presentational symbols, mirroring, and attunement

Freud's "paternal" account of "becoming conscious" involved "translation into words" (1915e, p. 202) of the thing-presentation and this required that words be "linked with" the thing-presentation and "remain attached to [it]" (1915e, p. 202). The link in this model is external—a straightforward conjunction of two elements which have no structural (analogical) affinity with each other. Although the thing presentation has certain image-like qualities (being derived from sensory perception), the word-presentation is a "pure" semantic symbol of objective language. Images have no part to play in this account of consciousness, for they constitute the "language" of the *primary process* and belong to the system Ucs. As Rycroft (1968) observed, Freud did not have a "place" for images which could mediate, or create, self-knowledge in his theoretical system; although dreams were regarded as the "royal road to the unconscious", they were emissaries of the unconscious domain and could only reveal their meaning when interpreted by the analyst.

In a more "maternal" account of "becoming conscious", images can be given a more salient role. Following Langer, I have argued that the image itself is a mediator of awareness, capable of presenting a structure of experience as a whole, without resort to detailed verbal description. This is something every analyst knows, and working with images is an integral part of normal practice. In psychoanalytic theory, however, the image has a less certain place, and in order to differentiate "working with images" from "interpretation" in the cognitive sense, I propose to regard it as a form of *mirroring*. While interpretation can be seen as belonging to the "paternal domain" (Wright, 1991), mirroring is rooted in the maternal world of two-person relationships and is thus part of the "facilitating environment" (Winnicott, 1953).

The term "facilitating environment" refers to the mother's adaptive function, which normally finds expression in the provision of "forms" moulded to the infant's expectation. The mother does not "tell" (i.e., dictate to) her infant how he should be, but responds to the infant's "gesture" (or way of being) in a way that feels intuitively "right". In the beginning, the adaptive response takes concrete form—a feed that is moulded or "shaped" by her reading of the situation.

At this stage, form is embedded in the concrete situation: in infant gesture and maternal response, in the timing, punctuation, and overall speed of the mother–infant transaction, and above all in the subtle modulations of maternal response.[16] But developing alongside this is the more specific interaction of *mirroring* (Winnicott, 1967), an affective resonance between mother and infant, in which the mother reflects in her facial expressions the affect expressed by the infant at any particular moment. Winnicott captured the essence of this in his metaphor of the mother's face as the infant's first mirror: "What does the infant see when he or she looks at the mother's face? I am suggesting that what the baby sees is himself or herself . . ." (Winnicott, 1967, p. 112).

For Winnicott, mirroring is related to holding and helps to lay the foundations of the self ("I am seen and recognised, therefore I am"). In the present context, however, I want to emphasise the *image* aspect of the process, the fact that the mother's "expression" provides an external *image* of what the infant is *like*. As well as being an affective response, each expression is also an image—a (maternal) *representation* or *symbol* of the infant's affective self—that is waiting to be recognised as such by the infant.[17]

In this original sense, mirroring is limited by the small number of biologically determined facial expressions, but *maternal attunement* (Stern, 1985) extends the scope of mirroring into the later pre-verbal period and greatly increases the range of maternal forms presented (Wright, 2009). Attunement is also a mirroring response, based on maternal identification and mediated by images, but the repertoire of maternal images is extended. An attuned response is a spontaneous, intuitive mini-performance (a rhythmic sequence of movements and sounds) that replicates in some way the "shape", or "affective contour" of the infant's behaviour, and is part of the mother's ongoing "conversation" with the infant (Trevarthen, 1979), in which she gives external form to fragments of infant "experience".[18] The infant might experience the mother's response in different ways, but, as with mirroring in the narrower sense, I am stressing the fact that *each maternal portrayal is an image, or external form*—a "motion picture" of the infant's vitality,[19] and potentially a pre-verbal representation of the infant's self.

The importance of mirroring and attunement to my present argument is twofold: first, it delineates an actual domain of preverbal experience (the maternal) and shows us what it is like, and second, it highlights a type of response in which "meaning" is conveyed through images. Such images can be visual, auditory, or multimodal, but their import is always conveyed through the form of the image which analogically replicates a form of feeling. I shall argue in the following section that such forms are important in organising experience, in making it available to conscious awareness and ultimately in creating mental structure. They are an essential part of the maternal mode of "becoming conscious" which is absent in Freud's account of the process.

From mirroring form to mental structure

"Mental structure" is a metaphorical term through which we attempt to imagine the nature of mind. We imagine a physical structure and the relationship between its parts, and then suppose that the parts of the mind are interrelated in a comparable way. Thus, we conceive of the mind as an "inner space" containing "objects". In psychoanalytic theory these "objects" are deemed to have quasi human characteristics, derived in part from an individual's earlier forms of experience with significant others, and since such "objects" are "human" in this sense, we think of them as doing things to each other, and communicating with each other. This is essentially a "content" approach to the mind—"internal objects" are characterised in a way that parallels our delineation of external objects. Thus, we might speak of an internal mother or father, a greedy baby, or a punitive superego. This approach is a legacy of classical psychoanalysis, which paid little attention to the mind as container or to the structure of the mental itself. Contemporary psychoanalysis has reversed this trend,[20] but understanding of the field is far from complete. In the last part of my chapter, I want to address certain aspects of this topic.

Let us suppose that at some point the infant's perception of the mother's attuned response begins to change and the infant *recognises himself* within the attuned maternal image; in a quantum leap, he sees the mother's performance in a new light. It is no longer just an exciting spectacle, or an aspect of the mother to be simply enjoyed; it acquires a new significance and begins to *mean* "Now I can *see* the connection: this pattern has the same rhythm as something I have just felt!" I would argue that, at this point, the external image (the attuned "performance") is "internalised" and transformed into "mental structure", a primitive symbol. The performance is no longer just a game but conveys *meaning*; it "speaks" to something just experienced and becomes a means of representing and remembering it. In this respect, the new "object" is strikingly similar to Winnicott's transitional object. Although the latter is external, and the newly formed "attunement structure" internal, both have primitive symbolic function, and both keep memory alive by means of reverberating sensory patterns.[21]

My discussion of mirroring has taken us a long way from Freud's paper on the unconscious, but emerging from it is a vision of mental structure in which the basic units are relational, and derived, at least in part, from early forms of communication between mother and infant. In some degree, therefore, it offers a vision of the matrix of the mind (Ogden, 1986), populated, at least in part, by preverbal symbolic structures. These are capable of holding elements of experience in mind, and relating them, by means of their patterns, to other structures of a similar kind—in other words, they make possible a primitive form of thinking. In Freud's view, by contrast, the "matrix" (in his terms, "the unconscious") was based on instinct, and populated by the "ideational representative[s] of instinct" (Freud, 1915e, p. 177), later called "unconscious phantasy" by Kleinian writers (Isaacs, 1952). Mental activity was, thus, confined to hallucinatory gratifications of a sexual or aggressive nature. In this view, "thinking with images" has no place.

The model I have sketched is at variance with this classical view. It suggests a relatively early development of image-based symbolic structures in which an internalised maternal form functions as container for remembered experience. In so far as it perpetuates an attuning "communication" between its parts (resonance, or reverberation of patterns), this structure could be said to be "alive", or to keep experience alive, in the same way as the mother–infant "conversation" from which it derives.

Different modes of consciousness

How, then, might this more relational view of the mind link up with Freud's account of consciousness? In the topographical model, "becoming conscious" is bound up with words—the essential, though perhaps not sufficient, condition is "translation into words" of the thing-presentation. In contrast, I have argued for a form of conscious awareness that is not dependent on words, but mediated through presentational images, which enable experience to be grasped as a whole, in its imminent and felt reality.[22] Such images *display* their meanings, all at once, but in order to become conscious in the cognitive sense (i.e., conceptualised and contextualised), they need to be "translated into words" and unravelled by means of them. In this view, there are two ways of becoming conscious and two modes of conscious awareness; neither is superior to the other, but each is valuable in different ways. The "paternal mode" is external and involves looking at experience from a distance and placing it in context; the "maternal mode" is more narrowly focused and based on identification: it creates a sense of being *in* the experience (though not really in it), which enables it to be contemplated and known, perhaps for the first time (Wright, 1991).

Freud did not have a place for such images in his theory of the conscious mind, and underestimated their value. He was a rationalist, taking his stand in a three-person world of separate objects, in which paternal law and organisation were the primary measures, and the "truth" lay in "scientific" description. Evocative images were the "language" of the unconscious—ambiguous, illusory, and wish-fulfilling, *unless or until* unravelled in a logical way.[23]

We might surmise that, from Freud's "paternal" perspective, images were an aspect of the "maternal" realm in which he felt uncomfortable and out of his depth; they were bodily, sensual, fluid, and unbounded, and created a world of shifting presences—"an aboriginal population of the mind"—that made him anxious and ill at ease. His attitude to art—another world of images—was ambivalent; while he sometimes idealised artists in general, he often diminished their achievements[24] and only admired art he could understand (i.e., "translate into words"). Music, which defies such translation, was beyond his aesthetic grasp (except for certain operatic arias which he knew by heart). And finally, images were intrinsically "unscientific"—my starting point in this chapter—though it now seems that his aversion to the image and his preference for the highly abstract might have had deeper roots.

Repression, from this perspective, is a means of keeping the "maternal" and its emissary images at bay. It is a mechanism of control, rooted in the world of the father (consciousness), and standing guard with an array of border guards (counter-cathexes) to combat forbidden incursions. Images, which link back to sensual memories of the mother's body, are turned away, and paternal words, which would give them a place in the conscious scheme of things, are withheld. As I hinted at the beginning, Freud's theory of the unconscious might itself be shaped by a process of this kind.

Concluding remarks

Freud's topographical theory (Freud, 1915e) will soon be a hundred years old, and although constrained by the range of its author's sensibility and the *Weltanschauung* of its time, it remains an essential starting point for any discussion of mind as dynamic organisation of experience. Freud, however, presented his theory in a "scientific" language of mechanisms and forces, and since we now think in a more relational way, we have to rethink his insights in order to integrate them better into contemporary thinking.

Although it might have been important to Freud that his theories wore the "paternal" garb of science, I have argued that deeper reasons—a fear of the "maternal"—led him to repress the non-verbal (image-based) elements of his understanding. If, to use Lacan's language (Lacan, 1977), his feet were firmly planted in the symbolic, then the imaginary—the realm of maternal images—was strictly out of bounds. In this sense, only words are "pure"; the sensory *body* of the word—the *image*—belongs to the realm of the repressed. From this "paternal" perspective, it is permissible to look—to be an observer–theoretician (Greek *therios*, spectator)—but not to touch, to engage with forms that reignite the conscious sense of bodily experience (Wright, 1991).

In this chapter, I have attempted to fill out Freud's theory of "becoming conscious" and explored how resurrecting the repressed "maternal" could affect our view of psychological structure. This opens up the imaginary—the world of maternal form—and recalls the power of images to organise and communicate emotional import without the mediation of words. It suggests an enhanced role for images in the analytic process (the process of "becoming conscious") and creates a new awareness of form. Considerations of form lead to aesthetics, and, thus, the *way* the analyst constructs his communications—the *form* they take—becomes as important as their content.

In his more idealising moments, Freud would sometimes feel that the artist had been there before him and accessed "truths" of human nature which he, the first psychoanalyst, was only then beginning to understand. Stumbling behind, in pedestrian "scientific" mode, he could not fathom the means by which this was achieved. We now can see that he was looking in the wrong direction—*the secret of maternal form would never yield itself to analytic dissection because it gave itself directly to the senses as pure expression.* Art is, and always has been, a different *way* of self-realisation, a *revelation* of the self and human nature. Its "means to meaning" (MacLeish, 1960), its *presentational* method, is direct: the work of art, with its complex articulation of forms and images, *shows* and makes manifest the way we are—either we *see* it or we do not.

The value of art theory to the psychoanalyst lies in its language; by looking in the right direction it has found a way of putting into words the "how" of the work of art. This has enabled us to see how emotional truth—the truth of experience—is revealed in the complex articulations of form, and, beyond this, how every work of art which "plumbs the depths" conveys its import directly, by means of these articulations, to the depths of the listening (i.e., receptive) "other". Finally, it enables us to see how every art object of worth is a small revelation of the structure of the human psyche because its articulations *are* the forms of that psyche, realised in the medium of the external world.

Notes

1. "If . . . the 'Papers on Metapsychology' may . . . be regarded as the most important of all Freud's theoretical writings, there can be no doubt that the . . . essay on 'The unconscious' is the culmination of that series" (Strachey, 1957, p. 161).

2. I am not suggesting that in writing this paper, Freud was specifically concerned to avoid the short story format of the *Studies on Hysteria*. I am referring to a more pervasive struggle that arguably informs all his work and reflects his aspiration towards scientific respectability. However, this might not be the whole story; a case can be made for this being one aspect of a deeper conflict in which his predominantly "paternal" personality (three-person, "Oedipal") caused him to repress the more "maternal" (two-person, pre-Oedipal) aspects of his makeup. I refer to this in greater detail below.

3. It has often been suggested that the richness of Freud's writing (he was awarded the Goethe prize for literature) has been partially obscured by a depersonalising bias in Strachey's translation. While this is almost certainly the case (we have, for example, the "ego" rather than the "I"), it is hard to believe that this is the only explanation. Freud began his professional life in a mainstream academic environment, and the internalised attitudes of his mentors, as well as a real fear of criticism from the scientific community, are at least plausible factors to take into account in trying to understand the final shape of his theories (but see footnote 2, above).

4. In calling my approach "relational", I am being deliberately vague to keep my options open. Creative thinking involves a freedom from constraint, and tying oneself to a specific set of relational constructs makes for precisely the kind of bias I want to avoid.

5. I use the phrase "newly appreciated" to emphasise the fact that insight comes and goes, and that Freud, particularly in this area, is struggling with something like repression in relation to the "body" of the word—the sensual, "maternal" aspect of the "thing-presentation".

6. In the terms of my later discussion, the external "atomic" link is "paternal", the link through affinity of "form" is "maternal".

7. Freud's terms *word-presentation* and *thing-presentation* are "objective" and experience-distant, but point to an important distinction between fully symbolic mental contents (words) and mental contents which are less clearly symbolic, non-verbal, closer to bodily experience, and not sharply differentiated from it (sensory imagos of objects). Contemporary discussions use a variety of terms for similar kinds of distinction, but much overlap exists between them. Langer's (1942, 1953) *discursive* and *presentational* symbols (discussed below) are a case in point, while the philosophers Lakoff and Johnson (1999), writing from a cognitive psychology perspective, refer to *linguistic symbols* (words) and underlying *image schemata* (abstractions from bodily experience).

8. There is an excellent discussion of language development in Vivona (2012) with responses by Bucci, W., Fonagy, P., Litowitz, B., and Donnel Stern.

9. I am assuming here that the referential function of symbols depends on the infant's growing capacity to tolerate separation from the object. The essence of a symbol as a mental structure is to represent the *idea* of an object, and this depends on a prior ability to conceive of the object in its absence.

10. In maternal attunement (Stern, 1985), the prosodic features of the mother's speech (the tones and rhythms of her "motherese") are an integral part of an attuned "performance". The speech element of an attunement thus shares the rhythmical pattern of the experience itself (see my discussion of maternal attunement, below).

11. Langer first put forward her ideas in relation to musical form (Langer, 1942), but later developed a general theory of art that included linguistic forms. It could be argued that musical form reveals the essential shape and texture of emotional life more clearly than other art forms, but, according to her theory, every art form reveals the "shape" of an emotional form in an analogical way (Langer, 1942, 1953).

12. It "contain[s] its sense as a being contains its life" (Langer, 1988, p. 38).

13. The same could be said of dream images, but while these are spontaneous creations of the mind that often seem meaningless to the waking subject, aesthetic symbols are intentionally created, often through laborious effort, and their import is more transparent and owned. Like dream images, they are closer to concrete experience than discursive language, but, being fully symbolic, they are exemplars of *form* or *type*. They are not wish fulfilments or simple memories, but show us what it is *like* to love, to be jealous, or to suffer loss, etc. In this sense, aesthetic symbols are concrete *and* abstract: concrete because they are sensory and embodied, abstract because they reveal the *form* of experience.

14. It would be no exaggeration to say that this polarity has shaped psychoanalytic theory and practice from the beginning (Wright, 1991). It is reflected in many pairs of words which attempt to capture different aspects of practice, emotional development, and/or mental structure: pre-Oedipal–Oedipal, dyadic–triadic, two-person–three-person, narcissistic–object-related, psychotic–non-psychotic, preverbal–verbal, maternal–paternal, holding–interpretation, imaginary–symbolic, to name just some of them. All are related in some way to the fact that the human infant is born in an immature state both physically and mentally, and spends the first two years of life immersed in a hugely formative maternal environment that for the most part is non-verbal.

15. I have used the somewhat vague term "structure" throughout this chapter precisely because it leaves the meaning open (to be filled as the reader wishes). I could have used the term "phantasy", but this is laden with too many precise meanings in psychoanalytic theory, and I like to think that the thoughts I am sketching could, in fact, be filled from a number of different psychoanalytic perspectives. In point of fact, many of the "structures" to which I refer will be relational structures which bear the imprint of transactions with, and feelings about, other people. As psychoanalysis has rightly understood, these are the central "stuff" of human life, and as such are foundational of self-structure, and, arguably, of the mind as well.

16. In a somewhat analogous way, there is a whole array of movements that the analyst makes during a session, largely outside of his awareness, that reveal in a non-verbal way the degree to which he is attuned and responsive to the patient: his breathing, the way he sits in his chair, the tilt of his head, the amount he fidgets, not to mention his yawning, picking his nose, and other such activities that he might wish to hide from the patient. A patient said to me the other day, "I felt dreadful in the last session. You were moving your legs all the time and I felt you were bored with me" (i.e., non-attuned).

17. In Langer's terms, it is a *presentational symbol*.

18. Stern uses the terms "vitality affect" (Stern, 1985) and "forms of vitality" (Stern, 2011) in his attempt to say precisely what the mother is tracking, and responding to, in her infant, but more important is the fact that throughout, and in an ongoing way, she is in touch with her baby, feeling what the

baby is "feeling" and playing this back to the baby as a quasi "musical" (i.e., essentially non-verbal) response (Malloch & Trevarthen, 2009).

19. Attuned responses are multi-modal and may include words. It is not, however, the meaning of the words that count, but their tone and prosodic shape that are interwoven into the reflecting image.

20. Bion was a pioneer in this respect with his papers on thinking (1962a) and containment (1962b, 1965).

21. A mental structure derived from attunement could also be likened to Bion's "container–contained" structure, though the background theory is different (Bion, 1962a,b, 1965).

22. The power of the image to mediate experience is beautifully expressed by the poet Archibald MacLeish (1960, p. 16): "The poet's task is to cage, to capture, the whole of experience, experience *as* a whole . . . in meaningful form . . . or shape . . . to which the emotions answer". Transference is also a means of 'capturing experience as a whole' but there is an important difference: the transference, when it becomes experientially active, is 'a form of remembering' (Freud), but not yet a symbol; it is waiting upon analytic transformation to achieve this *mental* level. By contrast, the presentational image is a purposefully created symbol.

23. It has often been noted that Freud had difficulty in understanding maternal areas of experience. One of the earliest and most radical critiques from this point of view was that of Suttie (1935) who argued that Freud had repressed the "maternal" in his personality, and that this "taboo on tenderness" had led to a systematic skewing in his theoretical work. To me, this argument is quite convincing; it is probable that every analyst and every theoretician has a limited range of sensibility determined by his makeup, and, although this might be enlarged by his own analysis, it will never cease to influence what he creates. In this sense, an analytic theory is autobiography, and a form of self-realisation (Wright, 1991), as well as a more or less valid description of certain aspects of "reality".

24. For example, in "Creative writers and day-dreaming" (Freud, 1908e), he argued that the artist was simply giving expression to forbidden fantasies in a roundabout way that brought him acclaim because it gave vicarious pleasure to others.

6

Complementary models of the mind in Freud's "The unconscious"?

Bernard Reith

Freud in his consulting room

When reading Freud, I like to imagine him in his consulting room, involved in an analytic session and pondering questions such as: What is going on here? How to understand it? How am I involved?

Reading "The unconscious" (1915e) with this picture of him in mind, I find in it something more than the topographical model of which this text is usually considered to be the supreme statement. Between the lines of the topographic model, Freud might have been trying to find his way to a transformational model of the analytic couple. This two-person transformational model would be complementary to the one-person topographic model and add an extra dimension to it. Of course, I am not suggesting that this was Freud's overt intention, but I do believe that with hindsight we can see it at work as an implicit theme.

Following some passages step by step, I shall try to show the interplay between the two models. The topographical model is described in parts II to VI of Freud's paper, but it is embedded in many other interesting thoughts and set between his introductory Part I and his exploration of psychosis in Part VII, like a jewel in a silk-lined box.

The jewel being so well known, I shall concentrate on the box and lining.

The opening paragraph of "The unconscious", linking it to "Repression" (1915d), the previous paper in Freud's series on metapsychology,

> We have learnt . . . that the essence of the process of repression lies, not in . . . annihilating . . . the idea which represents an instinct, but in preventing it from becoming conscious. When this happens we say . . . that it is in a state of being 'unconscious', and we can produce good evidence to show that . . . it can produce effects, even including some which finally reach consciousness. Everything that is repressed must remain unconscious; but . . . the repressed does not cover everything that is unconscious. The unconscious has the wider compass . . . (Freud, 1915e, p. 166)

can, of course, be taken as a straightforward announcement of what he will describe in Part II as the differentiation between the "systematic" and "descriptive" unconscious (pp. 172–173). But if we change perspective and listen to it as reflecting his private questions during his analytic work, then we may imagine him thinking that the theory of repression is not all there is to say about the analytic situation and that more needs to be understood, such as how the unconscious produces its "effects" and how it can "reach" consciousness. His very next sentence then reads like *the* fundamental question of what we can capture in the psychoanalytic situation: "How are we to arrive at a knowledge of the unconscious?" (1915e, p. 166).

Typically, Freud uses the first person plural, engaging his audience and including himself. The "we" has several functions throughout the text, from the rhetorical "we" of dialogue, through the "we" of introspection into our personal minds, to the "we" of the community of psychoanalysts, combining to convey a sense of profound reflection on our analytic function. Freud gives an eminently clinical answer to his fundamental question: "It is of course only as something conscious that we know it, after it has undergone transformation or translation into something conscious. Psychoanalytic work shows us every day that translation of this kind is possible" (1915e, p. 166).

The next sentence might give the impression that he thought of this "transformation or translation" mainly in terms of what happens in the patient, in a dynamic model of the individual psyche centred on repression: "In order that this should come about, the person under analysis must overcome certain resistances—the same resistances as those which, earlier, made the material concerned into something repressed by rejecting it from the conscious" (1915e, p. 166).

However, if we continue to think of Freud as being in a session with the patient, then we may hear the epistemological issues that he raises immediately afterwards, in Part I, "Justification for the concept of the unconscious", as his way of introducing his thoughtful answer to the clinical problem of *how* the analyst can help the "person under analysis" to "overcome" these resistances. He states that "the existence of something mental that is unconscious" is an "assumption" that is "*necessary*" (1915e, p. 166)[1] because

> . . . conscious acts remain disconnected and unintelligible if we insist upon claiming that every mental act that occurs in us must also necessarily be experienced by us through consciousness; on the other hand they fall into a demonstrable connection if we interpolate between them the unconscious acts which we have inferred. A gain in meaning is a perfectly justifiable ground for going beyond the limits of direct experience. When, in addition, it turns out that the assumption of there being an unconscious enables us to construct a successful procedure by which we can exert an effective influence upon the course of conscious processes, this success will have given us an incontrovertible proof of the existence of what we have assumed. (1915e, p. 167)

When Freud forcefully affirms himself as a practising psychoanalyst in the last sentence, this places his epistemological concerns in the context of his analytic work and suggests that his answer appeals not only to the patient's mind, but also to the analyst's mind working in collaboration with the patient's, in order to "construct a successful procedure" that goes "beyond the limits of direct experience" and involves "transformation", "translation", "interpolation", and "a gain in meaning". At least implicitly, Freud complements the topographic model that he is about to describe with another model centred on the analytic couple. I shall call this a *transformational* model, to use Freud's own notion of "transformation"[2] as adumbrated in his paper, before it was more specifically developed by Bion (1965) and Bollas (1979). As Freud emphasises, this working model is to be judged by the quality and success of the psychoanalytic procedure that it sustains.

A case vignette: finding thing-presentations for closeness

To illustrate what I mean by transformational psychoanalytic work, I shall condense a sequence extracted from a period spanning about six months in the analysis, at four sessions per week, of a young man (I shall call him John) who could not bear to establish intimate relationships of any kind. When he tried, he would inevitably become preoccupied with impressions that the other person would reject him and leave him out in the cold or, which was worse, overpower him and imprison him in a suffocating relationship. He could work, but most of his life was taken up with his efforts to allay his anxiety, which could take on extreme proportions bordering on depersonalisation. He hoped for help and understanding, only to be bitterly disappointed. Sexuality was an out-of-bounds topic. Often his anger and/or fear of being controlled would prevent him from talking for much of the session. When he did talk, it tended to be factual and repetitive.

I would interpret, for example, that: "To feel together you need me to hold you well in my mind, but then you worry that I will take over and influence you. So when you want to tell me what's on your mind, at the same time you are afraid to do so." John understood what I meant and was grateful that I could think about him in this way, but such work did not really change the dynamics between us. I had other misgivings about such interpretations, because, by talking like this, I was indeed taking over, telling him about himself instead of letting him discover himself, or working side by side to discover him together. I was being the one who could hold people and who had the strength to do so, while he believed that he could not hold anybody, because he projected all his capacities into others. Moreover, intervening like this could feel as if I was intruding, including sexually, on someone who had very fragile boundaries. Similarly, when I interpreted his resentment of the powers that he attributed to me, John seemed to understand intellectually, but did not seem able to own his resentment, as if he did not know where to locate it in himself.

Another problem was that I would become drowsy during sessions. Sometimes this felt as though I wanted to extract myself from our tense relationship, and other times as though I was identified with John's need to find a safe place where he could relax. One day, I slipped into such a dreamy state while he was complaining about how he could not afford to depend on others. For some reason, I had a picture of turning a sock inside out. I could not understand why, but as it was all I had, and still half in my hypnotic state, I blurted out, "It's like turning a sock inside out, isn't it? Everything that was inside ends up outside, and then you feel all over the place."

I was surprised and also worried, because he could take this as if I were calling him a dirty sock, or referring to his rectum and protesting against the projections he was submitting me to (and this might indeed have been one of the unconscious determinants of my remark). But John laughed, not his usual tense and defensive laugh, but a more relaxed one, like a giggle—a little bit as if I had tickled him. He said, "That's a funny idea but I can see how it makes sense." Then, after a short silence, "I'm thinking that one thing about socks is that if you turn one inside out, it almost looks like the same sock, although if you look closely you can tell the difference." I thought to myself that this was a fine idea of his, which had not come to my mind and which added a lot of meaning to the image. Later on, we could use it to talk about his sense of not quite knowing who he was.

Over the ensuing months, John would occasionally report that he thought about the sock image sometimes. Then, one day when I had again interpreted his wish for, and fear of, closeness, he said, "You know, the other day I was thinking about the sock idea again, and I thought that it *can* be good to turn a sock inside out, when you want to fold a pair of socks together to put them in a drawer. You turn half of one of the socks inside out to cover both of them and so hold them together." There could not have been a better way to describe being held, and being able to hold someone, with good and safe skin-to-skin contact, close together yet well differentiated.

It was after this episode that he became more self-reflective, better able to hold himself in his own mind to think about himself, and about his own place in his relationships. He also began to use more evocative imagery of his own. Not long after, he risked his first date in a long time.

Perhaps what had happened was that I had captured something unconsciously about his need for safe and differentiated skin-to-skin contact as a starting point for feeling in contact with himself, but for which I had not until then found an image (a "thing-presentation"[3]) that I could put in words. Instead, I was reduced to giving somewhat intellectual interpretations, based on our relationship and on my psychoanalytic theory, but too removed from his experience to enable him to make the connection. In my dreamy state, I seem to have made a better preconscious link between my theory and his experience, expressed in the image of the sock. He was able to use this for capturing yet other aspects of his unconscious experience, in a most interesting and creative way. Something unconscious was transformed, first into a "thing-presentation" that had so far been lacking, then into a network of "thing-presentations", and, ultimately, through linkage to "word-presentations", into a meaningful structure. I am not saying that this replaced the interpretative work, but I do believe that it gave it more flesh and meaning.

Possibilities and pitfalls of psychoanalytic understanding

To return now to Freud's paper, although the rest of his Part I might read like an abstract discussion of the scientific and philosophical status of the concept of unconscious mental activity, it becomes livelier if we continue to picture Freud at work, trying to pin down how it is that he can understand his patient, or fail to do so. We can take his typical rhetorical style of arguing with imaginary detractors as expressing his own inner debates about the possibilities and pitfalls of analytic understanding. It is worthwhile to follow his careful and detailed argument, which guides us towards the essence of the psychoanalytic position.

The first pitfall is extra-analytic knowledge. The problem of "latent memories" allows him to argue that it would be beside the point to explain them through "somatic processes" and that a "*psychical* process" must be understood in its own terms (1915e, p. 167). The attempt to equate "psychical" with "conscious", and "latent" with "somatic", can only be an artificial "convention" (p. 167) leading to an impasse:

> It disrupts psychical continuities, plunges us into the insoluble difficulties of psycho-physical parallelism, is open to the reproach that for no obvious reason it over-estimates the part played by consciousness, and that it forces us prematurely to abandon the field of psychological research without being able to offer us any compensation from other fields. (1915e, p. 168)

In other words, the search for understanding through extra-analytic knowledge can lead the analyst to "abandon the field" of the analytic relationship by over-estimating conscious understanding and, therefore, missing other "psychical continuities". It assigns patient and analyst to parallel worlds that cannot meet. Freud continues, about "the latent states of mental life",

> We shall therefore be better advised to focus our attention on what we know with certainty of the nature of these debatable states. As far as their physical characteristics are concerned, they are totally inaccessible to us . . .. On the other hand, we know for certain that they have abundant points of contact with conscious mental processes; with the help of a certain amount of work they can be transformed into, or replaced by, conscious mental processes . . . (1915e, p. 168)

There are "points of contact" between unconscious and conscious and, therefore, in the reading that I am proposing here, between patient and analyst. Note that Freud repeats the themes of transformation and "work". This is because the "points of contact" cannot be found *directly* in consciousness: to imagine that they could be is the second pitfall. He begins with "identification", in the sense of inferring that others are like us:

> The assumption of an unconscious is . . . a perfectly *legitimate* one, in as much as in postulating it we are not departing a single step from our customary and generally accepted mode of thinking. . . . without any special reflection we attribute to everyone else our own constitution and therefore our consciousness as well, and . . . this identification is a *sine qua non* of our understanding. (1915e, p. 169)

His discussion of animism allows him to warn us about the limits of this kind of unreflective "identification" with the patient—it can be projective and affords no secure base:

> . . . even where the original inclination to identification has withstood criticism—that is, when the 'others' are our fellow men—the assumption of a consciousness in them rests upon an inference and cannot share the immediate certainty which we have of our own consciousness. (1915e, p. 169)

Moreover, says Freud, certainty about our own consciousness is an illusion:

> Psycho-analysis demands . . . that we should apply this process of inference to ourselves also—a proceeding to which . . . we are not constitutionally inclined. If we do this, we must say: all the acts and manifestations which I notice in myself and do not know how to link up with the rest of my mental life must be judged as if they belonged to someone else: they are to be explained by a mental life ascribed to this other person. (1915e, p. 169)

If this is in the context of psychoanalytic work, then this "other person" is not the patient, of course, but our internal reaction to the patient, which we "do not know how to link up with the rest of [our] mental life" and which, moreover, we are disinclined to investigate:

> Furthermore, experience shows that we understand very well how to interpret in other people (that is, how to fit into their chain of mental events) the same acts which we refuse to acknowledge as being mental in ourselves. Here some special hindrance evidently deflects our investigations from our own self and prevents our obtaining a true knowledge of it. (1915e, pp. 169–170)

Freud then elegantly demonstrates that any attempt to circumvent this "hindrance" by trying to understand the "other person" in ourselves in terms of consciousness would lead to an impasse, either through the paradox of "an unconscious *consciousness*" (p. 170), or through an infinite regress of "an unlimited number of states of consciousness, all unknown to us and to one another" (p. 170). What we need to do is to admit that our reaction really *is* "alien", not just because it is in response to the patient, but because it has

> . . . characteristics and peculiarities which seem alien to us, or even incredible, and which run directly counter to the attributes of consciousness with which we are familiar. Thus we have grounds for modifying our inference about ourselves and saying that what is proved is not the existence of a second consciousness in us, but the existence of psychical acts which lack consciousness. (1915e, p. 170)

It is in these "psychical acts which lack consciousness" that the "points of contact" are to be found. These are at work in the analyst as well as in the patient, but can be "transformed" into conscious ones. Truly psychoanalytic "identification" begins at this level. Referring to Kant, Freud reassures us that it is possible to work in this zone ("beyond . . . direct experience"), but warns that it requires us to adapt our notions of reality:

> . . . psycho-analysis warns us not to equate perceptions by means of consciousness with the unconscious mental processes which are their object. Like the physical, the psychical is not necessarily in reality what it appears to us to be. (p. 171)

This, I believe, is the strange and surprising reality that I was thrown into when I found myself dreaming about socks while listening to John.

Entering a different reality

In Part II, Freud turns to his jewel, "The topographical point of view". He outlines it in three rapid steps. First, he clarifies the distinction between the "descriptive" and "systematic" senses of the terms "conscious" and "unconscious", unconscious processes in the latter sense standing out "in the crudest contrast" to conscious ones (pp. 172–173). Next, he formalises this in his account of the three "systems" *Ucs.*, *Pcs.*, and *Cs.*, separated by a "censorship" between each system (pp. 172–173). The third step, which is the insertion of the three systems in a metaphorical "psychical *topography*" (p. 173), is so familiar to us that it seems natural, although it is not logically required by the differentiation of three "systems". In fact, this step does not seem self-evident to Freud, who immediately raises an objection, expressed as a "doubt" about the "transposition" between the systems:

> When a psychical act (let us confine ourselves here to one which is in the nature of an idea) is transposed from the system Ucs. into the system Cs. (or Pcs.), are we to suppose that this transposition involves a fresh record—as it were, a second registration—of the idea in question, which may thus be situated as well in a fresh psychical locality, and alongside of which the original unconscious registration continues to exist? Or are we rather to believe that the transposition consists in a change in the state of the idea,

> a change involving the same material and occurring in the same locality? This question may appear abstruse, but it must be raised if we wish to form a more definite conception of psychical topography, of the dimension of depth in the mind. (1915e, p. 174)

What Freud recognises in this objection is that a "psychical act" can belong to two different psychical "systems", without having to be in two different "localities"; a "system" can be fully defined by the "*functional*" (p. 175) relationship between its components. A language can be used to tell a folk tale, for example, but one would not think of these two structures as being in a spatial relationship. Freud's most convincing argument in favour of the topographical hypothesis is

> . . . the possibility that an idea may exist simultaneously in two places in the mental apparatus—indeed, that if it is not inhibited by the censorship, it regularly advances from the one position to the other, possibly without losing its first location or registration. (p. 175)

However, this could conceivably also be understood in functional terms: an unconscious "idea" could remain unchanged and yet find ever-changing expression ("second registration") in dreams, daydreams, and object relationships, just as a folk tale can find expression in stories, pictures, or dance.[4] Freud's other key argument is worth close scrutiny because it is as much in favour of a transformational hypothesis as of a topographic one:

> If we communicate to a patient some idea which he has at one time repressed but which we have discovered in him, our telling him makes at first no change in his mental condition. Above all, it does not remove the repression nor undo its effects. . . . On the contrary, all that we shall achieve at first will be a fresh rejection of the repressed idea. But now the patient has in actual fact the same idea in two forms in different places in his mental apparatus: first, he has the conscious memory of the auditory trace of the idea, conveyed in what we told him; and secondly, he also has—as we know for certain—the unconscious memory of his experience as it was in its earlier form. Actually there is no lifting of the repression until the conscious idea, after the resistances have been overcome, has entered into connection with the unconscious memory-trace. It is only through the making conscious of the latter itself that success is achieved. On superficial

> consideration this would seem to show that conscious and unconscious ideas are distinct registrations, topographically separated, of the same content. But a moment's reflection shows that the identity of the information given to the patient with his repressed memory is only apparent. To have heard something and to have experienced something are in their psychological nature two quite different things, even though the content of both is the same. (1915e, pp. 175–176)

What Freud is saying is that while the "content" of both ideas may *seem* the same, in fact "the identity of the information *given* to the patient with his repressed memory is only apparent" (my emphasis); in other words, the "conscious idea" remains *the analyst's* idea unless it "has entered into connection with the [*patient's*] unconscious memory-trace". The analyst must find a way of working so that *his* "idea" is based on, and expresses, *the patient's* "unconscious memory of his experience . . . in its earlier form". If he proposes an intellectual "idea" too far removed from the patient's experience, he might even provoke "a fresh rejection". Freud's point that "To have heard something and to have experienced something are in their psychological nature two quite different things" is as valid for the analyst as it is for the patient! The challenge for the analyst, then, is how to enter this realm of the patient's experience in order to find images and words to express it. This, as we have already suggested, requires participation of the analyst's unconscious.

We might, perhaps, detect another reason for Freud's use of a spatial metaphor, apart from his wish to help us with "graphic illustrations" (p. 175). Although his neurological background might have played a role, he insists that his "psychical topography has *for the present* nothing to do with anatomy" (p. 175). Spatial and/or temporal metaphors abound in his work: the parts of an optical instrument, different rooms, archaeological discovery, prehistory, Biblical myth. My impression is that they are his way of conveying a sense of exploring a different reality. His evocative phrase "the dimension of depth in the mind" (p. 174)[5] does this with its suggestive image of plunging into an unsounded dimension. It can, indeed, be taken as referring to a stratified topographical representation of the psyche ranging from the most superficial *Cs.* to the deepest *Ucs.*, but it can also be taken—without contradicting the topographical model—as a representation of unconscious mental life as an imaginary *space* and not only as a series of "localities". Freud's metaphor of an extra "dimension" evokes the "alien . . . or even incredible" reality into which patient and analyst must delve in order to reach their "point of contact", comparable to the mythical underworld or deep-ocean exploration: a vast, dimly perceived space, populated by unfamiliar creatures, perhaps uncanny, perhaps strikingly beautiful. This is psychoanalytic space, standing out "in the crudest contrast" to the ordinary space of the consulting room.

Describing psychoanalytic space

We can, thus, read Freud's fine description of the topographical model, in Parts III to VI of "The unconscious", as being equally a description of the psychoanalytic space in which the analytic couple must work. It remains valid today, despite the forbiddingly abstract terminology (which I would not normally use) of his 1915 metapsychology.

In Part III, "Unconscious emotions", Freud relinquishes his earlier provisional limitation of a "psychical act" to an "idea",[6] in order to tackle the status of affect. To do so, he first establishes his well-known distinction between an instinct and its psychical representative:

> An instinct can never become an object of consciousness—only the idea that represents the instinct can. Even in the unconscious . . . an instinct cannot be represented otherwise than by an idea. If the instinct did not attach itself to an idea or manifest itself as an affective state, we could know nothing about it. When we nevertheless speak of an unconscious instinctual impulse or of a repressed instinctual impulse . . . we can only mean an instinctual impulse the ideational representative of which is unconscious . . . (1915e, p. 177)

The key, of course, is in the phrase "*or manifest itself as an affective state*" (my emphasis): affective states are *also* perceptible "psychical acts" that function as representatives of instincts. Freud now proceeds to describe how affects can be understood as the result of a more or less advantageous "*development*" (p. 178, my emphasis) in which, in the most favourable instances, the "quantitative factor in the instinctual impulse" (p. 178) reaches consciousness through linkage to representations. This "development" can be fallible or incomplete, with several other "vicissitudes" (p. 178):

- the "affective or emotional impulse" can be "perceived but misconstrued" by becoming "connected with another idea" (pp. 177–178);
- at the other extreme, if the "quantitative factor in the instinctual impulse" loses all links to representation, it can be completely "suppressed" or "transformed into . . . anxiety" (p. 178);
- in between these extremes, "where repression has [partially] succeeded in inhibiting the development of affects", they are restricted to an unconscious "potential beginning" (p. 178, my interpolation).

These poorly developed "affective structures" or "potential beginnings" in the system *Ucs.* press forward to consciousness as "processes of discharge" (p. 178):

> The whole difference arises from the fact that ideas are cathexes—basically of memory-traces—whilst affects and feelings correspond to processes of discharge, the final manifestations of which are perceived as sensations. (p. 178)

Today, we would add that "memory-traces" might equally fail to find representations, and, therefore, remain unavailable for the development of affective structures; we would furthermore propose that defence mechanisms other than repression, such as splitting and denial, as well as developmental circumstances like trauma, can hinder representation. Nevertheless, the implications of Freud's description for psychoanalytic work are clear: the analyst must help the patient to find or evolve adequate representations ("ideas") for instincts (as well as for memory traces). Only this will ease the "constant struggle for primacy over affectivity . . . between the two systems *Cs.* and *Ucs.*" (p. 179).

One reason why this can be so difficult becomes clearer in Part IV, "Topography and dynamics of repression", where Freud introduces the *economic* (p. 181) point of view of his metapsychology. Repressed ideas (and presumably also the consequently poorly developed "affective structures"), which have "remained cathected or [have] received cathexis from the *Ucs.*", constantly "renew the attempt to penetrate into the system *Pcs.*" (p. 180). They are countered by "an *anticathexis*, by means of which the system *Pcs.* protects itself from the pressure upon it of the unconscious idea" (p. 181). The implication is that the Pcs. reacts as if it were threatened with disturbance by what arises from the Ucs., in spite of the fact that "(pre)conscious cathexis" [belonging] to the system Pcs." (p. 180) is needed to hold the "idea" (or "affective structure") in mind and work with it.

The resulting balance and interplay between Ucs. and Pcs. forces lead Freud to formulate the economic point of view which "endeavours to follow out the vicissitudes of amounts of excitation and to arrive at least at some *relative* estimate of their magnitude" (p. 181). Simply stated, what this means for analytic work is that the analyst can feel disturbed, threatened, or overwhelmed by the representations and/or affective states arising from his unconscious identification with the patient, and so unconsciously or preconsciously defend against them by repression (or other defence mechanisms).

Freud will have more to say about the specific characteristics of the three "systems" in the last three parts of his paper, but by now we are already enabled to translate the three metapsychological points of view in terms of the analyst's position in analytic space. I shall reformulate them as the three questions which I imagined Freud asking himself at the beginning of my chapter:

- *The dynamic point of view:* What are the psychic movements (the instincts and their vicissitudes) that are at work at this point in the session? (What is going on here?)
- *The topographical point of view:* How are these movements experienced and/or expressed (by my patient and/or by me), that is, through what sort of (or paucity of) representational or affective "psychical acts"? (How to understand it?)
- *The economic point of view:* How am I affected or perhaps disturbed by these "psychical acts", and how can this influence my participation in their more or less favourable "development"? (How am I involved?)

For example, my own sense of being threatened by John's need for closeness might have led me to become a bit too distant and intellectual in my interpretative work. Part of the threat might have been due to my own inability to represent his need, which left me feeling that he was getting under my skin because I was not fully able to think about him. My image of turning the sock inside out might have been my way of trying to throw him back out, as much as a first representation of the problem, which we were progressively able to use to allow the more favourable "development" of his unconscious "potential beginning".

Psychoanalytic resources in psychoanalytic space

Fortunately, psychoanalytic space has specific resources that aid us in our task. Freud turns to these in Parts V and VI.

To begin with, his description of "*primary psychical process*" (p. 186) in Part V, "The special characteristics of the system *Ucs.*", reminds us that because *Ucs.* "cathectic intensities . . . are much more mobile", allowing "*displacement*" and "*condensation*" (p. 186), they are creative, as in humour (p. 186). Their "*replacement of external by psychical reality*" (p. 187) can make them a precious play-space which we can access "under the conditions of dreaming . . . when processes of the higher, *Pcs.*, system are set back to an earlier stage by being lowered (by regression)" (p. 187). Thus, the analyst can capture something, preconsciously, of this creative resource through formal regression in the analytic setting.

Referring to Breuer's differentiation between "freely mobile" and "tonically 'bound'" "states of cathectic energy" (p. 188), Freud describes how the "system *Pcs.*" can hold on for a moment, as it were, to the instinctual representatives through "an inhibition of [their] tendency . . . towards discharge", and, hence, "make communication possible between the different ideational contents so that they can influence one another" (p. 188). Thus, "the system *Ucs.* operates . . . as a preliminary stage of the higher organization" (p. 189).

This creative and elaborative interplay between the systems *Ucs.* and *Pcs.* is further underscored in Part VI, "Communication between the two systems":

> . . . the *Ucs.* is alive and capable of development and maintains a number of other relations with the *Pcs.*, amongst them that of co-operation. In brief, it must be said that the *Ucs.* is continued into what are known as derivatives, that it is accessible to the impressions of life, that it constantly influences the *Pcs.*, and is even, for its part, subjected to influences from the *Pcs.* (1915e, p. 190)

Freud is careful to show the limits to this co-operation, pointing out that "to every transition from one system to that immediately above it (that is, every advance to a higher stage of psychical organization) there corresponds a new censorship" (p. 192), and that there are unconscious ego defences that form "the strongest functional antithesis to the repressed" (pp. 192–193). Supervision, intervision, and self-analysis reveal how painfully true these limitations are of our own analytic functioning.

Nevertheless, the substance of Freud's discussion is that by exploiting the interplay of psychical forces, analysis can overcome these obstacles at least to some extent and allow the *Pcs.* to bind the derivatives from the *Ucs.* into "higher" states of "psychical organization". He repeats this important idea about the integrative function of psychical work as a built-in aspect of the topographical model when he writes that "becoming conscious is no mere act of perception, but is probably also a *hypercathexis*, a further advance in the psychical organization" (p. 194).

Lest we had any remaining doubts about the analyst's part in this process of helping the patient to overcome "censorship" and other obstacles to "further advance in the psychical organization", it is at this point that Freud, after stating that the Ucs. is "affected by experiences originating from external perception" (p. 194), makes his well-known observation about unconscious communication:

> It is a very remarkable thing that the Ucs. of one human being can react upon that of another, without passing through the Cs. This deserves closer investigation, especially with a view to finding out whether preconscious activity can be excluded as playing a part in it; but, descriptively speaking, the fact is incontestable. (p. 194)

Although Freud does not go quite so far, it is fair to spell out the obvious implication of this assertion, which is that the analyst's *Ucs.* will react to the patient's *Ucs.*, without necessarily "passing through" the analyst's *Cs.* The converse, of course, is just as true. This, I believe, is the ultimate "point of contact". It means that one of the routes to psychoanalytic elaboration is through the analyst's receptivity to unconscious communication or identification with "derivatives" originating in the patient's *Ucs.*, followed by their preconscious "hypercathexis" and integration in the analytic collaboration.

This hypothesis would give full force to Freud's description of how pathological mental functioning can be changed in analysis, in the last paragraphs of Part VI. Referring to the systems *Pcs.* (or *Cs.*) and *Ucs.*, he writes,

> A complete divergence of their trends, a total severance of the two systems, is what above all characterizes a condition of illness. Nevertheless, psycho-analytic treatment is based upon an influencing of the Ucs. from the direction of the Cs., and at any rate shows that this, though a laborious task, is not impossible. The derivatives of the Ucs. which act as intermediaries between the two systems open the way, as we have already said, towards accomplishing this. (1915e, p. 194)

Remembering his discussion of failed interpretations in Part II (pp. 175–176), we can now see that when the patient's "experience . . . in its earlier form" and "the conscious idea" remain "in two forms in different places" (p. 175), this is because the "derivatives of the *Ucs.*" have not been sufficiently enabled to "act as intermediaries" and to "open the way" (p. 194). The transformational hypothesis is that this "way" might have to be through the *analyst's* psyche, working in collaboration with the patient's, and provided that the analyst's resistances (his "censorship") against emergence of the *Ucs.* derivatives into his *Pcs.* are less strong than the patient's. The analyst might then be able to find representations for the patient's *Ucs.* derivatives that, at some point, the patient's *Pcs.* can use. This may be the "situation" to which Freud refers in his next paragraph:

> Co-operation between a preconscious and an unconscious impulse, even when the latter is intensely repressed, may come about if there is a situation in which the unconscious impulse can act in the same sense as one of the dominant trends. The repression is removed in this instance, and the repressed activity is admitted as a reinforcement of the one intended by the ego. The unconscious becomes ego-syntonic in respect of this single conjunction without any change taking place in its repression apart from this. In this co-operation the influence of the *Ucs.* is unmistakable: the reinforced tendencies reveal themselves as being nevertheless different from the normal; they make specially perfect functioning possible, and they manifest a resistance in the face of opposition which is similar to that offered, for instance, by obsessional symptoms. (1915e, pp. 194–195)

I think that in the last sentence Freud might be referring to moments of grace in mental functioning, as in humour or artistic creation, or in analytic collaboration, as in "Aha!" moments of insight into some important *Ucs.* truth. Many such small moments would be necessary to achieve real integration and change. We would hope that his comparison with the "resistance in the face of opposition . . . offered . . . by obsessional symptoms" is to contrast such new developments with the former pathological rigidity, but, with his usual subtlety, he might also be pointing towards the profound ambiguity of mental life—and of analytic work. What appears like an insight at one moment might turn out to be defensive at the next; what can seem a perception of psychic truth might be perilously near to delusion. However careful we are, and as was my case with John, there are moments in interpretative work when one has to say something that feels a bit mad, but turns out to be useful; at other moments, we come to recognise that we were not, after all, in contact with the patient's unconscious, but astray in our own defences. We never know for sure: only the patient's progress over time will tell.

Words, things, objects, and symbols: the missing link

This momentary incursion into madness might not be inappropriate for the last stretch of our trek through Freud's sometimes stark and sometimes beautiful landscape in Part VII, "Assessment of the unconscious".[7] Here, he completes a missing link between the *Pcs.* and the *Ucs.* in the topographical model, and provides us with a clue about how to fill in a corresponding missing link between patient and analyst in the transformational model.

Although today many analysts would disagree with aspects of Freud's descriptions of psychosis and narcissism, many would also find enduring value in his sensitive observation that in neurosis "object-cathexis persists in the system *Ucs.*" (p. 196), while other patients (psychotic, narcissistic, or otherwise) can suffer terribly from "a primitive objectless condition" (p. 197)—not, we would say today, because object-cathexis is lacking, but because it has not been bound in integrated self- and object-representations.

Indeed, Freud's further profound observation, that in these states "a great deal is expressed as being conscious" but that "to begin with we [are] not able to establish any intelligible connection between the ego-object relation and the relationships of consciousness" (p. 197), remains highly relevant. Something is missing that would be needed to "establish [an] intelligible connection" between the patient's conscious experience and the dynamics of the "ego-object relation". Without this link, conscious experience and unconscious derivatives cannot find their place in a common "higher organization" (i.e., self- and object-representations) that can give them meaning in the minds of both patient and analyst; in other words, they cannot be "identified", to use this translation of Freud's word *Agnoszieren*.[8] In such situations, more than ever, it is the analyst who must work to provide the missing link.

Freud's relation of the case of Victor Tausk's young woman patient "who was brought to the clinic after a quarrel with her lover" (pp. 197–198) demonstrates, if we listen to what she has to say with an ear for the transference, that her difficulty has to do with a failure to find a differentiated position in the object relationship:

> [She] complained that *her eyes were not right, they were twisted*. This she herself explained by bringing forward a series of reproaches against her lover in coherent language. 'She could not understand him at all, he looked different every time; he was a hypocrite, an eye-twister, he had twisted her eyes; now she had twisted eyes; they were not her eyes any more; now she saw the world with different eyes.' (1915e, p. 198)

She is saying that her mind does not work and that she cannot identify Tausk as an individual (her eyes are not right, he looks different to her every time); after projective identification of her disturbance into him, it is he who has becomes an eye-twister who twists her eyes, so that she cannot see. As a result of this confusion, she experiences her impulses and attitudes as being controlled by him: "She was standing in church. Suddenly she felt a jerk; she had to *change her position, as though somebody was putting her into a position* . . ." (p. 198).

Analytic work (like any object relationship) is, therefore, experienced as a threat to identity:

> He was common, he had made her common, too, though she was naturally refined. He had made her like himself by making her think that he was superior to her; now she had become like him, because she thought she would be better if she were like him. He

> had *given a false impression of his position*; now she was just like him (by identification), 'he had *put her in a false position*'. (1915e, p. 198)

In situations where subject–object (i.e., self-object) differentiation and integrated self- and object- representations have not been established, words can only represent part-objects, afloat in an undifferentiated psychic space. What Freud calls "organ-speech" (pp. 198, 199) is what we would call today "symbolic equations" (Segal, 1957). As with my patient John, long, careful work is required to establish self–object differentiation, the precondition for a symbolic space in which subject and object can work side-by-side to find sensations, images, and words for the experiences arising in the analytic relationship. Such work takes place at a level where representations and "affective structures" are not yet available. It is the analyst's task to delve into his preconscious experience, informed by unconscious derivatives arising at the "point of contact" with the patient, in order to find representatives of "instincts" and "memory-traces" that the patient might be able to use. The converse is equally true: that this process of finding meaningful representatives is part of the progressive establishment of subject–object differentiation.

Freud discusses such disturbances in terms of his fundamental distinction between "word-presentations" and "thing-presentations".[9] His argument is,

> If we ask ourselves what it is that gives the character of strangeness . . ., we . . . realize that it is the predominance of what has to do with words over what has to do with things. . . . If now we put this finding alongside the hypothesis that in schizophrenia object-cathexes are given up, we shall be obliged to modify the hypothesis by adding that the cathexis of the *word*-presentations of objects is retained. What we have permissibly called the conscious presentation of the object can now be split up into the presentation of the *word* and the presentation of the *thing*; the latter consists in the cathexis, if not of the direct memory-images of the thing, at least of remoter memory-traces derived from these. (1915e, pp. 200–201)

Where we would differ with his analysis today is that "object-cathexes" have not been "given up", but that subject–object differentiation has not succeeded, and so "thing-presentations" (or "object-presentations") have not been developed on a secure basis. It is this, and not a withdrawal of cathexis from objects or "things", which leads to the *apparent* "predominance of . . . words". As discussed above, the difficulty of transformational analytic work at this level is to help the patient to *find* "thing-presentations" for the "remoter memory-traces" of object relations, at a level where "direct memory-images" are unavailable. To my mind, these considerations do not detract from Freud's differentiation of "thing-" *vs.* "word-presentations"; on the contrary, they confirm its lasting value for the understanding of psychotic and deeply disturbed narcissistic states.

These concepts provide Freud with the final key to the solution of his "doubt" as to whether the passage from the "system *Ucs.*" into the "system *Pcs.*" should be explained as "a second registration" or as "a change in the state of the idea" (p. 174). It is a combination of both:

> We now . . . know . . . what the difference is between a conscious and an unconscious presentation. The two are not . . . different registrations of the same content in different psychical localities, nor yet different functional states of cathexis in the same locality; but the conscious presentation comprises the presentation of the thing plus the presentation of the word belonging to it, while the unconscious presentation is the presentation of the thing alone. The system *Ucs.* contains the thing-cathexes of the objects, the first and true object-cathexes; the system *Pcs.* comes about by this thing-presentation being hypercathected through being linked with the word-presentations corresponding to it. It is these hypercathexes, we may suppose, that bring about a higher psychical organization and make it possible for the primary process to be succeeded by the secondary process which is dominant in the *Pcs.* Now, too, we are in a position to state precisely what it is that repression denies to the rejected presentation in the transference neuroses: what it denies . . . is translation into words . . . attached to the object. A presentation which is not put into words, or a psychical act which is not hypercathected, remains thereafter in the *Ucs.* in a state of repression. (1915e, pp. 201–202)

There are only two qualifications that we would add today to this extraordinarily precise description. The first is that, as I have already argued, "the thing-cathexes of the objects, the first and true object-cathexes", simply might not be available for linking to words because they have not yet been developed. The second is, consequentially, that the missing "translation" of "thing-cathexes" "into words . . . attached to the object" can result not only from repression as in the transference neuroses, but also in other forms of psychic organisation, from other defence mechanisms and/or developmental circumstances that obstruct the development of "thing-presentations". This is where the analyst's transformational work is most needed, beginning at the unconscious "point of contact" with the patient and passing through the analyst's unconscious and preconscious capacities for object-relatedness and symbolisation. Relying on these resources and on the patient's collaboration, the analyst's task is to help the latter to find "thing-presentations" and "word-presentations" that he or she may be able to use. When this succeeds, the "development of affects" becomes possible again, moving on from their "potential beginning" (p. 178), together with the elaboration of adequate, symbolic representations to "bind" affects and memory-traces in an enriched preconscious experience. This process of finding "thing-presentations", also called "primary symbolization" (Roussillon, 1999), is an essential precondition for the "secondary symbolization" of meaningful linkage to "word-presentations". It is, I believe, the process that John managed to pursue when he took my image of the sock in meaningful directions that I could have not imagined when it first came to me.

Thus, though we might disagree with some aspects of Freud's account of psychosis in the first pages of Part VII, it is in clear continuity with the rest of his extraordinary paper and remains highly relevant to the psychoanalytic understanding and treatment of poorly symbolised mental states.

Freud's legacy

There is always a risk of reading into Freud's writings psychoanalytic theories that were developed on the basis of his work, but which he would not recognise or accept. My contribution might be an example of this and my natural concerns about that cannot be fully assuaged by appealing to *après-coup* understanding: this is why I have added a question mark to its title. The enduring clinical relevance of

Freud's paper is what encourages me to propose this reading of it. My hope is that I have managed to propose some "thing-" and "word-presentations", perhaps with a "a gain in meaning", for one of the hidden treasures in Freud's legacy,[10] which we are enabled to recognise today because generations of analysts have helped it to bear fruit.

If so, we might see the seeds sown in Freud's study of "The unconscious" taking root in the work of his successors, beginning with that of Melanie Klein (1926, 1930), whose psychoanalytic play technique could arguably be seen as a way of helping her patients to find "thing-presentations" for their unconscious experience. Following her work, two main branches of the legacy are found in the work of Bion (1962b, 1965) and of Winnicott (1971). Bion's (1962b) concept of an α function transforming β elements into α elements could be compared to finding "thing-presentations" for "memory traces" and for the "quantitative factor in the instinctual impulse",[11] while his (1965) concept of transformation in O could be compared to the unconscious identification and collaboration between patient and analyst at the "point of contact", which I have argued is at least implicit in Freud's paper. Winnicott's (1971) concept of transitional space might be seen in a similar way. These two branches lead to contemporary transformational models of psychoanalytic work, as in, to mention only two, the developments through Bion and the Barangers (2008) to the work of Ferro (1999, 2009), or through Winnicott to that of Roussillon (1999, 2008).

I do not see premonitions in Freud's paper of intersubjective work in the wider sense of the term, in that I see no indications there of total co-creation of intersubjective phenomena between analysand and analyst; Freud's thinking seems to me to be totally centred on how to find expression and meaning for the analysand's unconscious experience, warranting only a concept of co-creation in a limited sense as discussed by Hanly (2007). This being said, I do see in it a basis for intersubjective work in a more specific sense as described for example by Brown (2011). However, given the multiple meanings of "intersubjective", my own preferred term for this kind of transformative work would be "interpsychic", as used, for example, by Bolognini (2011), and which would seem closer to Freud's original usage.

Notes

1. Unless otherwise specified, emphases in the quoted material are those introduced by James Strachey, but which do not exist in the original German text.

2. Freud's original German word is *Umsetzung*, which can mean "transformation", "conversion", or, as in music, "transposition".

3. My use of Freud's terms "thing-presentation" and "word-presentation" will become clearer in what follows.

4. Indeed, this is how Freud describes unconscious phantasies on pp. 190–191.

5. In German, "der psychischen Tiefendimension", *GW*, *X*, p. 273.

6. German *Vorstellung*, or "representation".

7. "Assessment" is Strachey's translation for the German *Agnoszierung* (*GW*, *X*, p. 294), which might be better translated as "recognition"; the French translation is "identification".

8. See note 7, above.

9. From here on, Strachey no longer translates *Vorstellung* as "idea" but as "presentation", perhaps to convey the pre-symbolic nature of "thing-" and "word-presentations", but in French, for example, *Sach-* and *Wortvorstellung* are translated, respectively, as "représentation de chose" and "représentation de mot".

10. Brown (2011) would call it our genetic heritage!

11. This is the one point where I disagree with Brown (2011), who compares "thing-presentations" to β elements.

7

The unconscious in work with psychosomatic patients[1]

Marilia Aisenstein

Speaking about the manifestations of the dynamic unconscious in psychosomatic patients calls for a few preliminary remarks. Since the 1950s, different schools of psychosomatics, defending various theoretical models, have argued about the question of the unconscious meaning of somatic symptoms. Groddeck was the first to attribute an unconscious significance to every organic manifestation. Freud reproached him in a letter dated June 5, 1917 for making no real difference between the somatic and the psychic (Freud, E. L., 1960, pp. 316–318). In 1963, at a Congress for French-speaking analysts held in Paris,[2] Angel Garma and Michel de M'Uzan took up contrasting positions, the first arguing that the treatment of physical illnesses must seek to unearth the unconscious fantasy underlying them and interpret it as in a classical analysis, while, for the second, "the somatic symptom is stupid", precisely because it has no meaning, but is evidence of a traumatic excess that overwhelms the capacities of the psychical apparatus for elaboration, thus obliging the subject to find other paths of discharge for excitation, whether behavioural or somatic.

The Chicago School has highlighted the importance of emotional factors, but has mainly sought to discover the specific conflicts involved in each somatic pathology, stipulating the existence of a neurophysiological mechanism linking emotions to organs, whereas for the Kleinians somatic illness is determined by a psychical process involving fantasy activity from the very beginning of life. The theoretical models of psychosomaticians have been described and studied by Smadja in *Les modèles psychanalytiques de la psychosomatique* (2008), while Elsa Rappoport de Aisemberg and myself have presented these schools of thought through clinical illustrations in *Psychosomatics Today: A Psychoanalytic Perspective* (Aisenstein & Rappoport, 2010).

The aim of this introduction is to show that whether or not we think of illness as having an unconscious meaning radically changes the understanding of the symptom as well as our interpretative technique.

The drive as the foundation of a psychosomatic, or, rather, somatopsychic theory

My choice of the term somatopsychic rather than psychosomatic is based on the idea of an ascending direction that goes from the body to the psychic according to an imperative of increasing complexity.

Psychoanalysis existed before the definition of the drives, and yet the notions of excitation and drive do not stand in a relationship of continuity. We can see "a radical caesura" in Freud's thought before and after the conception of the concept of the drive.

Here, I am defending the idea that the whole approach of the Paris School of Psychosomatics, to which I adhere, is already present in embryo in the Freudian construction of the concept of the drive.

Let me recall the famous definition of the concept:

> If now we apply ourselves to considering mental life from a biological point of view, an 'instinct' appears to us as a concept on the frontier between the mental and the somatic, as the psychical representative of the stimuli originating from within the organism and reaching the mind, *as a measure of the demand made upon the mind for work in consequence of its connection with the body*. (Freud, 1915e, p. 121, my emphasis)

The demand comes, then, from the body, which imposes on the mind a measurable and, I would add, indispensable amount of work for its protection and, thus, for its survival. I am reminded of André Green's fine formula: "The psyche is, so to speak, worked by the body, worked in the body" (Green, 1973, p. 170). The body demands a labour from the psyche (elaboration comes from labour). Green continues,

> But this demand cannot be accepted in its raw state; it must be decoded if the psyche is to respond to the body's demand, which, in the absence of any response, will increase its demands in force and in number. (p. 170)

The word drive (in the English translation we read "impulse") is mentioned for the first time in the *Letters to Fliess* in 1897 (25 May 1897 and 31 May 1897; see Masson (1985)). But the German term *Trieb* only appears in his writings as a metapsychological category in 1905, in the *Three Essays on the Theory of Sexuality* (Freud, 1905d, "The sexual instinct in neurotics", pp. 163–165, and "Component instincts and erotogenic zones", pp. 167–170). Freud writes,

> By an instinct[3] is provisionally to be understood the psychical representative of an endosomatic, continuously flowing source of stimulation as contrasted with a stimulus which is set up by single excitations coming from without. The concept of instinct is thus one of those lying on the *frontier between the mental and the physical*. The simplest and likeliest assumption as to the nature of instincts would seem to be that in itself an instinct is without quality, and, so far as mental life is concerned, is only to be regarded as a measure of the demand made upon the mind for work. (Freud, 1905d, p. 168, my emphasis)

The *Three Essays* is a text in which Freud reflects on human sexuality, and it was in this context that the conception of the drive emerged. The psychoneurosis must thus be related to the force of the drive. The energy of the sexual drive constitutes a portion of the forces that sustain pathological manifestations, but this contribution is the most important source of energy and the only one that is constant.

I would like to stress two points: first, it seems to me that Freud sees a drive force (or rather the alloying of two drives), which, on account of its excess, paves the way for psychic pathologies. He says nothing about the reasons for this excess, thereby suggesting that it is constitutional.

My second point concerns the notion of continuity; the thrust of the drive is continuous, or, rather, it should be. Now one of the major contributions of the Paris School of Psychosomatics is to have drawn the attention of the psychoanalytic world to the discontinuities of mental functioning. Thus, we may make the assumption that a failure of the "demand for representation" occurs that is linked to excess.[4]

If the notions of source, object, and aim were defined in 1905, it was not until 1915, in "Instincts and their vicissitudes" (1915c) that Freud grouped them together with the idea of "pressure" (*Drang*), an economic quantitative factor, to give a general definition of the drive.

The characteristic of exerting pressure is common to all drives, and even their very essence (Freud, 1915c, p. 122). However, Freud links the constant nature of the pressure with the demand to represent. From the body there arises a demand to represent.

Where is the "demand" to be located in topographical terms? Should it be seen as a principle transcending the agencies? This question will lead me to compare the two essential texts, "The unconscious" (1915e) and *The Ego and the Id* (1923b).

An attentive reading reveals a crucial change from one topography to the other: in the first, the accent is placed on the unconscious ideas always combined with "pressure", whereas in the second topography, the id, a reservoir of instinctual impulses, is constituted on the one hand by the repressed unconscious of the first topography and, on the other, by a space open to the body, which consists only of forces that are sometimes contradictory and without representations. Here, we can see that force has primacy over representation. This has important technical consequences. Would it not be reasonable to suppose that if the treatments of neurotics aim to transform unconscious material into preconscious material, those that we conduct with somatic and borderline organisations *have the goal of transforming id into unconscious?*

The unconscious and the id

I am now going to read again, attentively, Freud's description of the unconscious in the first topography. This text is of particular concern to us for several reasons. It is fundamental in itself, but, above all, a large number of "difficult" patients—non-neurotic, borderline, and somatic cases—are described as patients for whom free association does not exist, making access to unconscious material problematic. It is often said that "they present deficiencies in preconscious functioning", and I would like to try to understand this statement better in the light of the text of 1915.

The repressed does not include the whole of the unconscious, but is part of it. The essence of repression is to prevent ideational representatives of the drive from becoming conscious, but its specific aim is *to suppress the development of affect*: "the work is incomplete", writes Freud, "if this aim is not achieved" (1915e, p. 178). Affect cannot be repressed, but its suppression is the aim of repression.

The hypothesis of the separation of the systems unconscious and preconscious implies that an idea or presentation may exist simultaneously in both places—the thing-presentations in the unconscious, thing- and word-presentations in the preconscious—and "advance from one position to the other", Freud writes (1915e, p. 175). The drive can only be represented by the representative that is attached to it, otherwise it appears in the form of affect. At the beginning we have to imagine an indissociable pair consisting of the instinctual psychic representative arising from the body and the object-presentation arising from perception. Two vicissitudes follow from this: one towards the ideational representative of things and words, the other towards the affect representative and differentiated affect. The question of affect is a complex one; indeed, what I am interested in here is its avatars between the unconscious and the preconscious.

If the repressed idea remains in the unconscious as a real formation, Freud writes, the unconscious affect is but "a potential beginning which is prevented from developing" (1915e, p. 178). Strictly speaking, then, there are no unconscious affects, but formations charged with energy which seek to break through the preconscious barrier. Moreover, Freud compares affect with motility, both of which are governed by the conscious mind and have discharge value. Freud writes,

> Affectivity manifests itself essentially in motor (secretory and vasomotor) discharge resulting in an (internal) alteration of the subject's own body without reference to the external world; motility, in actions designed to effect changes in the external world. (p. 179, fn. 1)

In my view, this gives an indication as to the importance of the actual presence of the bodies of both protagonists in the treatment.

Thus, preconscious affects of the psychoanalyst can be perceived by the patient and meet in him or her an unconscious "potential beginning" which seeks to break through. *This is only qualified in the transfero–countertransferential process, where it acquires its status of affect as a result of being processed by the analyst's preconscious.*

Moreover, in Chapter Six of "The unconscious", Freud studies the "Communication between the two systems". Every passage from one system to the other implies a change of cathexis (or investment). Yet, this does not suffice to explain the constancy of primal repression. He is obliged to postulate a process that sustains the latter. The preconscious protects itself, in effect, against the pressure of thing-presentations by means of an anti-cathexis nourished by energy withdrawn from word-presentations.

To speak of the "deficiencies of the preconscious" is to remain on a phenomenological level. I think it is more interesting to imagine in our patients *a preconscious emptied of its forces by such a drastic anti-cathexis that it paralyses this system and isolates the other. I imagine this anti-cathexis to take the form of a vast mechanism of repression.* For, let us not forget that, of course, the unconscious is alive; it communicates with the other systems and remains subject to the influences of the preconscious and external perception.

Now, Freud does not say that perception is unconscious (in fact, he never developed a theory of unconscious perception), but it none the less underpins the whole dream-theory (without it, Section 7 becomes incomprehensible). "It is a very remarkable thing", he writes further on, "that the *Ucs.* of one human being can react upon that of another, without passing through the *Cs.*" (p. 194). Freud then wonders how preconscious activity can be excluded from "this incontestable clinical phenomenon".

Eight years later, in *The Ego and the Id* (1923b), we are given some formidably complex and interesting answers, which I shall attempt to summarise succinctly here.

The second topography gives us the anthropomorphic and psychodramatic vision of a boundless ego which has become a psychical quality, and which is also an agency of repression whose defensive operations are to a large extent unconscious. It is up against an id which Freud describes as "a chaos, a cauldron full of seething excitations. We picture it as being *open at its end to somatic influences*" (Freud, 1933a, p. 73, my emphasis). The subject is an unknown and unconscious psychical id on the surface of which an ego is formed which is the portion of the id modified by the influences of the external world, that is, the sensory perceptions coming from the outside. In *The Ego and the Id*, we can read,

> We have come upon something in the ego itself, which is also unconscious, which behaves exactly like the repressed—that is, which produces powerful effects without itself being conscious and which requires *special work* before it can be made conscious. From the point of view of analytic practice, the consequence of this discovery is that we land in endless obscurities and difficulties if we keep to our habitual forms of expression and try, for instance, to derive neuroses from a conflict between the conscious and the unconscious. (1923b, p. 17, my emphasis)

Very different from the first, the second topography passes from the qualitative to the structural and privileges force, the instinctual impulses, to the detriment of ideational contents. This seems to indicate a change correlative to the introduction of the second drive theory, which was conceived to account for a hitherto unrecognised dimension of destructivity. That is the essential difference between the unconscious and the id: while the unconscious of the first topography remains in the register of pleasure, the id is inhabited by contradictory *instinctual impulses including those of destruction* = chaos.

From comparing these two articles, we can see a decline of the concept of representation in favour of the notion of instinctual impulse. Now, this turn towards the economic implies *a promotion, new in Freud's thought, of affect.*

Freud had had a premonition of the immense clinical implications of this shift of emphasis from representation to affect. With certain patients, among whom are somatic patients, though not exclusively, the whole work of analysis will be focused, I believe, on gaining access to affects and on their metabolisation.

In the analyses of psychoneurosis, the guiding thread that allows us to gain access to unconscious material is free association. In analytic work with non-neurotic patients, actual neuroses, borderline, and somatic cases, one is frequently faced with "non-associativity". The discourse is not, or is no longer, "alive"; psychic functioning can prove to be *opératoire* or "mechanical", and affects are apparently absent. Psychic energy is not elaborated, manifesting itself more through acts or, as I maintain, through soma. Neither resistances, nor derivatives of the repressed, nor compromise formations can be detected; it is as though there was no conflict between opposing psychic forces. Often, the only guiding thread is anxiety, the affect of anxiety as Freud calls it. An affect of unpleasure, anxiety is a flight in face of the libido which is at once an outcome and an alteration. A rudiment of unconscious affect seeking to break through might appear, transformed into anxiety.

Affect: the only means of access to the unconscious of the ego[5]

I would now like to illustrate this type of work with some brief clinical vignettes.

A woman of about fifty was referred to me at the Paris Institute of Psychosomatics for severe eczema, which was troubling her a lot. Mrs X gave the impression of being a very worthy and courteous, though austere, woman, and was dressed like a nun in plain clothes. She had an administrative job. It took me months to understand that this eczema was located "at the bottom of her back" and on the inside of her thighs, which she called "the top of my legs". The eczema had begun after the marriage of her only daughter. I tried desperately to explore her relations with her daughter and with her husband. Mrs X replied politely that she did not think, did not dream, did not have those sorts of ideas, and added, "I am not sentimental. Questions are useless; in life, it's better to act than to think." She told me in great detail about her days at the office and commented on the weather. Her discourse was not associative; I suspected the existence of a drastic and long-standing suppression bearing on affect and representation. I was both touched by this patient and driven to despair by the sessions with her. On one occasion I had the flu, and was feeling feverish and tired. She noticed and was visibly anxious; indeed, she was so agitated that I was prompted to ask her what was wrong with her. She said she was feeling bad; she felt sick and wanted to end the session. I refused and said, "Imagining that I am ill seems to make you feel sick, as if from disgust." This she denied, and then she suddenly doubled up to stop herself from retching. I insisted that it was important for us to speak about this and for the first time she mentioned a childhood memory. She told me how she had felt disgusted at seeing her mother's sick, exhibited body. Her mother had died when the patient was twelve, leaving her alone with an absent and exciting father who spanked her to "calm her down" and punish her. We were then able to make the link between the spanking and her eczema "at the bottom of her back", and to understand later on how much her daughter's marriage had upset her, assuming the significance of a trauma. Having been brought up as a model little girl, her daughter was very idealised and narcissistically invested by the patient, who had always experienced sexual relations as a distressing obligation. On the wedding day, she had had the thought that she was handing her daughter over to a rapist. Her eczema had appeared shortly after, in the days following.

Another younger and single woman,[6] aged forty, presented with severe asthma, which prevented her from working. Her psychic organisation was typically borderline, but there were long periods during which she would function in a very "mechanical" (*opératoire*) mode.

For months she had been clinging to my gaze and would either launch into factual descriptions of her life or into furious diatribes against the weather, the government, the social security, doctors, and so on.

One day, after complaining about her allergist, her secretary, and my silence, she started to describe at great length a new and violent intercostal pain she had been having; since the weekend, she had been diagnosed with a cracked rib due to her bouts of coughing and the strong doses of corticoids she was taking.

This made me think of a dear friend who had died from an embolism. Being a doctor herself, she had not sought advice about the pain she was having, thinking it was an intercostal fracture. I was overwhelmed by powerful feelings of sadness. A few seconds later, the patient started to be agitated and was breathing noisily; she was starting to have an asthmatic attack. She got up, as if to leave, and shouted at me, "You see, it's your fault . . . you've abandoned me."

I asked her to sit down again and spoke to her at some length. I told her she was right; I had indeed been thinking of someone else she had made me think of, but that we needed to understand together why she could not tolerate not having complete control over someone else's thoughts.

At that moment, the patient started breathing more easily, and I proposed to her a construction to the effect that it was probable that she was making me experience what she had suffered from in the distant past (feelings of being invaded and the sense that her thoughts were being controlled). She cried for the first time.

Once the dimension of the "third" and of history had been introduced, analytic work could begin.

In both cases, these were patients whose discourse was actual and factual. For each of them it was a question of a rare moment in which affects of anxiety emerged. These turned out to be fruitful moments in both treatments, and I think it will be useful to reflect on the way in which they appeared in the transference.

Transference compulsion and repetition compulsion

In both these examples, the affect of anxiety could be qualified and, thus, become an object of construction or interpretation thanks to the transfero–countertransferential work. I am referring to countertransference in the broad sense of the analyst's mental functioning as a whole during the session, as employed by André Green in many of his seminars. But there is a transference, even if not a classical and interpretable transference, as in a transference neurosis. Now, some of our patients who suffer from a somatic illness and who arrive for a consultation at the Institute of Psychosomatics come "with a prescription". They say they are not interested in the "psychic" or in introspection; however, generally speaking, they continue coming, and often for years. This may seem very mysterious.

The classical answer, according to which they continue their treatment because for them it is supposedly "non-conflictual", has never convinced me. I think that they come and continue to come *because there exists within the human psyche a "transference compulsion"*. Small children fall in love with a doll or a lorry, etc., which are already transferences. Classical transference is the most evolved form, but includes the transference on to language and into language, as well as the first form of transference: from the somatic to the psychic. *The demand of the drive for representation is an obligation to transfer from the somatic to the psychic.*

Freud adopted two successive theories of the transference: the first runs from 1895 (*Studies on Hysteria* (1895d)) to 1920 (*Beyond the*

Pleasure Principle (1920g)); the second covers the period from 1920 to the end of his work. The first has often been called the "libidinal theory of transference", an outmoded term, but one he explained clearly in "The dynamics of transference" (1912b). The motor of the transference is the eternally renewed need for instinctual satisfactions within the framework of the pleasure–unpleasure principle.

The second takes shape after 1920; it sees the transference as a fundamental tendency to repeat which is "beyond the pleasure principle". In the chapter devoted to the transference in his book, *La Cure Psychanalytique Classique*, Bouvet (2007) writes,

> As the traumatic situation, or the experience responsible for the complex, has resulted in unbearable tension, we cannot say that the subject transfers under the sign of the search for pleasure; rather, it must be due to an innate tendency to repeat. (p. 227)

These two conceptions of the transference do not contradict each other and can co-exist; none the less, they each drew on different clinical material, for it was the clinical failures that led Freud to think again about the opposition between the drives, topographical questions, anxiety, and masochism. There is one conviction, though, that Freud never reneged on until the end, and this was that the transference is the most powerful motor of the treatment.

I think, though, that one can distinguish *two phases* in Freud's work. In the first, all the clinical material and the theoretical elaborations Freud makes from it have as their reference or matrix the psychoneurosis of defence, which he also called the "transference neuroses", for which the principal model is hysteria. The work of analysis aims essentially to gain access to latent material through mechanisms such as displacement and condensation. Here, we are in the domain of representation and under the aegis of the pleasure principle.

Transference manifestations are the symbolic equivalents of desire and unconscious fantasies.

In the second phase, Freud was faced with clinical material in which negative narcissism, destructiveness, action, and discharge played a predominant role; the transference here is no longer "libidinal" and under the aegis of the pleasure–unpleasure principle, but under that of pure repetition compulsion. What is its texture? There is a compulsion, an appetite, for the object, which condenses the tendency to inertia and the regulatory mechanisms aimed at reducing or calming instinctual tensions progressively, by degrees.

The object/analyst is invested according to a mode of repetition compulsion, but the work of countertransference consists in transforming anxieties into affects so as to put history in the place of repetition. This first transference can be followed up by a classical transference with displacements from one object to another, which will finally actualise the patient's history, thus making regression possible.

By way of summary and conclusion

For me, the somatic symptom has no symbolic meaning, but can acquire one secondarily in the aftermath of analysis. It is, thus, not interpretable in itself as a direct manifestation of the unconscious, but is evidence of an excess of excitation which cannot be elaborated by psychic work alone.

My psychosomatic approach is based on the Freudian paradigm of the drive: the question of representation, or the failure of the system of representations, is, thus, crucial in my view.

The model of neurosis cannot account for the somatic symptom.

The change of topography in 1923 seems to me to have its roots in Freud's research in response to his experience with non-neurotic cases, where free association no longer provided a path of access to the unconscious. A careful reading of these texts shows how much the id is different from, and cannot be superposed on, the unconscious of 1915. I think one can see in them a decline in the importance of representation and a promotion of the question of force, of the instinctual charge. As a result, affect becomes the key concept, for it alone is capable of linking a charge to a representation or to a chain of representations.

In my two clinical examples, an element concerning the analyst, though perceived by the patient as "coming from outside" and not counter-cathected, is felt to be a source of anguish or unbearable. It can be tolerated thanks to the transference, and transformed into affect by virtue of the analyst's work of linking a charge to a representation. In both cases, this moment inaugurates real psychoanalytic work, for it establishes alterity, that is, the forced recognition of the object's own psychic life.

Notes

1. Translated by Andrew Weller.
2. 23rd Congress for French-speaking psychoanalysts, Paris, 20–23 July 1963. Published in the *Revue française de psychanalyse*, *28*, special edition, 1964.
3. Strachey chose to translate *Trieb* by "instinct" rather than "drive", but in the German text the term used is "drive" and not "instinct".
4. In 2010, I wrote a Report for the Congress of French-Speaking Psychoanalysts entitled "Les exigences de la répresentation", published in the *Revue française de psychanalyse* (Aisenstein, 2010b). Here, I am developing passages already elaborated in this Report.
5. "And this *Ucs.* belonging to the ego is not latent like the *Pcs.*; for if it were, it could not be activated without becoming Cs., and the process of becoming conscious would not encounter such great difficulties" (Freud, 1923b, p. 18).
6. This case was published in a paper on representation (Aisenstein, 2010b).

8

The unconscious and perceptions of the self

Ira Brenner

Freud's seminal monograph on the unconscious (Freud, 1915e) has been a wellspring of ideas which, almost a century later, continue to inspire us to elaborate upon his insights. In this essay, I will extend his ideas on the role of the unconscious upon a specific aspect of perception. While his thinking about perception, the central component of mental functioning, evolved over the half-century of his writing and some theoretical contradictions were left to later writers to reconcile (Beres & Joseph, 1970; Schimek, 1975; Slap, 1987), it is now universally accepted that unconscious processes influence how and what we perceive.

Perception has been defined as "1. the state of being or process of becoming aware or conscious of a thing, *spec.*, through any of the senses" (*The New Shorter Oxford English Dictionary*, 1993, p. 2156). Therefore, the emphasis in perception is on external stimuli and bringing the outside world into the mind primarily through the eyes, ears, nose, mouth, and skin. We therefore speak of perceiving the animate as well as the inanimate world. We also refer to the perception of abstract phenomena such as "b. the intuitive or direct recognition of a moral, aesthetic, or personal quality, e.g., the truth of a remark, the beauty of an object; the instance of this" (*The New Shorter*

Oxford English Dictionary, 1993, p. 2156). The well-known saying "Beauty is in the eye of the beholder" exemplifies the subjective nature of perception, which also is not an arguable point.

In psychoanalytic theorising, constant attention is paid to how the ego's perceptual capacities are affected, compromised, and altered by influences from the unconscious. Both what is perceived and what is not perceived come under the purview of such consideration. And, the perception of both external and internal realities is seen to be coloured by covert antecedents. The assessments of texture, nuance, timbre, hues, angulation, and, to a lesser extent, of even the "harder" qualities such as height, weight, and age is viewed as in part unconsciously determined. The same is true of internal assessments of an object's emotional value, a self-representation's place in one's heart, the hierarchy of moral values, and the passage of time. The last-mentioned may be studied in virtually every analytic session and provides enormous information about unconscious mental functioning. Major disturbances in this aspect of perception, especially "losing time", might indicate disturbances in other aspects of the psyche that are more elusive, but if able to be examined, might shed more light on our overall enterprise.

As advancements in psychoanalytic technique have enabled more difficult patients to benefit from psychoanalysis, patients generally thought to be untreatable have provided opportunities to re-examine basic concepts. For example, the conscious aspects of self observation have been overvalued, and unconscious aspects of self-perception have been minimised. The influence of these unconscious forces on self-perception, however, may be re-examined in those patients who employ defensive altered states of consciousness and the preponderance of periodic irruptions of dissociated, unconscious aspects of the self. As a psychology major, I witnessed someone having a "bad trip". A young woman's repeated utterance made such an indelible impression upon me that, over forty years later, her simple but haunting words continue to disturb and fascinate me. She was standing a bit ahead of me in line with her friends at a cinema. This coed suddenly blurted out repeatedly, "I'm here and I'm not here—and I'm here and I'm not here . . ."

The townspeople noted her confusion and silently registered their mixed feelings of concern and disdain. Her friends tried to quiet her down but to no avail. She only became more insistent and persistent in her disorientated wonderment. Her voice became more hollow and eerie-sounding as she was overheard repeating her mantra while her entourage embarrassedly escorted her away. Clearly, she was in no condition to watch the film as she apparently experienced an abrupt change in her mental state, which altered her perception of her self and her surroundings.

Seeing this young woman decompensate remained memorable. I have asked myself why my perception of this woman's disturbance of perception made such an impression upon me. Here was a real, live demonstration of a mental aberration I could ponder over. I had known this young woman slightly and was struck by her shyness and almost secretiveness. Superficially friendly, she exuded a type of aloofness that could have easily been mistaken for being snobbish or conceited. I had heard that on the evening in question she had smoked marijuana for the first time. The likelihood of it being contaminated with a toxic hallucinogen was quite low. In perhaps one of my first psychodynamic formulations, I speculated that there was some underlying vulnerability in her psyche that made her especially sensitive to losing contact with her ability to know where she was. I wondered where she "went to" when she exclaimed that she was "not here", as she gave the impression that she had somehow left her body. She might have experienced a sense of her body as being quite different from her usual feelings about her overall self.

This disturbance in her perception had a certain quality to it that one might indeed attribute to depersonalisation, or derealisation (Arlow, 1966; Guralnik & Simeon, 2010), and could be diagnosed as a "dissociative" experience. An extreme of the dissociative continuum would be those cases of dissociative identity disorder (DID), or multiple personality. Those who live with such phenomena, also described as a lower-level dissociative character (Brenner, 1994, 2001, 2004, 2009), can feel that, in addition to being "here and not here", it is "me and not me", as well as "know and not know" a painful truth, quite often of a traumatic nature. Becoming aware of one's own mental processes, Freud likened "to the perception of the external world by means of the sense organs" (Freud, 1915e, pp. 170–171). He thereby provided an avenue for comprehending what might have happened to this temporarily deranged young woman. She probably experienced alternating awareness of her unconscious mental processes and, thus, took leave of her usual senses. Freud stated,

> Just as Kant warned us not to overlook the fact that our perceptions are subjectively conditioned and not to be regarded as identical with what is perceived though unknowable, now psycho-analysis warns us not to equate perception by means of consciousness with the unconscious mental processes which are their object. Like the physical, the psychical is not necessarily in reality what it appears to be. We shall be glad to learn, however, that the correction of internal perception will turn out not to offer such great difficulties as the correction of external perception—that internal objects are less unknowable than the external world. (Freud, 1915e, p. 171)

As Freud lays out his understanding of the unconscious and reminds us that the nature of mentation follows different principles associated with primary process thinking, he attempts to diminish the significance of those ever problematic cases of multiple personality in the following way:

> . . . analysis shows that the different latent mental processes inferred by us enjoy a high degree of mutual independence, as though they had no connection with one another, and knew nothing of one another. We must be prepared, if so, to assume the existence in us not only of a second consciousness, but of a third, fourth, perhaps of an unlimited number of states of consciousness, all unknown to us and to one another. In the third place—and this is the most weighty argument of all—we have to take into account the fact that analytic investigation reveals some of these latent processes as having characteristics and peculiarities which seem alien to us, or even incredible, and which run directly counter to the attributes of consciousness with which we are familiar. Thus we have grounds for modifying our inference about ourselves and saying that what is proved is not the existence of a second consciousness in us, but the existence of psychical acts which lack consciousness. We shall also be right in rejecting the term 'subconsciousness' as incorrect and misleading. The well known cases of '*double conscience*' (splitting of consciousness) prove nothing against our view. We may most aptly describe them as cases of a splitting of the mental activities into two groups, and say that the same consciousness turns to one or the other of these groups alternately. (Freud, 1915e, pp. 169–170)

The question of these "different latent mental processes [which] enjoy a high degree of mutual independence, as though they had no connection with one another, and knew nothing of one another" has continued to vex theoreticians and clinicians ever since. This is especially so when there are more than "two groups", which is often the case in this population. In an effort to reconcile classical theory with findings in self-psychology and relational theory, Slap and Slap-Shelton (1991) describe pathogenic, sequestered schemas as residues of early childhood traumata which colour perception, function on the level of the dynamic unconscious, and then reappear. In their view, their reappearance accounts for the repetition compulsion. They consider night-time mental processes as "the product of the interaction of the sequestered schemas with a current day event or situation". For them,

> the sequestered schema is understood as an organization of the mind, having at its core traumatic impressions and situations of the past which have been separated from the generally interconnected mass of ideas and which function at a primitive cognitive level in which assimilation prevails over accommodation. (Slap & Slap-Shelton, pp. 79–80)

Thus, they account for disturbances in perception in terms of "anachronistic templates", which colour the input.

In the following vignette, a patient with one of these "well known cases . . ." with several splits in her "mental activities" could not accept her psychical reality of sequestered schemata and dissociated selves. Her non-acceptance resulted in a serious surgical mishap.

Case report

Cindy had contemplated getting laser eye surgery to permanently correct her near-sightedness. She was especially low on funds at this time, so her sense of urgency to undergo such a procedure was notable and brought to her attention. Despite her conscious intention to see better than ever and no longer need her spectacles, deeper forces were simultaneously at play which were determined to obscure her delving into her incestuous relationships with key male relatives. Having been in analysis for several years at this point, and having observed profound changes in her demeanour, identity, and memory, as well as episodic self-destructive behaviour, there was much clinical evidence to support her having a severe dissociative disorder (Brenner, 2001).

As I listened to her rationalisation about the forthcoming surgery, I was reminded of the fact that in another of her states of mind "Candy" wore a different pair of glasses that had a different prescription. In this state of mind, Candy, a rather carefree, capricious, seemingly separate, and hypersexual self would exude a very different air about herself and berate Cindy for her old-maid-like behaviour. She had her own relationships as well as a separate wardrobe that Cindy had no recollection of buying. Moreover, "Candy" could know Cindy's mind but not vice versa—like a one-way mirror. Candy also had knowledge of the inner population. Cindy was loath to acknowledge her amnesia about such times when this other self had ascendancy, but the clues about her secret life that were left behind became a source of analytic enquiry. In yet another state of mind, her vision was reportedly perfectly fine and she wore no glasses. At such times, she cross-dressed and hid her long hair under a baseball cap. This transgender self was prone to paranoid violence.

In addition to the already complex and devastating situation, Cindy, when dressed as a man, was quite menacing in the transference. This "male" self tried to acquire a penis and absolutely hated being trapped in a female body. It occurred to me that her wish to permanently change the structure of her eyes might have also been an upward displacement of a wish to change her genitals. This symbolic solution would adversely affect the overall human being's capacity to see clearly. Although I had observed this phenomenon of fluctuating visual acuity in other patients, I could not find any reports in the literature and surmised that the changes in acuity were not of a hysterical nature, but rather more of a psychophysiological fluctuation of extraocular muscles of accommodation.[1] At this point in her therapy, Cindy was confronting yet another level of very painful truths about the traumatic nature of her background and severe abuse which were not well tolerated in her usual state of mind. Suicidal impulses re-emerged. Clearly, I interpreted that there were things that she wanted to see and did not want to see about her past that greatly affected how she saw herself. A personification of her superego was vicious and punishing. In a desperate moment, she sought an external, concrete solution to her internal problem. However, this interpretation had no effect on the patient, as she continued headlong into her medical misadventure. Not surprisingly, after the procedure, her vision was blurred for well over a year. Her ophthalmologist was alarmed and puzzled. While she became depressed, despairing, and withdrew, her new preoccupation with this visual fog seemed to diminish her suicidality.

Discussion

It could be argued that the heart of the psychoanalytic enterprise is the exploration of unconscious influences upon perception. We see what our minds enable us or need us to see and do not realise it unless we understand what is going on out of our awareness. With regard to seeing oneself, Jacobson described it this way:

> By a realistic image of the self we mean, first of all, one that correctly mirrors the state and the characteristics, the potentialities and abilities, the assets and the limits of our bodily and mental self: on the one hand, of our appearance, our anatomy, and our physiology; on the other hand, of our ego, our conscious and pre-conscious feelings and thoughts, wishes, impulses, and attitudes, of our physical and mental functions and behaviour.
>
> At present it may suffice to point to the enormous and rather disruptive influences which the process of infantile denial and repression exert upon the formation of the images of the self in the object world . . . [t]he cutting out of a considerable sector of unpleasurable memories by infantile repression eliminate a large amount of unacceptable amounts of both the self and the outside world. The effects caused by the work of repression may be filled in by screen elements, distortions, or embellishments produced by the *elaborate* maneuvers of the ego's defense system. (Jacobson, 1964, p. 21)

Cindy was unable to tolerate her psychical reality of having multiple, dissociated selves. She needed to maintain an illusion of cohesion, which, apparently, was quite limited and subject to dynamic influences. In her flight from seeing the state of her self-organisation, she severely damaged her capacity to see the external world. This extreme example of reciprocity between inner and outer perception, once better understood, helped explain seemingly bizarre and quasi-psychotic symptomatology. In less complex, more mundane cases, such a principle is axiomatic.

From transient distortions of basic sensory experiences to analysis of the transference, the basic question is how all of our unique dynamics affect "what we see". While this viewpoint is hardly new or original, the fact that it is so well known is perhaps why there seems to be diminishing interest in the topic among analysts. An emphasis on perception was primary in Freud's early work as the Pct.-Cs was a central tenet of topographic theory (Freud, 1900a). In the original model, perception was seen as accurate and non-conflictual, as has been pointed out (Slap & Slap-Shelton, 1991). As Freud's thinking evolved and the primary process of mental functioning was recognised as manifesting itself in derivatives (Freud, 1915e), the distinction became less clear. Also, with the introduction of structural theory (Freud, 1923b), where perception was relegated to an important ego function, there seemed to be less concern over the conscious–unconscious differentiation. Then, Arlow's 1960 study of unconscious fantasy, with its central organising influence upon ego functioning, undoubtedly included perception, but his emphasis was more on mental creation and instinctual influences. The Kleinian object-relations perspective, which focused on the crucial importance of splitting and projective identification (Bion, 1959; Klein, 1946), also enlarged our understanding of how unconscious factors might affect what we perceive. But here, too, the emphasis on the defensive operations seemed to get more attention.

In my experience with adults who have sustained severe early trauma, there may be a preponderance of defensive structures organised around altered states of consciousness and amnesia which might resemble "very deep" repression and a division of the psyche which Breuer and Freud described as splitting of consciousness (Freud (with Breuer), 1895d). In this type of mental organisation, those who dissociate and who suffer from major disturbances of self-constancy might have alternating, seemingly separate, self-organisations that appear to take over the conscious and utilise secondary process mentation, not unlike what was described in the legendary case of Anna O. They also manifest a "cutting out of a considerable sector of unpleasurable memories . . . and *elaborate* maneuvers of the ego's defense system" (Jacobson, 1964, p. 21). Freud retreated from such cases subsequently, convincing subsequent generations of analysts that this condition was either easily explained, unimportant, or so mysterious that analysts had nothing to offer (Brenner, 2009). In the following vignette, I describe the clinical challenge of addressing a patient's rather sudden and dynamically meaningful change of self-perception. This raises some technical questions for contemporary analysts.

Case Report

Minh, a tall, thin, strikingly beautiful but aloof Asian-American woman, was in her fifth year of a five-times-a-week analysis. As she lay on the couch in the middle of an hour, she was sobbing over the forthcoming anniversary of the untimely death of her uncle. They had had a problematic and extremely ambivalent relationship that came to an abrupt end just as he was beginning to recognise his niece's importance to him. Since her father was absent much of the time due to military obligations, her maternal uncle served as a father surrogate. Struggling with her bitterness and grief over having lost him again—this time permanently—she then turned on her side and tucked her head under her arm. Her crying stopped and she became perfectly still and completely quiet. Attuned to her states of mind, I felt a sudden rupture of our connection at this moment. I then waited quietly for what might ensue, be it an extended silence or more outpouring of emotion. Shortly, she started speaking in a different tone of voice, but one with which I was familiar. It had a playful, sing-songy quality and she addressed me formally as Dr Brenner. In her usual states of mind, she never addressed me by any name, careful to avoid being too formal or informal, a longstanding theme that had come up not infrequently. This cautiousness appeared to be a derivative of her effort to achieve optimal distance (Mahler, Pine, & Bergman, 1975) and reflected her attempt to rework in the transference a healthier, pre-Oedipal, maternal relationship. Her relationship to her mother had been profoundly disturbed throughout her childhood, and separations were often characterised by rageful protests punctuated by prolonged ruptures of our rapport of the type described above. Periods of chaos and altered states of consciousness were suggestive of adult manifestations of a disorganised, disoriented attachment.

So, upon hearing how I was being addressed, it immediately signalled and confirmed my intuition that another self, one seemingly separate from her "regular" self, had emerged and taken over the executive functioning of her ego. She spoke differently, often with more colourful, raw, and direct phrases consistent with a precocious adolescent who was rather street smart and wise beyond her years. In sharp contrast to Minh's extreme politeness, correctness, and great sensitivity about not offending others, she often appeared timid and easily frightened. This other self was extremely devaluing of Minh, calling her an idiot for being so emotional, naïve, and trusting of others who quite often took advantage of her good nature and her fear of antagonising others. In addition, she was extremely jealous of Minh, who spent so much time "out" and had seemed to have become stronger as a result of analysis, thus making it more difficult for her to "push through" and take over.

However, there were still times when Minh would be so overwhelmed with intolerable affects, such as grief and deep sadness, as well as instinctual anxiety over libidinal and aggressive currents, that she would take leave either by literally exiting the office or taking leave of her body and dissociating. At such times, this self, Linh, would most likely take over following a prodromal symptom of debilitating vertigo. The patient had consulted several ENT specialists in the past for this mysterious symptom, which could literally cripple her and render her unable to function for periods of time. Diagnosed as benign positional vertigo and reproduced in the specialist's testing centre, Minh was incredulous to discover that it also heralded a change in her self states.

Other selves less regularly involved in therapeutic process but having an enormous influence on the process none the less included an intellectual, rageful self with a lesbian predilection who would scream and yell about how she hated and mistrusted me. She would leave furious telephone messages for me, calling me by my first name, and pronouncing it in a slow, mocking, and derisive way. Together with Linh, this dyad appeared to have the power to internally persecute and punish Minh, causing her to lose her balance and trip, accidentally burn herself on hot appliances, or in other ways cause her to be clumsy and get hurt. From a vantage point outside the patient, such accident-proneness and bungled actions would be entirely consistent with the "psychopathology of everyday life" (Freud, 1901b). As though this were a personification of a punitive superego, as with Cindy, such times were clearly associated with unconscious motivation and attributed to repressed wishes for punishment due to unrecognised guilt. Minh, whose longstanding awareness of these selves had been very private and contentious, was laden with deep shame and embarrassment. She had more or less "known and not known" about them for years, but could not allow herself to articulate the problem to herself, let alone to an outsider, such as her analyst. Like elusive floaters in the eye that quickly disappear into peripheral visual fields when trying to focus upon them, Minh likened these selves to this phenomenon. They were just out of reach of consciousness and she could not see herself as sharing her body with other selves. However, she would dream about having a tea party with four empty chairs and fully understand the symbolism. Significantly, Linh had access to the patient's inner population and spoke freely about the problem, offering insight and detailed historical information about the uncle's perverse, incestuous violations of her young body that often foreshadowed Minh's progress in treatment. At first, Minh could only acknowledge a very aberrant relationship with her uncle, which she could not put into words. Instead, all she could really say for the first several years was "I can't think about what I remember!"

Linh could not only remember such things, but she could think about them and talk about them. She protected Minh and took over when, as a child, the pain had become too much to bear. Linh was unable to acknowledge that she shared the same physical fate with Minh and essentially wanted my help to eliminate Minh.

Over time, the rivalry between Minh and Linh became quite palpable and real for the patient in both states of mind. Extremely jealous of all my patients, especially the female patients, her possessiveness was apparently represented and played out both internally and externally. So, when I heard the patient call me "Dr Brenner", it confirmed that a significant, defensive shift had taken place, probably due to affect intolerance associated with grief, as it was now Linh's turn to be out. At such times, the clinician is presented with a technical dilemma, which has enormous implications for the analysis. Does one acknowledge the dissociated self and engage with the patient at that level? Does such an approach "play into", reinforce, and perhaps reify a quasi-delusional belief about other people inhabiting someone's mind? Or would that stance be empathic and respectful of the patient's psychical reality? Does such a direction introduce iatrogenic complications into the treatment? Or should the analyst simply listen to the patient's utterances like any other associative material and treat the patient as he or she would any other analytic patient (Gottlieb, 1997)? If the patient has the requisite ego strength for analysis, would she eventually simply give up such a defensive stance for more adaptive, healthy defences? Are we dealing with a fantasy of multiplicity, or are the structural changes of such a deep nature that additional work in addressing these selves is warranted? Is this a disturbed self perception or a perception of disturbed selves?

Discussion

Psychiatrists in training are generally taught not to confirm or play into the schizophrenic's delusions for a number of reasons, not the least of which is the concern about further weakening of the patient's grasp on reality. Instead, the clinician is instructed to tactfully listen and not aggressively confront the psychotic thinking, as further decompensation and violent or suicidal repercussions might ensue. Such a shibboleth has often been applied to the situation in those with "multiple personality", as even today those with little experience (Taylor & Martin, 1944) with the condition might conflate schizophrenia and DID. Since Bleuler's term "schizophrenia" is derived from root words meaning "split mind", and since Freud made short shrift of it, DID continues to have an identity problem of its own (Brenner, 1999) and is, ironically, often seen as outside the realm of psychoanalysis.

So, given these historical circumstances and the particular dynamics of the patient in question, the technical challenge over how to listen to and how to respond to the patient's dissociated and unconscious perception of herself was critical. Failure to acknowledge that a change had occurred would have insulted and enraged the patient, whereas undue attention and favouritism might have had negative repercussions also. Linh had revelled in her capacity to slip in and out of sessions with "their" former psychotherapist who, despite his good intentions and considerable overall clinical experience, was apparently clueless about these shifts and made little headway after almost a decade of treatment.

In my view, the idea that if the analyst does not acknowledge or recognise such shifts they will eventually cease and not be problematic is tantamount to behavioural therapy masquerading as psychoanalysis. One would be wittingly or unwittingly employing the treatment strategy of trying to "extinguish" an unwanted behaviour by ignoring it rather than analysing it! In addition, since many such patients have a significant history of early sexual trauma (Brenner, 1994, 2001, 2004; Kluft, 1986) and were threatened with serious consequences if they told anyone and/or were brainwashed (Shengold, 1989) into thinking nobody would ever believe them, they had become quite adept at reading others and sensing when essentially to shut up, hide, and become like a chameleon. From a Winnicottian perspective, their pseudo-compliant, false selves would prevail (Winnicott, 1955).

The issues of observing ego, self-awareness, self-perception, and perception of the self are critical here, as quite often there may be considerable cohesion within a given self or a "narcissistic investment in separateness" (Kluft, 1986). At the same time, by definition, such patients are sorely lacking in self-constancy. This seeming contradiction appears to ward off deep annihilation anxiety through this illusion, whereas, ironically, the presence of other selves might at times provide company or companionship for the patient and defend against separation anxiety. Not unlike imaginary playmates in this regard, such selves serve multiple functions in the psyche. Such a complex psychical arrangement serving multiple functions (Wälder, 1936) must be dealt with carefully, as the extent of internalised aggression could precipitate a suicidal regression. In the following case, the clinician did not appreciate such a nuanced approach and a near-fatal catastrophe occurred.

Case report

While a colleague was providing inpatient coverage for a severely traumatised patient many years ago while I was on vacation, she complained to him about how she had become more aware, or "co-conscious", of another self trying to take over her mind. She feared such a takeover would consign her to getting lost somewhere in her mind forever, which was associated with profound abandonment anxiety. Seriously underestimating the extent of her conflict, he made the bold pronouncement that he would try to get rid of this particular self who was harassing her. Mistakenly believing that such a psychological exorcism was indeed possible by this imposing, authoritarian presence, the intervention reactivated a malevolent, paternal, internalised object. The patient panicked and retreated into her bedroom where, in a dissociated state, she found a razor blade which she had smuggled in and severed her radial artery in the bathroom. As conflicted as she was over staying alive, she had intended to exit the bathroom, turn right, and bleed to death on her bed, but instead, turned left and promptly fell on the floor in the hallway. An alert member of the nursing staff rushed to her side and applied direct pressure to stop the spurting of arterial blood. Emergency vascular surgery saved her life.

Following my return and careful exploration of this disaster, it appeared that the patient's sense of abandonment in the transference left her feeling unprotected and vulnerable to the covering doctor's intrusive directive. Just as her mother retreated into her nightly alcoholic stupors and enabled her father's vicious sexual attacks to occur with impunity, so, too, her protective analyst disappeared and left her at the mercy of the substitute doctor.

Reviving fear and old memories of her father's repeated violent sexual intrusions into her unprotected young body, this schema became enacted by an internal perpetrator in the form of a dissociated self who, out of fear of being caught, brought to justice, and subsequently eliminated, had reverted to suicide. Here, the patient's unconscious, disorientated, self-perception was of being a hunted, sexual criminal who, backed into a corner with no escape, gave into a desperate, life-threatening impulse. The question of perception of the self becomes rather complicated when there is an organisation of multiple, dissociated selves who may, alternately at times, or at times conjointly, become, as it were, conscious or take over consciousness.

Perception of the bodily self

As Freud reminded us, first and foremost, the ego is a "bodily ego" (Freud, 1923b) and, therefore, the somatic basis of the self is generally accepted to be sensory–motor in origin. The infant's growing awareness of bodily position and muscular co-ordination as well as sensory and perceptual input is organised into schemas (Piaget & Inhelder, 1969; Schilder, 1950). Multiple schemata and perceptions of bodily image are then created which, under normative conditions, blend more or less seamlessly into a cohesive sense of self (Kohut, 1971). A nodal point of development, erroneously thought by Lacan to occur at eight months in his "Mirror Stage" (Lacan, 1953), is the recognition of one's self in a mirror. This stage is in contrast to Kohut's "mirror stage" (Kohut, 1971), where the infant basks in the gleam of the mother's eye. Although infants might react to their image at such an early age, more recent research concludes that this capacity is more likely to be achieved between the ages of fifteen to eighteen months (Asendorpf, Warkentin, & Baudonnière, 1996).

Coinciding with other crucial milestones at this time, such as anality and rapprochement along with their affective and cognitive accompaniments, this acquisition appears to have a very important organising quality to it. While studies have concluded that other species such as chimpanzees (de Veer, Gallup, Theall, van den Bos, & Povinelli, 2003), Asian elephants (Plotnik, de Waal, & Reiss, 2006), and bottlenose dolphins (Marten & Psarakos, 1995) may also acquire the capacity to recognise themselves in a mirror, the obvious language barrier between humans and these animals precludes a deeper understanding of the full implications of this achievement in these species.

Our fascination with our reflection quite probably predates the myth of Narcissus, as even Palaeolithic cave art from almost 30,000 years ago has revealed reflections of actual human hands in the form of colourful, stencil-like representations carefully applied to the wall. Much more recently, it has been incorporated into many genres of literature. For example, this theme is found in fairy tales with magic mirrors, as in *Snow White*, where the wicked, vain queen reportedly asks, "Magic mirror on the wall. Who is the fairest of them all?" It is also seen in preternatural stories, such as the story of Dracula, the vampire, who did not have any reflection in the mirror. In the sequel to *Alice in Wonderland,* entitled *Through the Looking Glass, And What Alice Found There* (Carroll, 1871), Alice found a bizarre and wondrous world on the other side of the looking glass. Stepping through the mirror on her fireplace mantel, she encountered a land of opposites, reversals, and time travel. A clinical correlate to this fictionally fanciful account is seen in the following case.

Case report

During a particularly anxiety-laden session with Christine in which she became very aware of my presence in the room, I made a statement to her that in some ways I was like a mirror, listening to and reflecting things that she was saying. Much to my surprise, shortly thereafter, there was a change in her affect, in her syntax, in her tone of voice, and in her body language, and a very young self emerged, giggly and saying, "You're a mirror?" I was aware of this change in her self-state, and continued to listen. What emerged was a series of recollections in this child's voice and, later on, in the patient's usual voice, of experiences as a young girl. Following painful, sexualised torture at her mother's hands, she would retreat into the bathroom and see her tear-streaked face in the mirror. Looking at her reflection in the mirror, she saw a girl there whom she did not perceive as herself. In her depersonalised state, she then experienced herself going into the mirror, looking for help and solace from the girl whom she believed lived in the mirror. A period of amnesia would then result, which was relieved during the session. As we attempted to reconstruct what had happened to her when she was young, it appeared that another self, called the "Mirror Girl" or the "Girl in the Mirror", would emerge dissociatively, take over, and absorb the pain. The patient was very confused and it took a number of weeks for her to find words and make sense of this aspect of her experience. Her relationship to her reflection in the mirror and her attempts at flight into the world inside the mirror to get help from her dissociated reflection seemed to be an autohypnotic effort on her part to escape an intolerable affectively and physically painful situation.

Closing comments

In *Don Quixote* (de Cervantes, 1605), the master and his servant encounter the Knight of the Mirrors, a neighbour who uses mirrors to obscure his own identity and hopes to trick the Don into giving up his quest and returning home. Ultimately, Don Quixote was to be cured of his madness by being forced to see himself realistically in the mirror so he would give up his delusional self perception, which emerged from his unconscious. The mirror as a symbol of realistic perception is also seen in Shakespeare's philosophy of the theatre. It was expressed through Hamlet, who insisted that it hold the "mirror up to nature" and reflect life as it is. The great Italian playwright, Pirandello, a contemporary of Freud, whose deep understanding of human nature informed his writing, also considered the mirror to be essential to his work:

> When a man lives, he lives and does not see himself. Well, put a mirror before him and make him see himself in the act of living, under the sway of his passions: either he remains astonished and dumbfounded at his own appearance, or else he turns away his eyes so as not to see himself, or else in disgust he spits at his image, or again clinches his fist to break it; and if he had been weeping, he can weep no more; if he had been laughing, he can laugh no more, and so on. In a word, there arises a crisis, and that crisis is my theater. (Pirandello, in Bassanese, 1997, p. 54)

A monologue by the character, Laudisi, in *It Is So! (If You Think So)* offers a theatrical illustration of the emergence of disowned aspects of the self:

> LAUDISI [walking around the study for a while, smiling derisively to himself and shaking his head; then he steps in front of the large mirror over the mantelpiece; he looks at his image and starts speaking to it]: Oh, so there you are! [He greets his image by raising two fingers, giving a cunning wink of the eye, and laughs sarcastically] Tell me, old friend, which one of the two of us is crazy? [He raises a hand and points his index finger at his image that, in turn, points a finger at him. Another sarcastic laugh, then] Ah yes, I know: I say 'You' and you with your finger point at me. Come on now, let's admit it, just between the two of us, the two of us know each other quite well, don't we? The trouble is that other people just do not see you the way I do! And so then, dear friend, what becomes of you? As for me, I can say that here in front of you I can see myself and I can touch myself—but you, what do you

> become, how do other people see you? A ghost, my friend, a ghostly image! And yet, you see all these crazy people? Paying no attention to that image they carry around with them, inside themselves, they run around full of curiosity, chasing after the ghostly image of others. And they believe that it is something different. (Pirandello, 1995, p. 173)

In closing, while such concepts as observing ego focus our attention on the conscious perceptions of the self, unconscious, dissociated influences must be considered in order to "really" see ourselves in the mirror. It also must be considered that I might have strayed so far afield from Freud's original 1915 contribution that I have used it as a jumping-off point and little more. After all, I do not think that the word "self" even appears anywhere in the text, as he seems to be more interested in exploring the qualities of the unconscious, the metapsychology of repression, and the relationship of the unconscious to the preconscious. So, perhaps it would be useful to remind the reader that, at the time, Freud believed that

> The content of the *Ucs.* may be compared with an aboriginal population in the mind. If inherited mental formations exist in the human being—something analogous to instinct in animals—these constitute the nucleus of the *Ucs.* Later there is added to them what is discarded during childhood development as unserviceable . . . (Freud, 1915e, p. 195)

He therefore contended that the unconscious was inhabited by the evolutionary heritage of our species in some state of personification. So, it would follow that a better understanding of not only what but "who" is residing in those dark recesses of our mind could promote a better integration of the psyche.

Note

1. The eyes and their surrounding structures are quite reactive to affective states. Changes in eye colour have also been observed. One such patient whom I treated in the hospital insisted upon meeting in a darkened room lest I know that a change had occurred and another self "was out".

9

"In spite of my ego": problem solving and the unconscious[1]

Stefano Bolognini

As often happens, this topic has mobilised a series of reflections in me of various kinds—reflections that go beyond the specifically theoretical and clinical field of psychoanalysis.

In wandering through my associations, influences, and memories, I was struck by the internal perception of an acute feeling of envy in calling to mind some figures acting as part of my personal experience, figures characterised in some way by a strikingly intuitive attitude and by an instinctive capacity for facing up to and resolving problems of various kinds.

Certainly a well-justified envy, in my opinion—a physiological and "secret" envy of which I am not ashamed and about which I do not feel guilty, and that, when all is said and done, even leads me to feel a certain sense of solidarity within myself. How does one *not* envy, in fact, persons who seem endowed with the gift of not having to look for solutions to certain problems, persons for whom the solutions instead seem to seek *them* out . . . and find them?

I will try to explain myself.

Some people are characterised as "endowed with practical sense", in the broad definition and not necessarily in reference to concrete or manual abilities. Others are summarily described as "intuitive";

still others as capable of instinctively regulating themselves in more complex situations, giving the impression not of puzzling over things in a reasoned, obsessive way, but of inventing useful solutions with a certain quick and fluid creativity.

And if, in many cases, one manages to observe a conscious, well-functioning central ego at work in these persons, one capable of effectively focusing on the problem, of not losing its way or getting worked up in a counterproductive manner in facing the task at hand, in other cases, one observes something more surprising and less comprehensible. That is, certain people actually seem to bypass the normal processes of getting one's bearings, of analysis, and of working out the facts of the problem, and instead land smoothly and directly on the solution, who knows how.

We can take for granted that in this description of mine, there is a certain idealising emphasis due to the intent to highlight this kind of impression and phenomenon; we can also agree, then, that I might be exaggerating a little in establishing a separate category for this type of mental functioning in the realm of problem solving.

Nevertheless, there seems to be some truth here, in that there is widespread recognition of the phenomenology I have described, even though it is certainly somewhat rare. Moreover, precisely the feeling of envy to which I refer has allowed me to reflect on this topic with greater curiosity and with more motivation, in search of the "secret" of these surprising abilities—to the point that, for all intents and purposes, I consider it the driving force of these considerations.

* * *

In Chapter VI of "The unconscious" (1915e), "Communication between the two systems", Freud makes a very important comment on the psychic work carried out by the unconscious:

> It would nevertheless be wrong to imagine that the Ucs. remains at rest while the whole work of the mind is performed by the Pcs.—*that* the Ucs. is something finished with, a vestigial organ, a residuum from the process of development. It is wrong also to suppose that communication between the two systems is confined to the act of repression, with the Pcs. casting everything that seems disturbing to it into the abyss of the Ucs. On the contrary, the Ucs. is alive and capable of development and maintains a

> number of other relations with the Pcs., amongst them that of co-operation. In brief, it must be said that the Ucs. is continued into what are known as derivatives, that it is accessible to the impressions of life, that it constantly influences the Pcs., and is even, for its part, subjected to influences from the Pcs. (p. 190)

And later:

> It is a very remarkable thing that the Ucs. of one human being can react upon that of another, *without passing through the Cs*. This deserves closer investigation, especially with a view to finding out whether preconscious activity can be excluded as playing a part in it; but, descriptively speaking, the fact is incontestable. (p. 194, my emphasis)

Of these two Freudian passages, I would highlight, then, two fundamental concepts.

1. *The unconscious, too, "works"* (and, as Freud says, it sometimes "collaborates").
2. *The unconscious can be activated*; for example, it can combine with the unconscious of another, "eluding" the conscious mind.

Many authors have explored the work of the unconscious, focusing in particular on dream work, understood differently from classical "oneiric work", which is overall destined to mask latent content. Almost all the authors whom I will cite have been fascinated, in fact, by the variability of the *combination of primary process and secondary process* that sometimes seems to be created in the dream, produced in a sort of *"joint venture" between the unconscious and the preconscious, in the absence of the conscious ego*. It would, therefore, seem appropriate to differentiate these two activities of the unconscious, designating this activity "oneiric working through".

We will see along the way how this work of the unconscious in collaboration with the preconscious can more easily be manifested when there is a certain internal psychic arrangement, which usually includes the subject's *conscious ego being "put in stand-by mode"*, or the ego having *a very discrete, peripheral presence, not an invasive one*.

This is the subject of the second part of my paper. In the first part, I try to describe some processes that I think might be fundamental in at least a partial comprehension of the creativity of the unconscious and its problem-solving capacities.

The unconscious as an area of active transformation

In *Secret Passages: The Theory and Technique of Interpsychic Relations* (2011), I summarised some inspirational contributions of that time that are very different among themselves, though all are orientated toward the perspective of a "sensible" unconscious, one that is "at work" and potentially transformative:

> Adler (1911) spoke of the dream's "functions of premeditation"; Maeder (1912) spoke of a *fonction ludique* [playing function] of the dream, as a preparatory exercise to subsequent operations in external reality; Grinberg (1967), describing "elaborative" dreams in phases of integration, highlighted the patient's growing reparative capacity as he begins to know how to take care of himself; Garma (1966) outlined a "broad" way of thinking during dreams—an archaic-type thinking, intensely visual, but one in which judgements, reflections, criticisms, and other mental processes exist, belonging to the same type as those of being awake; the theoretical line that starts with Winnicott and extends to Bollas placed value on the experiential dimension of the dream; De Moncheaux (1978) hypothesised a reintegrating function of the dream with respect to trauma; and Matte Blanco (1981) reexamined a possible aspect of displacement in dreams, like an opening—at times, a creative one—onto possible new places, times, and representations, and saw condensation as an attempt at integration of different spatiotemporal categories.
>
> There are still others: Kramer (1993) was concerned with the effects of dreamlike activity on the mood-stabilsing function, and Greenberg and Perlman (1993) with the increase in REM sleep in situations of complex learning. Fosshage (1997) brought out the generally synthetic function of primary process, which emphasises, through highly intense sensorial and visual images, the affective colouring of the experience. [p. 140]

I mention this overview of contributors—who are certainly not homogeneous among themselves, and only partially relevant to the topic under examination—because I consider them to be united, at any rate, by their interest in a mysterious component of working things out that exists at a deep oneiric level: *something unknown to the ego works, combines, assembles, conceives, creates, transforms*.

Furthermore, the history of philosophy and the history of science are rich in famous examples of dreams that opened the way to a solution to the dreamer's extremely difficult problems (one thinks of Bohr's dream on the composition of the atom). Even ancient literature and mythology make frequent reference to an intense unconscious activity that is the bearer of unexpected solutions that can take the subject's conscious central ego by surprise. It is especially in the dream that the gods appear to mortals and convey to them what to do in crucial moments of their experiences: apparently "magical" solutions springing up from deep sources rather than from conscious reasoning by the subject's ego.

At a less abstract level, I maintain that the well-known fairy tale *Puss in Boots* may aptly represent in metaphorical form what we are considering here.

The story, of popular origin but narrated in different eras by Giovanni Francesco Straparola (in the fifteenth century), and then by Giambattista Basile and Charles Perrault (eighteenth century), by Ludwig Tieck in 1797, and finally by the Brothers Grimm in the nineteenth century, tells of the youngest of three sons of a miller. On the death of the father, this young man inherits only a cat from him, while his brothers receive more substantial benefits.

Left alone with the cat, the boy is anxious because he does not know how to get himself out of unfortunate and apparently impossible situations; his mind is constricted by desperation, and he sees no way out. And then it is the cat (an undervalued but extremely intelligent animal, and also one held in high esteem by the boy's father) sets about inventing appropriate solutions!

After having ably engineered an excellent rapport with the king on his master's behalf, making him believe that the boy is in the service of a noble gentleman, the cat carries out his *tour de force*, inducing an evil ogre to transform himself into a mouse and then eliminating him. In this way the boy will acquire the ogre's castle, and with it a correspondingly high social status.

"What" is the cat? It is an instinctive part of the boy, endowed with an unexpected genius in the area of problem solving that takes everyone by surprise.

The boy (in turn a metaphor for the conscious central ego) is too constrained and weighed down by his difficulties, and perhaps also by a basic feeling of inadequacy, to be able to think or to act accordingly. The cat, by contrast, intuitive and open-minded, bypasses any anxiety about insufficiency with a healthy dose of omnipotence (after all, he wears "seven-league boots") and turns the situation upside down, transforming the invincible ogre into an easy-to-deal-with mouse, and in this way bestowing power on the boy ("the ogre's castle"), so that the boy will be able to marry the princess.

But wait a moment: kudos are due to the extraordinary cat, yes, but we should take off our hats to the boy as well—the boy who was not opposed to these developments, who did not feel himself to be diminished by the unusual roles played by the two of them, and who tolerated his own passivity in relation to the cat's initiative; he was not blinded by envy of the cat's intelligence.

The conscious central ego (the boy) knew how to recognise and respect the occasional superior creativity of the whole of the unconscious–preconscious (the cat) in these difficulties, giving it space without narcissistically opposing it and without allowing his desires for control to prevail over what happened at this juncture.

All this was unforeseen. We find ourselves observing not a single unit, gifted and capable, but instead *a couple who collaborate well, thanks to the fact that one of them lets the other work in areas where the other works better*.

Perhaps something of this sort—here played out on the level of internal objects and parts of the self—had already happened long ago between the child (then playing the part of the cat) and a figure who was crucial to his life experience. Had someone allowed the child to carry out explorations and to develop areas of competence? Had someone really understood a natural, existential talent of his?

As you will already have noticed, I am describing a *favourable situation in the internal relationship between an individual's ego and his self*, and I am alluding to *interpsychic parental styles* and to originary formative events that, *once introjected*, can then produce just such a positive situation later in the individual's life as well, which can truly constitute a very precious "inheritance".

We will return to this point later on, since for now I wish to limit myself to hypothesising about and describing *a potentially and occasionally creative oneiric area, which is based on the possibility of representation, of decomposition, and of recombination of the elements at play in the subject's internal world, thanks to the reliable and reconnecting effect of primary process, and to the reorganisation permitted by secondary process*, which alternate in varying degrees.

The work of the unconscious proceeds in this way. The ego can agree with it or oppose it.

The little Guatemalan dolls

There is a delightful Central American custom in this regard that seems to me to provide an illustrative, metaphorical representation of what I have just outlined in metapsychological terms, and that was described to me many years ago by an analytic patient who had just returned from a trip to Guatemala.

To better contextualise this metaphor, I will mention in advance a bit of clinical information that is not incidental; indeed, it is quite consistent with the fact that the patient brought to her session precisely this associative material, and that she engaged in a small example of acting out: she gave me a gift (a concrete one).

The patient had been in analysis for four months and was going through a felicitous, distinct, and benign regression of the analytic "honeymoon" type. In my belief, she was reproducing a positive primary experience of fusion and nursing (her traumatic problems had occurred subsequent to that phase).

Quite significantly, the patient gave me a little treasure: a Guatemalan lucky charm that consisted of a little box with six dolls in it, each different from the others. The popular custom, she explained to me, was that of placing the six little dolls at one's bedside in the evening. One then recounted a different problem to each doll, turned out the light, and went to sleep.

During the night, the six little dolls would talk to each other, and in the morning one would have a different view of one's problems!

This custom fascinated me, and—in addition to considering the meaning this story had for the patient—I set about reflecting on the advantages that this custom could offer to those who practised it. For example, it can allow one to sleep more soundly because one's problems have been entrusted "to someone else". Furthermore, it is established that more than a certain number of problems (in this case, six) cannot be dealt with at one time, thus setting a standard limit on a possible flood of anxieties and disturbances, establishing a container.

Overall, a basic trust is established in the existence of an unconscious, working-through process of transformation, which takes place in the absence of the conscious central ego (while the subject sleeps) and can produce substantial changes in one's vision of things.

With the defensive vigilance of the ego lowered, the containment of anxieties—represented by the story and entrusted to "someone/something" else (the dolls)—and the creative recombination of contents (a "solution" in the double etymological meaning of "release" and "resolution") due to primary process seem to be happily condensed in this private little ritual. The work will take place in the dreamer *with the partial unawareness of the conscious ego, but with its agreement*, given acceptance of the ritual.

The overall atmosphere of this turn of events is, at any rate, a comfortable one, intimate and on a human scale. Here, the work is entrusted to the unconscious, which is implicitly understood as a natural resource that can be drawn upon without fear.

Intuition

Let us take a step back, for a moment, and return to the phenomenological aspect of the processes that we are exploring.

The concept of "intuition" (from the Latin verb "*in-tueor*": "a look inside") designates that type of apparently immediate knowledge that does not pass through cognitive reasoning or a sensate process, and that seems, instead, to spurt miraculously from somewhere deep down.

Intuition has had a long development and a very tumultuous course in philosophy, starting with the era of the great thinkers of Ancient Greece, who gave it multiple readings and definitions. In considering intuition, they sometimes focused on sensorial functioning, but more often on that of the intellect, with a strong tendency towards the description of transcendent experiences and the idea of immediate perception of "first principles" (as in Plato and Aristotle).

My personal impression, in going back over those ancient journeys through philosophy texts, is that, in general, philosophers decisively intended to place a high value on intuition, attributing special characteristics and functions to it (usually contrasting it with an insistence on mere sensorial perception). However, one cannot extract much interesting information on the nature of the psychic processes implied from the study of these philosophers.

Much more stimulating for the study of this phenomenon, even if not as useful for the comprehension of underlying processes, are the contributions of cognitive psychology, it seems to me. In 1926, Graham Wallas, who had studied the processes leading to creative solutions to problems, described four typical stages of these processes:

- *preparation of the task*, in which one tries to describe and understand the problem in its various aspects;
- *incubation*, a sort of decanting period in which the subject does not think about the problem and instead devotes himself to other things;
- *illumination* (or "*insight*"), when the solution to the problem is suddenly revealed in an unexpected way (something analogous to the "Aha! *Erlebnis*" of phenomenologists).
- *assessment*, when the cognitive ego is placed at the passageway to the intuitive parts, providing an integrating explanation of what has been acquired.

An example of this process could be furnished by the testimony of the French mathematician Poincaré, who usually dedicated a couple of weeks to the phase of "preparing the task" and then refrained from it, dedicating himself to other pursuits. He would then be the recipient of an "explosion of illumination" in an unexpected way, while he was busy with geological excursions and other studies.

This pattern brings to mind analysts' analogous capacity for suspension, which I like to define as their being "happily resigned"—from a certain point in their professional development onward—to letting themselves be surprised by the spontaneous and unplanned emergence of interpretative solutions and empathic intuitions (Bolognini, 2004). This can occur for the analyst after he has ceased all intentional acts of investigation and instead entrusted himself to evenly hovering attention.

Metcalfe and Wiebe (1987) demonstrated that *problems requiring a creative solution can be resolved effectively quite suddenly*. Their interesting study involved asking researchers who were subjected to a problematic situation, at four-minute intervals, how much they felt they were advancing towards a solution to the task. The results showed that an awareness of progress was very much present in processes that involved strategies aimed at reproducing experientially verifiable situations, while it was absent in processes characterised by intuitive "leaps".

Moreover, as early as 1959, Wertheimer had hypothesised, from a gestalt point of view, that *creative intuition* might emerge *when the individual grasps new relationships between elements of a problem*. De Bono (1970) traced this back to the "capacity for lateral thinking", a special mobility of the observing centre of gravity based on the assumption of a potential multiplicity of points of view in considering a problem.

By contrast, among the obstacles to the operation of these intuitive processes would be the complex phenomenon described in psychology as "subjective formulation" ("Impostazione soggettiva", Rumiati, 2006), related to problem-solving patterns that are so repetitive and habitual for an individual that they impede him from considering alternative pathways. This concept calls to mind the idea of "functional fixedness" (Duncker, 1945), which is more connected, however, to the repetitive consideration of objects' characteristics.

Continuing to draw from the field of psychological research, I would like to mention last a noteworthy concept that has had extremely productive applications in very different spheres: the concept of "brainstorming" (Osborn, 1962), especially interesting when it is connected to a group setting. If a portion of co-participants' mental work undoubtedly takes the form of a simple expansion of the operative capacity of the various "working egos" in the group, in many ways and on other levels, it is, none the less, undeniable that brainstorming produces something more than a simple summation of cognitive resources.

Perhaps the phenomenon of brainstorming resonates with Freud's comment quoted earlier: "It is a very remarkable thing that the Ucs. of one human being can react upon that of another, without passing through the Cs." (1915e, p. 194).

Here, I think, we are in the realm of the work carried out by the six little dolls in the Guatemalan ritual. It is only that, in brainstorming, the individuals are awake and are real people. But is there something similar here, something that depends on a shared lowering of ego defences? Is the interpsychic a factor?

Connections between cognitive theories and the psychoanalytic view of intuition

As a psychoanalyst, I am led to revisit these stimulating contributions from cognitive theories, which, in a certain sense, predict and describe the production of exclusionary effects related to the subject's usual viewpoint, and I would like to integrate these theories with certain psychoanalytic concepts that seem invaluable to me in shedding light on some aspects of intuition.

I am referring, for example, to functional derivatives of the *processes of partial identification* (Grinberg & Grinberg, 1976), which can be produced in a physiological way in the internal world, if there have been *multiple, adequate introjections of useful and positive objects and of their functions*. These internal objects are the intrapsychic equivalents, if you will, stable and structured ones, of the six Guatemalan dolls.

Expressed in other terms, it is easier for the subject to be capable of assuming multiple and different points of view—which are, none the less, co-ordinated among themselves, with an adequate synthesis—if he has experienced, to the point of solidly introjecting it, a similar way of being in some of the figures who have been significant for him, now present and accessible in his internal world.

In order for this process to take place, however, it is necessary that such intense identifications are not total ones, and that they do not substitute for the individual's self. There must be a structure and a usual way of functioning in which there is a certain degree of internal separateness. *That is, the subject must be able to consult his objects*, placing himself partially and temporarily in their shoes, but "with a round-trip ticket", so to speak, identifying with the objects and their points of view, but also managing to reclaim his own observing and organising centre of gravity. In this way, he retains both a sense of self and an adequate internal mobility in relation to the other objects, *without "fixing" on an identification with any one of them.*

This internal mobility, not conscious and not intentional, which actually unfolds in a natural, syncretic way and in a very brief period of time, could perhaps be "unmasked" in the following self-directed questions: "How would they see these things . . . my father? . . . my mother? . . . my teacher? . . . my friend?" Etc.

And the plurality of the "consulted" objects could be connected to the integration and cohabitation of more family figures who enrich the child's reality. In my language (Bolognini, 2011), I consider these processes to be "the Central Ego's capacity to consult internal objects"; in this way, the central ego can draw on the creativity and richness of these internal sources and on their diverse perspectives.

An even more detailed analysis of the levels of interiorisation (a general term with which to group together all the processes through which an object is brought from the outside to the inside) requires clarification with respect to some basic questions.

1. "Inside" what? In the Ego or the individual's Self?
2. What is "inside"? And how does it come to be there?

Following the criterion of a certain functional equivalence between bodily processes and psychic ones, we can describe the various degrees and types of interiorisation in this way.

- *The object is taken into the mouth*, savoured, controlled (it is not swallowed and it is not spat out until the subject decides to carry out one of these two actions that would lead to his no longer having control over it), and in this way one can know some of its characteristics, such as form, consistency, taste, etc.

  This level ("incorporation") is at play in *imitation*: the subject can experience some of the object's characteristics and mentally reproduce some aspects of them in a conscious way, detaching from them, however, without difficulty, and without lasting modifications in the subject's own internal world.

  Professional actors—especially comedians, specialists in caricature—develop a certain degree of psychological mastery and technique in deliberately carrying out these operations when they imitate another person.
- *The object is swallowed, but not digested*. In this way, the object is "taken inside", occupies an internal space (concretely, in the stomach) and can no longer be voluntarily controlled, except in the intentional vomiting of anorexia, but it remains inside as an internal object and does not become part of the individual's self (literally, of the organism's cells). It is other than the self, even though "inside".

  The object is "internalised." Processes of *projective identification with the internalised object* are possible (the subject, identifying with it, "becomes" the object), but *at the price of a certain replacement of the self* with that object.

  In general, this situation is pathological. Partial introjective identifications are not accomplished with individual functions (see the following paragraph).

In these cases, the person does not succeed in consulting his internal objects, both because—being in a state of projective identification with one of them—he sees the world and tends to function only according to the perspective of the object with which he is identified, and because, in the absence of any internal separation, he cannot dialogue with any internalised object.

- *The object is digested and goes on to become part of the bodily self*. The psychic equivalent of that is the acquisition of characteristic partial functions received from the object, which begin to authentically become part of the subject's self and ego through introjection of the nuclear self (Wisdom, 1967).

We are then in the area of *partial introjective identifications*.

But a part of this picture is also the *internal relationship with whole objects* (for example, the father, the mother, or a teacher) who are well preserved as a memory, a representation, and an affect, with whom to relate without their replacing the subject's ego with actual identifications. Hosted within the self, distinct from the subject's conscious central ego, they can become objects for consultation.

I maintain that, on this basis (deriving, substantially, from object relations theory), the *specific obstacles to the consultation of internal objects* can be responsible for the phenomenon of "subjective formulation" described by Rumiati (2006), pertaining to repetitive patterns of problem-solving that interfere with the consideration of alternative pathways. Duncker's (1945) previously cited concept of "functional fixedness" can be a further consequence of these obstacles to the consultation of internal objects.

These psychological concepts effectively describe the dysfunctional result of psychic arrangements that impede creative intuition and "fishing" for solutions from the unconscious–preconscious area. Psychoanalytic object relations theory allows us to portray the internal scenario that makes in-depth consultations either possible or impossible, as well as the alternation of different points of view and a certain part of the work of the unconscious.

To review, I hypothesise that, in their rigidity, "subjective formulation" and "functional fixedness" implicitly reveal *a clear, extreme bond of identification that has taken the place of the central ego* (which, in general, would be more wide-ranging, if healthy), *to the point of colonising it*. This object is not infrequently a parental "occupant" figure with whom the subject's ego is projectively identified—totally so, to the detriment of his own authenticity, spontaneity, and curiosity.

Incidentally, this is precisely the problem of those analysts who have remained too intensely and exclusively identified with their own analyst, or—even more frequently—with their supervisors: these analysts have "become" their objects, who in this way replace their selves, and in reality they cannot truly consult them.

Deidealising intuition

The foregoing paragraphs have been dedicated to the study of "subjective formulation" and "functional fixedness" from a psychoanalytic point of view. Now I would like to address another particular aspect of intuition, connected not so much to the problem of the *variety* of points of view as to the *rapidity*, or lack of it, of the process.

We owe to Heinz Kohut some interesting comments—disenchanted ones, and not at all idealising—on the phenomenon of intuition, comments that can further our progress in this regard. According to Kohut (1971), *the mental processes that appear to be intuitive*, and that typically impress the observer to the point of making him believe he is in the presence of very special powers, different from ordinary ones, in fact differ only in the speed with which the mental operation is carried out—that is, the operation that has so struck us as to make us assume the presence of extraordinary ways of functioning.

In addition, Kohut observes:

> Talent, training, and experience will at times combine to produce results, in a variety of areas, which strike us as intuitive; thus we might find intuition at work not only in the empathic observation of the field of complex psychological states (such as is employed by psychoanalysts) but also . . . in medical diagnosis, or in the strategic decisions of a champion chess player, or in the planning of a physicist's experiments. (1971, p. 303)

This comment about the speed of the process—among other things rather tangential, since Kohut relates it almost incidentally in a chapter actually dedicated to empathy—seemed at first a little reductive to me, but with the passage of time, I have re-evaluated it (probably also because it implicitly limited the enviability of the "magical" resources demonstrated by intuitive subjects . . .).

I believe that Kohut might have been viewing the situation accurately here, and that it might be worth exploring the problem from another point of view. For example, if this hypothesis is well founded, what could cause a loss of that speed of mental functioning? Expressed in other terms, what can obstruct, weigh down, or gum up the thinking processes? And, to continue our exploration, what useful acquisitions can come to our aid, in this sense, from the comparative study of neurotic pathology and psychotic pathology?

The wasting of energy and ego functioning

The study of the neuroses from an economic point of view has revealed that there is a characteristic wasting of energy in repression: that is, the counter-attacks necessary to keep conflict-generating content repressed involve an increased economic cost, of which general fatigue, convolutedness, and a functional retardation of thinking can at times constitute symptoms accompanying those more specific to the neuroses.

In my manner of speaking, *the neurotic "travels with his entire load of baggage* (symptomatic, oneiric, economic) *as hand luggage*", in a system of ever-more precarious and costly repression into the dynamic unconscious, and the self's assets are not detached and projected far away.

Continuing on a metaphorical level, *neurotics do not lose their assets* (the self's legacy is repressed, but not split); *they must, however, manage to support very high expenses in order to continue repressing* and maintain within the unconscious *caveau* the conflictual elements that would upset the arrangement of the self's "day-zone". Exhausted by the demands on their energy, they have very deep eye sockets, so to speak, and extreme fatigue—neurotic symptoms, in fact.

The complications, the convolutedness, the inhibition of any retardation of thinking can result from continual, counterproductive interference on the part of internal conflicted components that prevail upon the ego, limiting its normal capacity for work, and from the wasting of energy that takes strength away from the ego. The slower rate of mental processes would make rapid, "intuitive" moments very rare, according to Kohut's observation.

My additional hypothesis is that, in many cases, the ego's capacity to give space to the creative contributions of the preconscious and the unconscious might also be damaged. In a state of internal alarm and a consequent increase of ego control and of functional contracture, the subject does not allow himself to make use of enriching intrapsychic consultations with internal objects, and he does not experience their points of view or their ways of being, virtually getting stuck in the "subjective formulation" described by Rumiati and in Duncker's "functional fixedness".

In terms of equivalent metaphors, the neurotic would then regulate himself intrapsychically in the manner of those persons who, in their defensive mode, "no longer listen to anyone" externally and avoid any interpsychic exchange. Alternatively, we could describe this dynamic by imagining that the miller's youngest son did not welcome the help of Puss-in-Boots, or that the Guatemalan subject did not want to know about the dolls that worked for him by night, but here we are already distancing ourselves from the economic aspect of the "wasting of energy" that is necessary to repress the creativity of the unconscious–preconscious area, a wasting that stems from conflict.

By contrast, *patients who are capable of marked splitting and projections of internal parts of the Self end up simplified, in a manner of speaking—impoverished as much in content as in the articulation of the Self, and are consequently "lighter"* (I would say that they "travel without hand luggage"). They are relatively asymptomatic, and, if anything, they are basically inclined toward a maniacal tendency. Economically speaking, they *lose a portion of their assets* ("assets" as the legacy of the internal world, as the basic endowment of the self, and as an abundance of the presence of, and connections with, internal objects)—disconnecting from these and, in a certain sense, renouncing them, given that in this way they avoid conflict.

In common language, these are the people, for example, who "don't worry about it", who "cut to the chase", and who—like Alexander the Great facing a Gordian knot—do not waste time trying to undo the knot, but instead simply cut it out with a sword in a single stroke.

In a specific way, *when important splits of the vertical type enter the scene* (to the point of dissociation, understood in a psychoanalytic sense and not in a phenomenologically psychiatric one), which have the effect of "compartmentalising experience", the mental functions and contents tend to be organised according to a simplified arrangement of personality structure. In these split states, the subject "travels without hand luggage", having renounced the "weight" of a part of the self—more or less as a lizard does when, exposed to danger, it detaches the end of its tail in order to leave it to the aggressor and run away faster.

In this compartmentalised condition, with the self simplified and impoverished, the subject is, however, basically asymptomatic, and he experiences less stress and bother precisely because he avoids, at least in part, the economic wasting involved in conflict, and very often he delegates someone else to represent and projectively experience the internal parts of the self.

The picture I have described with regard to the use of splitting can fall within frank pathology or, alternatively, when limited in quantitative terms and confined to a simple tendency, can characterise a certain personality type, circumscribed but decisive (and we must not forget that the etymology of "to decide" refers back to the Latin verb *de-caedere,* "to cut away from").

On the other hand, in a case quite compatible with good health, that of *functional specialisation of the professional self*, the fact that a person at work is organised in a relatively split way, can even be necessary and useful. If all surgeons identified with the people whom they operate on, for example, they would not succeed in doing their job; if all attorneys were not advocates of their clients but instead retained a minute-by-minute, fully integrated sense of humanity, they would lose too many legal battles—and so on.

Subjects do specialise, with temporary functional splits aimed at carrying out a task, and often a white coat, a black gown, or a pair of overalls worn on the job is the correlate of a *suitably split internal set-up*, learnt and then consolidated with society's full consensus.

The economic advantage of this internal simplification, with which the person is functionally transformed into a highly specialised character and is focused with intense investment on certain selected functions, *can produce an associative fluidity and a speed of traversing mental passages that are compatible with the functional rapidity of an intuitive type of person*.

If this optimal reduction of the wasting of energy is then combined with an a-conflictual possibility of contact and of internal consultations with significant objects, it generates, in turn, an increased richness in the mobility and variety of points of view, with a true "kaleidoscope effect" and accelerated functional time.

Conclusions

I have tried to indicate, with a rapid cinematic running shot between physiology and pathology, some psychic processes that demonstrate the participation of unconscious and preconscious levels in the work of problem solving. I have also briefly explored the area of intuition, proposing some hypothetical connections between the phenomenological observation of it and some aspects of how one might understand it psychoanalytically.

I would like to devote some final, broad reflections to the different perspectives with which the contribution of the unconscious to problem solving has been more or less explicitly considered in diverse cultural spheres, in order to close with an abbreviated formulation of a possible psychoanalytic vision of this subject.

With extreme brevity, one could say the following.

1. Many cultures of Eastern origin seem to converge in considering the subject's ego as an obstacle to the free expansion of potential internal knowledge. At times, they recommend extremely refined modalities of gradual deactivation and functional suspension of the central ego, through meditative practices, technical rituals, exercises in abstinence, thought control, diffuse fusionality with the environment, or "piloted" regression to functional conditions of pre-separation. In these cultures, the central ego is not fundamentally suppressed, but is partially marginalised and placed in a condition of "stand-by", impairing the subject's agency.
2. Cultures of a psychedelic Western type tend to openly devalue the central ego's function and to "force" a suspension of the ego through its functional suppression, based on the ingestion of substances. In practice, here the ego is intentionally stunned via pharmacology. These persons emphasise a presumed wisdom-producing feature in this deregulated experience, sufficient unto itself, with aspects of a demand (narcissistically invested) for the right to omnipotently regress to an intrauterine psychic state—in effect an "oceanic" state of pre-separation.

3. Cultures of the craftsman and the artist traditionally assign a more dignified status to action than to thought. In craftsmanship, competence in the manual accomplishment of the task is especially valued; in art, the work of art itself is what is highly valued, being strongly invested with narcissistic libido. The central ego, however, is the project adviser and the auxiliary assistant to the craftsman, whose more invested part is usually the hands; the unconscious of the craftsman engaged in working is especially the procedural unconscious, the seat of skills and abilities that have become automatic.

   In the artistic field, one aims ideally towards a level of "mastery" that relieves the conscious central ego of control functions. For example, the great violinist establishes a direct bridge between "heart" and "hands", given that his technique is no longer for him a problem to be regulated and monitored by the central ego's surveillance.
4. Psychoanalysis never intends to eliminate, deactivate, intoxicate, or pharmacologically stun the central ego. Since its inception, it has renounced manipulation of the attentional state and thought control in the way of hypnosis, which Freud abandoned very early on. Psychoanalysis is not interested in paralysing the gaoler (the defensive ego, when it is such), but in transforming it in its relationship with the other parts of the self.

One of the aims of contemporary psychoanalysis is that of permitting a *co-operative harmonisation between the various parts of the Self*, repairing and restoring the internal functional synergies that are missing in psychopathology. Such synergies, by contrast, are established naturally during development, when the child and his relational objects have a way to experience *forms of co-operation* (in sucking, in learning, in interpsychic interchange) that *are then introjected*, and are gradually structured into a way of functioning that also becomes intrapsychic.

When the developmental and formative process takes place harmoniously, the subject's internal demands co-operate with equal participation in situations of suffering or conflict as well, maintaining an internal sense of cohesion and reducing splits to a minimum.

A benevolent central ego—faithful, capacious, and tolerant, heir to the primary objects that have formed its capacities and functional articulations—knows how to intervene when it is useful, and how to step aside when other parts of the self demonstrate superior creativity and competence equal to the task. The ego is then called on again, at the end of the process, to provide a central, integrative contribution to what was produced from the contributions of the internal parts.

The cohesiveness, atmosphere, style, and fluidity of these internal relationships allow us to perceive the greater or lesser harmony that characterises the various persons who cohabitate with the self and with others. I think that precisely the perception of this internal complexity might have led the poet and philosopher Fernando Pessoa (1888–1935) to write, "My soul is a hidden orchestra; I know not what instruments, what fiddle strings and harps, drums and tamboura I sound and clash inside myself. All I hear is the symphony" (Pessoa, 2002).

Note

1. Translation by Gina Atkinson, MA.

Epilogue

Mary Kay O'Neil

> "Great works of art are only great because they are accessible and comprehensible to everyone"
>
> Leo Tolstoy, *What is Art?*

Freud's "The unconscious" is a great work of art. What an assertive and bold statement! Can it be substantiated? Is Freud's notion of the *unconscious* available and understandable to everyone?

Certainly, Freud's creative and unique model of the *unconscious* mind has formed the basis of psychoanalytic theory, practice, and research. Psychoanalysis, largely based as it is on the *unconscious*, has also stimulated exploration into the mind–brain relationship and has permeated and "profoundly changed the intellectual and cultural life of at least Western man, creating both obvious and subtle changes in our views of ourselves and our relationships to each other, our children, and our society" (Cooper, Kernberg, & Person, 1989, p. 1). Freud's notion of the unconscious is accessible to all who are interested. Even those who are not interested or disparage the presence of an unconscious give it attention—however negative or critical.

Freud began his discovery of unconscious mental processes as he struggled to understand the pain and suffering of his patients and how illnesses related to the workings of their minds (*Studies on Hysteria*, 1895d). With his brilliant work, *The Interpretation of Dreams* (1900a), he believed he had found the royal road to the unconscious. *The Psychopathology of Everyday Life* (1901b) grounded the notion of the unconscious influencing the daily lives of all of us. By 1915, Freud had developed much of psychoanalytic theory from his clinical experience, leading to numerous papers, to the point of being able to enunciate his early *topographic* model of the mind (unconscious, preconscious, conscious), while paving the way for further development of models both by himself and those who followed. By then, he had outlined most of the major concepts that continue to characterise psychoanalysis today, one of the most important (if not *the* most important) being *the unconscious*. As is well known, Freud worked to elucidate the characteristics of the *unconscious*, exploring its relationship with the preconscious and the conscious aspects of the mind. He came to find that the *unconscious* comprised at least two other dimensions besides the topographic—the dynamic and economic—to develop his metapsychology. Subsequent psychoanalysts and, indeed, non-analysts have addressed the task of expanding Freud's notion of the unconscious, reformulating and resolving the inconsistencies in his ideas, collecting new data, and generating further concepts and theories.

Is Freud's *unconscious* understandable today to psychoanalysts and interested others, whether in agreement or not with his ideas? Numerous articles, essays, and books have been written by analysts and others explaining, developing, debunking, and even reifying the *unconscious*.[1] Why then this book? Yet another volume on the *unconscious*! Why so soon after the 2007 IPA volume edited by Calich and Hinz, *The Unconscious: Further Reflections*? The only plausible explanation is that understanding the *unconscious*, making it comprehensible to everyone, is an ongoing process, a work in progress, both for and by psychoanalysts and others. A work of art is not considered great when observed by one or several persons just when it is produced. The attribution of greatness develops and continues over time as observers (for images) and readers or teachers (for ideas) delve into the work. The search for depth of meaning in a great work of art never ends. Hence, this new reflection of thought on Freud's "The unconscious" (19125e).

Here, it is useful to determine what our contributors have added to contemporary accessibility and comprehension of Freud's "The unconscious".

We begin with Peter Wegner, whose history of when and in what context Freud wrote "The unconscious" sets the stage for the reader.

It is 1915, the First World War has begun and Freud, unable to work as much in his consulting room, is in the midst of developing his metapsychology in five papers, "The unconscious" being the last. Wegner reviews how Freud's understanding of the *unconscious* developed. A contemporary thinker, Wegner maintains, like Freud, that the *unconscious* of the analyst is as involved as that of the patient and that *unconscious* communication between the patient and analyst is an integral part of the psychoanalytic endeavour. Such *unconscious* communication of the analyst, a highly valuable component of the process that might eventually come into awareness, derives from multiple influences. No two analysts learn and develop in the same way. Despite common parameters and knowledge of accepted theory and technique, each has his or her own way of working. Just as no two people are alike (including their *unconscious*), no two analysts work alike. The mind of each analyst combines individual life experience with particular training. The inevitable uniqueness contributes to uncertainty within the profession and within the analyst. Wegner recognises that the capacity to tolerate uncertainty while continuing to analyse is essential to our work. His forthright clinical illustration demonstrates his struggles to help his patient learn experientially the effect of her *unconscious* on her relationship with herself and others. Analysts' ways of working develop over time as they come to understand their use of self in being an effective analyst.

Mark Solms takes us away from the historical and plunges us right into current research. As a neuropsychologist, he explains what is now thought about the brain–mind relationship—knowledge that was unavailable to Freud. Accepting that the mental comprises conscious, preconscious, and *unconscious* elements, Solms summarises information about the brain–mind interface that Freud tried hard to understand but could not. First, Solms calls attention to the division within current neuropsychology between cognitive and affective neuroscientists. Cognitive neuroscientists do not accept the Freudian notion of the id being the deepest part of the *unconscious*, whereas affective neuropsychologists, notably Panksepp (Solms also places himself there), accept the id, primary process, and instinct as components of the *unconscious*. Yet, Solms and colleagues do not agree that the core content of what Freud calls the system Ucs.—the deepest stratum of the mind—is truly *unconscious*. For them, unlike for

Freud, the instincts are "the very font of consciousness". Solms asserts that it is now known that consciousness derives from the reticular activating system in the upper brainstem, information that undercuts Freud's "corticocentric fallacy". For Solms, the classical conception is turned on its head. Consciousness is not generated in the cortex; it is initiated in the brainstem. Moreover, consciousness is not inherently perceptual; it is inherently affective. When it comes to affect, Freud and today's neuropsychologists do agree. Freud's pleasure–unpleasure principle is consistent with Damasio's "I feel like this about that" (e.g., I feel good or bad about that)—the basic unit of core consciousness. Therefore, following recent neuropsychological findings, consciousness must come from below, because one cannot speak of awareness of pleasure and unpleasure without speaking of consciousness. Solms goes on to suggest that Freud's model needs significant revision for three reasons: (1) the core of the system Ucs. is not unconscious, it is the font of consciousness, which is primarily affective; (2) the systems Pcpt.-Cs. (Freud's later ego) are *unconscious* in themselves, and by inhibiting the Ucs., they aspire to remain so; but (3) they borrow consciousness as a compromise measure, and tolerate consciousness, in order to resolve uncertainties (and to bind affect).

Why offer this summary of Solms' chapter, the reader might ask? His is a rich but difficult chapter and it seems relevant to put forward its main points as current understanding of the mind–brain relationship. Further research will suggest further revisions of what is now known. We can only speculate about how Freud's thinking and his models might have changed had he had such neuropsychology knowledge. Psychoanalysts today need to remain cognisant of the latest emerging knowledge to put Freud's model in context.

Remarkably, Linda Brakel finds Freud's "The unconscious" relatively brief, but packed and amazingly contemporary. She notes that Freud suggests a link between the biology and psychology of the *unconscious*, and she highlights aspects of his metapsychological framework and offers an effective philosophical argument against his detractors. She continues in an astute though dense argument to discuss two main areas "The biological unconscious" and the "Conflict", that is, the "problems arising for any notion of an essentially biological unconscious". These problems have to do with time and reality. Brakel confronts the difficult question: "how can any biological system survive without regard to time and other aspects of reality?" No biological organism would be capable of adapting to its environment without built-in registrations and adjustments due to considerations of time and reality. She carefully weighs empirical evidence which demonstrates that Freud's *unconscious* processes are sensitive to time and reality and asks, "can this conflict about the unconscious, its potential biological relevance, and the biological factors of time and reality be resolved?" In her careful academic way, Brakel looks closely at Freud's views on the timelessness of the unconscious, yet uses an everyday example of how, without much awareness, hunger grows over time in herself and her dog. The increased drive to eat—the drive intensity—serves as a biological/psychological clock. When she talks about not feeling hunger—putting it aside—she asks the questions many of us ask. Is that really repression—*unconscious*–preconscious? Is awareness the process of making the *unconscious* conscious? Also are instinct and unconscious synonymous? We continue to seek answers.

Brakel then turns to her final topic—the reality conflict. She does so by offering a dual view (biological and social) of Freud's ideas. Her resolution of the problem with time and reality is to bring them together and to suggest another kind of time awareness and a different reality, "both mediated, not by biological imperatives, but by socio-cultural norms". Socially, she suggests, there is a time for certain behaviours as well as external availability (food is needed to eat and a toilet is used to urinate). This becomes complicated when drives/wishes are considered as primarily psychological. Socio-cultural norms can either forbid or facilitate such wishes. Brakel is not claiming that Freud, in "The unconscious", intended this dual view. Rather, she underlines that she and Freud maintain "psychoanalysis in its full psychological essence to be a theory and discipline that is essentially biologically based". Carefully, Brakel has moved towards resolution of the time and reality conflict in Freud's model. Yet, we are left with questions (such as, would Freud agree?) Brakel stimulates us to look further—to study her ideas and reconsider Freud's.

With Brakel's introductory sub-title "Freud, the biological philosopher", she offers us a bridge to Madhusudana Rao Vallabhanneni's (Rao for short) "a Hindu reading of Freud's, "The unconscious" in which he compares Freud's model of the *unconscious* with Hindu philosophy. Rao reminds us that "Freud's view is clinical and psychoanalytic. Hindu philosophers' view is meditative and metaphysical" and Rao's presentation is philosophical and spiritual but not religious. Strachey had noted that although Freud did not take a philosophical but a biological view of the *unconscious*, philosophical issues are present. As we have seen in the two foregoing chapters and as Rao notes, Freud's belief that a neurological explanation of mental phenomena would eventually be found has been borne out by discoveries in neuropsychophysiology (referencing Kaplan-Solms). Rao acknowledges a tension between the Hindu perspective and that of Freud, but before addressing this tension, he provides the main theses of the two viewpoints. For the Western reader unfamiliar with Hindu philosophy, this is a valuable contribution. His explanations of both views are lucid and engaging. Differences and similarities are noted.

To summarise the differences, "In Freud, word representation is necessary for the thing representation in the *unconscious* to become conscious, but for the Hindu philosopher, meditation on *OM* is very helpful in experiencing the ineffable, the absolute truth, and the Brahman. In Freud, the thing belongs to the unconscious, which needs to find attachment to the word representation to experience the phenomenal world, but to the Hindu philosopher, the experience of *OM*, the thing is transcendental and spiritual, which is the ultimate goal of life". The similarities are also brought together in the following excerpt: "for both the Hindu philosopher and Freud, the mind and intellect (the psychosomatic complex) is the seat of perception and action (reaction). The stimulus for desire—the instinct—arises from input from the object, through the five organs of perception, and forms the drive—a mental representation (the impression of latent memories, *vasanas*) that again is expressed in its pursuit of satisfaction from the object. Without the stimuli from the object world, there is no present experience of activation of previous memory impressions, both for Freud and the Hindu philosopher". Rao believes that the similarities are "due to the common goal of these two disciplines, which is to understand the human being and human behaviour". In his helpful "Summary and conclusions", Rao reiterates his main points. In fact, the reader unfamiliar with Eastern philosophy might want to examine these points first and then fill in with reading the rest of the paper. To understand something of the usefulness of Hindu philosophy to the practice of psychoanalysis, a reading of Symington's "How belief in God affects my clinical work" (2009) is helpful. Further understanding of Freud's work and its interface with Hindu philosophy can also be gained from Nagpal (2011).

Repression, the *sine qua non* of the dynamic *unconscious*, is addressed directly in Kenneth Wright's "The repressed maternal in Freud's topography of mind". Freud's view of repression is contained in these words, "the essence of repression lies simply in turning something away, and keeping it at a distance, from the conscious". According to Wright, Freud unconsciously repressed the maternal, and, by extrapolation, the relational in his model of the unconscious mind. "A relation perspective is more in tune with contemporary psychoanalysis than Freud's mechanistic account . . ." Wright asserts that the word—the verbal form—introduces the idea of shape. It is here that he brings us into the shape of the mother–child relationship and infers similarities with the analyst–analysand relationship. Freud, a man of his time, was more paternal–cognitive than emotional–maternal. Referring to the work of Langer and Ogden, the maternal is associated with experience and its "lived qualities" rather than the paternal way of naming and talking about it, of telling rather than allowing the patient to experience and, thereby, become aware of what lies beneath. Stern's maternal attunement that reflects the intonation, the rhythm, the intensity and vitality of the child's experience is coupled with Winnicott's notion of "mirroring", the experience of being seen and recognised, laying the basis of the self ("I am seen and recognised, therefore I am"). He goes further, to say that the mother's expression gives an external image of what the child is like. Of necessity, Wright brings in art and artistic expression, stating that "its presentational method is direct: the work of art, with its complex articulation of forms and images, shows and makes manifest the way we are".

Seeing for the first time one of Picasso's seated figures with size exaggerated arms and legs, I understood that he painted how it feels to sit with one's legs drawn up in front—he painted the physical experience that could be seen and felt by the viewer. Even though Freud could not directly discuss "the maternal", as unacceptable and repressed as the image was for him, it is not far-fetched to suggest that his intuitive grasp of human experience was sensitively (maternally?) active even in his early studies on hysteria. Lucy and Katarina come to mind; Freud recognising a young woman's love and yearning for the love of her employer, he helped Lucy to become aware of her wishes and accept that which was, at the time, not possible; also Katarina, horrified by what she had seen, pushed away what she knew, until, with Freud's assistance, she could find the words to describe the images that she saw. His words to these women, whether or not he was aware of it, evoked emotional experience and truth. The two sides of Freud—the external paternal and internal maternal—are present because even if the maternal is repressed, it has to have been there in the first place. Wright ends, "every art object of worth is a small revelation of the structure of the human psyche because its articulations are the forms of that psyche, realised in the medium of the external world". He affirms the creativity in Freud's "The unconscious".

Bernard Reith takes us into Freud's consulting room and imagines him asking "What is going on here? How to understand it? How am I involved? Immediately, he reads beneath the surface of the *unconscious* and proposes that "the something more than the topographical model" is the "two-person transformational model". This might confirm the notion that, although Freud might have repressed the maternal–relational model by not putting it into words or images, he nevertheless left enough evidence for Reith to delve beneath and imagine an implicit theme. Although Freud's topographical model is a construct about the mind of one person, that is, an intrapsychic model, it is his use of the word "we" that kindles Reith's idea that there is more than one person in the consulting room, that the analyst (Freud) is very much involved. Reith emphasises that the analyst is there to help the analysand overcome resistances and, thereby, to make conscious (transform, translate) what was repressed in the *unconscious*. To illustrate what he means by "transformational psychoanalytic work", Reith provides a well-integrated case vignette: "finding thing-presentations for closeness". He takes us into his consulting room; he shows us how his image of "turning a sock inside out" spoke to his patient in a way he could not have anticipated. His image evoked more than an intellectual understanding—the inside-out sock spoke to the patient's *unconscious* experience. Here is a superb example of the transformational work—the *unconscious* of two people working together. It also exemplifies an analyst, though uncertain, trusting his *unconscious*. This was a transformational moment. With the following paragraph, Reith not only recalls Wegner's points about psychoanalytic work needing time and patience and the bearing of uncertainty, but helps the reader understand what other authors have alluded to—differentiating "thing-presentation" and "word-presentation". Reith writes,

> Perhaps what happened was that I had captured something unconsciously about his need for safe and differentiated skin-to-skin contact as a starting point for feeling in contact with himself, but for which I had not until then found an image (a "thing-presentation") that I could put in words. . . . Something unconscious was transformed, first into a "thing-presentation" that had so far been lacking, then into a network of "thing-presentations", and, ultimately, through linkage to "word-presentations", into a meaningful structure. I am not saying that this replaced the interpretative work, but I do believe that it gave it more flesh and meaning.

Returning to Freud's paper, he imagines how Freud must have debated with himself (his imaginary detractors?) to find a way to understand his patient. He follows Freud's careful and detailed argument, explaining the various pitfalls that an analyst can encounter. For example, "latent memories", "points of conscious and unconscious contact", "identification with the patient", and "certainty about our own consciousness" are helpfully discussed in the light of Freud's paper. Reith recognises that the "other person" is the analyst's internal reaction to the patient. Reith has referred to Freud's topographical model as a *jewel*—placing Freud's paper in the realm of art. He continues to delve and read deeply, acknowledging that Freud has given us a lasting psychic model that does not have to be in a physical space. In fact, an idea, like a folk-tale, can remain the same but have different expressions. Analysts have often argued as to whether or not Freud proposes unconscious emotions. Reith puts this to rest by carefully discussing the presence of emotions in both participants in the analytic work.

Reith now reformulates for the reader his initial three questions that he imagined Freud asking himself and does so from the three metapsychological points of view (dynamic, topographic, and economic). After discussing these questions in the light of Freud's work, while integrating his clinical example, he also notes that Freud's legacy does not presage intersubjective work in the wider sense of the term. Rather, after recognising that Freud's legacy has been developed further by analysts such as Klein, Bion, Winnicott, Baranger, Ferro, and Roussillon, and discussed by Hanly, Reith concludes that "given the multiple meanings of 'intersubjective', my own preferred term for this kind of transformative work would be 'interpsychic', as used . . . by Bolognini (2011), and which would seem closer to Freud's original usage".

Bernard Reith, having brought us into Freud's and his own consulting room, paved the way for our next three authors (Aisenstein, Brenner, and Bolignini) whose clinical acumen especially speaks to today's analysts.

Marilia Aisenstein takes us into her work with the *unconscious* of psychosomatic patients. She begins with a history of the meaning of the dynamic *unconscious* in psychosomatic patients and outlines the different schools of psychosomatics. From her vast experience in working with somato-psychic patients whose problems go from the body to the psyche with increasing complexity, she maintains that her approach—that of the Paris School—"was present in embryo in the Freudian construction of the concept of drive". She has no doubt that mind and body are inextricably linked, but stresses that the demand or pressure comes from the body and assumes that the discontinuities of mental functioning for psychosomatic patients leads to the assumption that a failure of the " 'demand for representation' occurs that is linked to excess". Comparing "The unconscious" with *The Ego and the Id*, Aisenstein asserts that analysts working with "somatic and borderline organisations *have the goal of transforming id into unconscious*". Reading Freud's first topography, like Reith, she addresses the question of affect being part of the unconscious by elucidating the difficult notion that affect cannot be repressed, but suppression of it is the aim of repression. Similar to other authors in this volume using the two-person model, she maintains that psychoanalytic work with somato-psychic patients involves both analyst and analysand. Aisenstein states, "preconscious affects of the psychoanalyst can be perceived by the patient and meet in him or her an unconscious 'potential beginning' which seeks to break through". This is only qualified in the transference and countertransference process, where it acquires its status of affect as a result of being processed by the analyst's preconscious. Moving beyond "The unconscious" and *The Ego and the Id* to Freud's later work on the structural model and his second theory of anxiety, the reader is brought to see the difference between work with patients with neurotic problems and patients with somatic problems. She speaks of a "transference compulsion" but, like children, and unlike the hysteric capable of an interpretable transference neurosis, somato-psychic patients form less complex and less verbalised transferences. Her clinical examples vividly demonstrate that persons with somatic problems have no interest in the "psychic" or "introspection", but "mysteriously" continue coming to their sessions until eventually an emotional connection between analyst and analysand emerges. For her, somatic symptoms have no symbolic meaning, but only acquire one after analysis.

What can we, as clinicians, glean from Aisenstein's understanding of patients with somato-psychic problems? Her cogent and useful points are as follows: the analyst needs to be physically (bodily) and emotionally present; the analyst needs to acknowledge and validate a patient's perceptions and then link these to past experience. These points she illustrates clinically with her second example, in which she admits to her patient, "I had indeed been thinking of someone else . . . but that we needed to understand together why she could not tolerate not having complete control over someone else's thoughts". She followed with an historical interpretation, ". . . it was probable that she was making me experience what she had suffered from in the distant past", and this led to anxiety changing to experienced feeling. For Aisenstein, affect is the key concept capable of linking a charge (drive) to a representation or to a chain of representations. The patient's breathing calmed and she cried for the first time. With this "forced recognition of the object's (analyst's) own psychic life true analysis can begin". That is, after a long time of the analyst being there, the analysand can begin to explore with feeling his or her psychic life. Wegner's "patience and time" and Reith's "a sock turned inside out" agree with Aisenstein's approach. Indeed, all the contributors to this volume agree that the *unconscious* of the analyst is as involved as that of the analysand.

Ira Brenner acknowledges that Freud's seminal monograph, with its wellspring of ideas, continues to inspire elaboration of his insights. Brenner offers his own thoughts on the role of the *unconscious* in perceptions of the self. He firmly maintains that perceptions of both external and internal realities are significantly influenced by *unconscious* forces. Major disturbances, especially in "losing time", might indicate elusive disturbances in other aspects of the psyche, but, if examined, might shed more light on psychoanalytic work.

Drawing on his clinical experience, Brenner sheds light on work with patients who suffer from severe disturbances in self-perception—those who today might be diagnosed as having dissociative or multiple personality disorders. His interest in understanding the role of the *unconscious* was triggered when, as a student, he observed a young woman under the influence of drugs lose a sense of where she was "I am here and I am not here". Reflecting later, he realised that Freud had provided an avenue for comprehending that this temporarily deranged young woman "probably experienced alternating awareness of her *unconscious* mental processes and thus took leave of her usual senses". Freud also set the stage for understanding that aspect of multiple personality that keeps separate the different selves, and Brenner notes that later analysts "describe pathogenic, sequestered schemas as residues of early childhood traumata which colour perception, function on the level of the *dynamic unconscious*, and then reappear". Brenner discusses four different clinical vignettes, each of which demonstrates a different self-disturbance due to unconsciously influenced perception. In the first, an extreme example of the reciprocity of internal and external perception, he showed how inability to tolerate the psychic reality of having multiple, dissociated selves determined self-destructive behaviour. Brenner, recalling Freud and Breuer, attributed her "very deep" repression to sustained severe early trauma. His second case report describes the clinical challenge of addressing a patient's rather sudden and dynamically meaningful change of self-perception (she became a totally different person who, in that state, did not recognise her other self and vice versa). In his discussion of the technical problems, he notes that psychiatry has often confused schizophrenia with multiple personality, resulting in a failure in allowing the person to tell what had been hidden and then assisting them to understand their other self (selves) by analysing. The deleterious effect of this failure is illustrated with a third case. Turning to perceptions of the bodily self, he reminds us that Freud held that the ego is a "bodily ego" and that "the somatic basis of the self is accepted to be sensory-motor in origin". This is linked to the mirror stage, where the infant sees himself in the mother's eyes and then in a mirror—the fascination with one's reflection remains throughout life. Brenner's fourth case report illustrates graphically how his use of the word mirror—referring to himself—triggered a regression to a childish voice and memories of childhood torture.

Ending with references to great literature, Cervantes, Shakespeare, and Pirandello, Brenner comments, "In closing, while such concepts as observing ego focus our attention on the conscious perceptions of the self, *unconscious*, dissociated influences must be considered in order to 'really' see ourselves in the mirror". Admitting that he might have used Freud's paper as a jumping-off point, but the word "self" does not appear in the text, Brenner notes that Freud "contended that the unconscious was inhabited by the evolutionary heritage of our species in some state of personification. So, it would follow that a better understanding of not only what but 'who' is residing in those dark recesses of our mind could promote a better integration of the psyche".

Finally, we come to Stefano Bolognini's paper. His topic—"In spite of my ego": problem solving and the unconscious" mobilised for him "reflections that go beyond the specifically theoretical and clinical field of psychoanalysis". Bolognini begins with a self-observation—"envy" of those who seemingly resolve problems quickly, intuitively, with little effort, fuss, or bother. To introduce the "creativity of the unconscious", he quickly moves to two important points made by Freud: the *unconscious* "works"; the *unconscious* can be activated; for example, it can combine with the *unconscious* of another, "eluding" the conscious mind. It is the intuitive person's unconscious that works at a deep level, "something, unknown to the ego, works, combines, assembles, conceives, creates, transforms".

To illustrate his thesis of a working unconscious in metaphorical form, Bolognini creatively uses (with an amusing effect) the fairy-tale *Puss in Boots*. The boy (ego) becomes passive, and allows the non-anxious, healthily narcissistic cat (unconscious) to do the work. The work results in a favourable situation, from an internal relationship between the ego and the self that emanates from positively introjected interpsychic parental styles. After clarifying his understanding of Freud's terms, Bolognini hypothesises about "a potentially and occasionally creative oneiric area, which is based on the possibility of representation, of decomposition, and of recombination of the elements at play in the subject's internal world, thanks to the reliable and reconnecting effect of primary process and to the reorganisation permitted to secondary process". That is how the *unconscious* works and the ego can agree or oppose. Again creatively, the "little Guatemalan dolls" are used to demonstrate how solutions to problems can be reached unconsciously. Imaginatively, the dolls talk together and find solutions, while the person sleeps. On waking, these solutions become conscious and can be useful as long as the ego does not block them. That is, the ego (the conscious) has to give space to the preconscious and unconscious to be used creatively.

Returning to, and exploring, the notion of intuition, the reader is taken from the great thinkers of ancient Greece, to the 1926 cognitive psychologist (Wallas), who described the four typical stages of the intuitive process, to the 1987 work of Metcalfe and Wiebe, who demonstrated that problems requiring a creative solution can be effectively resolved quite suddenly. Those cognitive psychologists who studied the "capacity for lateral thinking", subjective formulation, functional fixedness, and brainstorming are also referred to.

What of the connections between cognitive theories and the psychoanalytic view of intuition? Bolgonini makes the connection by elucidating such psychoanalytic concepts as "multiple, adequate introjections of useful and positive objects and of their functions". In his words, complex concepts, such as identification, introjection, incorporation, imitation, partial introjective identifications, internal relationship with whole objects, etc. become understandable and clinically meaningful. Intuition, especially its rapidity, can be idealised; the reader, through reference to Kohut, is assisted in de-idealising speedy mental functioning. Turning next to the economic point of view, Bolgonini demystifies the energic cost of repression. Imaginatively, neurotics do not lose their assets, they protect themselves by using much energy to repress their conflicts and avoid genuine interaction. By contrast, those who are capable of marked splitting and projections of internal parts of the self lose a portion of their assets; they are lighter because they have renounced the weight of a part of the self. However, splitting can be temporarily functional, as one must do to do certain jobs. Economically, splitting for selective functions can result in rapid, intuitive problem solving.

In his conclusions, Bolognini briefly refers to cultural and psychoanalytic views of problem solving through intuition. He recognises that psychoanalysis permits co-operative harmonisation between the various parts of the self, and that a child who experiences forms of co-operation that are introjected most often develops a benevolent central ego—faithful, capacious, and tolerant, heir to the primary objects that have formed its capacities—to intervene or step aside when parts of the self are creatively superior. His final quote, "My soul is a hidden orchestra; I know not what instruments, what fiddle strings and harps, drums and tamboura I sound and clash inside myself. All I hear is the symphony" underlines this creative paper. Bolognini's words are so replete in images that his chapter is well worth reading and rereading.

To return to Salman Akhtar's lucid "Introduction" and the twelve major propositions he derived from "The unconscious". No one of our contributors has referred to all twelve. However, taken together, these authors, from their own fresh perspectives, cover one or more at a time and collectively address all twelve. Some support Freud's ideas, others are critical or, in certain areas, strongly disagree. Few ideas have been overlooked. All agree, as do I, with Akhtar's assertion that there is much more to be discovered about the *unconscious*. Freud has led us and he continues to stimulate.

The contributors—psychoanalysts and authors—have turned Freud's seminal monograph this way and that; they have delved into it from top to bottom, from bottom to top, and all around to reveal width, breadth, and depth. Their varying perspectives have not brought closure to the exploration of Freud's "The unconscious". Rather, their contributions have added to its accessibility and comprehension and opened doors for further learning. Eifermann (2007) summarises well the push and pull of such learning:

> The unconscious is a territory that will always remain to some extent unexplored, and its effects will persist alongside our continuous attempts to explore. . . . to deny its existence, or to neglect it through practical and theoretical innovations, blinds us to its constant influence on that which we can know. It strengthens our belief that we do know more than we do. Yet the pull towards denial and the temptation to conduct a psychotherapy in which suggestion replaces the development of the autonomy of the patient's mind is great. Delving into the unconscious mind is

> disturbing to its nature—to our nature. Therefore, the inner and outer conflicts over abandoning or persisting with this exploration will never cease.

To return to the qualities of "great art", these words of Tolstoy contain much of what Freud created for us in "The unconscious". "Art is the uniting of the subjective with the objective, of nature with reason, of the unconscious with the conscious, and therefore art is the highest means of knowledge" (Tolstoy, 1995).

Note

1. A rapid search of PEP revealed almost 700 articles in primary journals that had the word "unconscious" in the title.

REFERENCES

Aisenstein, M. (1993). Psychosomatic solution or somatic outcome: the man from Burma—psychotherapy of a case of haemorraghic rectocolitis. *International Journal of Psychoanalysis*, *74*: 371–381.

Aisenstein, M. (2008). Beyond the dualism of psyche and soma. *Journal of the American Academy of Psychoanalysis*, *36*: 103–123.

Aisenstein, M. (2010a). Clinical treatment of psychosomatic symptoms. *International Journal of Psychoanalysis*, *91*: 1213–1215.

Aisenstein, M. (2010b). Les exigences de la représentation. *Revue française de psychanalyse*, *74*(5): 1367–1392.

Aisenstein, M., & Rappoport de Aisemberg, E. (Eds.) (2010). *Psychosomatics Today: A Psychoanalytic Perspective*. London: Karnac.

Akhtar, S. (1999). *Immigration and Identity: Turmoil, Treatment, and Transformation*. Northvale, NJ: Jason Aronson.

Akhtar, S. (2009a). *Comprehensive Dictionary of Psychoanalysis*. London: Karnac.

Akhtar, S. (2009b). Metapsychology. In: *Comprehensive Dictionary of* Psychoanalysis (pp. 171–172). London: Karnac.

Akhtar, S. (2011). *Immigration and Acculturation: Mourning, Adaptation, and the Next Generation*. Lanham, MD: Jason Aronson.

Akhtar, S. (2013). *Good Stuff: Courage, Resilience, Gratitude, Generosity, Forgiveness, and Sacrifice*. Lanham, MD: Jason Aronson.

Alexander, F. (1947). Treatment of a case of peptic ulcer and personality disorder. *Psychosomatic Medicine, 9*: 320–330.

Amati-Mehler, J., Argentieri, S., & Canestri, J. (1993). *The Babel of the Unconscious: Mother Tongue and Foreign Languages in the Psychoanalytic Dimension*, J. Whitelaw-Cucco (Trans.). Madison, CT: International Universities Press.

Anderson, M., Ochsner, K., Kuhl, B., Cooper, J., Robertson, E., Gabrieli, S., Glover, G., & Gabrieli, J. (2004). Neural systems underlying the suppression of unwanted memories. *Science, 303*: 232–235.

Arieti, S. (1974). *Interpretation of Schizophrenia*. New York: Basic Books.

Arlow, J. A. (1966). Depersonalization and derealization. In: R. M. Loewenstein, L. M. Newman, M. Schur, & A. J. Solnit (Eds.), *Psychoanalysis—A General Psychology* (pp. 456–478). New York: International Universities Press.

Arlow, J. (1969). Unconscious fantasy and disturbances of mental experience. *Psychoanalytic Quarterly, 38*: 1–27.

Asendorpf, J. B., Warkentin, V., & Baudonnière, P.-M. (1996). Self-awareness and other-awareness. II: Mirror self-recognition, social contingency awareness, and synchronic imitation. *Developmental Psychology, 32*: 313–321.

Baranger, M., & Baranger, W. (2008). The analytic situation as a dynamic field. *International Journal of Psychoanalysis, 89*: 795–826.

Bargh, J., & Chartrand, T. (1999). The unbearable automaticity of being. *American Psychologist, 54*: 462–479.

Bassanese, F. A. (1997). *Understanding Luigi Pirandello*. Columbia, SC: University of South Carolina Press.

Beres, D., & Joseph, E. D. (1970). The concept of mental representation in psychoanalysis. *International Journal of Psychoanalysis, 51*: 1–8

Bergmann, M. S. (1993). Reflections on the history of psychoanalysis. *Journal of the American Psychoanalytic Association, 41*: 929–955.

Bernat, E., Shevrin, H., & Snodgrass, M. (2001). Subliminal visual oddball stimuli evoke a P300 component. *Clinical Neurophysiology, 112*: 159–171.

Bernstein, W. M. (2011). *A Basic Theory of Neuropsychoanalysis*. London, UK: Karnac.

Bettelheim, B. (1982). *Freud and Man's Soul*. New York: Vintage.

Bion, W. R. (1957). Differentiation of the psychotic from the non-psychotic personalities. *International Journal of Psychoanalysis, 38*: 266–275.

Bion, W. R. (1959). Attacks on linking. *International Journal of Psychoanalysis, 40*: 308–315.

Bion, W. R. (1962a). The psychoanalytic study of thinking. *International Journal of Psychoanalysis, 43*: 306–310; reprinted in Spillius (Ed.) (1988), Vol. 1, London: Routledge.

Bion, W. R. (1962b). *Learning from Experience*. London: Heinemann [reprinted London: Karnac, 1984].

Bion, W. R. (1963). *Elements of Psychoanalysis*. London: Karnac, 1984.

Bion, W. R. (1965). *Transformations*. London: Karnac, 1984.

Bion, W. R. (1970). *Attention and Interpretation*. London: Karnac.

Blau, A. (1955). A unitary hypothesis of emotion: anxiety, emotions of displeasure, and affective disorders. *Psychoanalytic Quarterly, 24*: 75–103.

Blos, P. (1985). *Son and Father*. New York: Basic Books.

Bollas, C. (1979). The transformational object. *International Journal of Psychoanalysis, 60*: 97–107.

Bollas, C. (1992). *Being a Character: Psychoanalysis and Self-Experience*. New York: Hill and Wang.

Bolognini, S. (2004). *Psychoanalytic Empathy*, M. Garfield (Trans.). London: Free Association Books.

Bolognini, S. (2011). *Secret Passages: The Theory and Technique of Interpsychic Relations*, G. Atkinson (Trans.). London: Routledge.

Bouvet, M. (2007). *La cure psychanalytique classique*. Paris: Presses Universitaires de France.

Brakel, L. A. W. (1994). Book review essay of *Rediscovery of Mind* (1992) by John Searle. *Psychoanalytic Quarterly, 63*: 787–792.

Brakel, L. A. W. (2009). *Philosophy, Psychoanalysis, and the A-rational Mind*. Oxford: Oxford University Press.

Brakel, L. A. W. (2010). *Unconscious Knowledge and Other Essays in Psycho-Philosophical Analysis*. Oxford: Oxford University Press.

Brakel, L. A. W., & Shevrin, H. (2003). Freud's dual process theory and the place of the a-rational. Continuing commentary on Stanovich and West (2001), Individual differences in reasoning: implications for the rationality debate, in *Behavioral and Brain Sciences, 23*: 645–666. *Behavioral and Brain Sciences, 26*, 527–528.

Brenner, C. (1976). *Psychoanalytic Technique and Psychic Conflict*. New York: International Universities Press.

Brenner, C. (1973). *An Elementary Textbook of Psychoanalysis*. Garden City, NY: Anchor/Doubleday.

Brenner, I. (1994). The dissociative character: a reconsideration of "multiple personality" and related phenomena. *Journal of the American Psychoanalytic Association, 42*: 819–846.

Brenner, I. (1999). Deconstructing DID. *American Journal of Psychotherapy, 53*: 344–360.

Brenner, I. (2001). *Dissociation of Trauma: Theory, Phenomenology, and Technique*. Madison, CT: International Universities Press.

Brenner, I. (2004). *Psychic Trauma: Dynamics, Symptoms, and Treatment*. Lanham, MD: Jason Aronson.

Brenner, I. (2009). *Injured Men: Trauma, Healing, and the Masculine Self*. Lanham, MD: Jason Aronson.

Brown, L. J. (2011). *Intersubjective Processes and the Unconscious*. London: Routledge.

Bruner, J. (1983). *Child's Talk: Learning to Use Language*. New York: Norton.

Bunce, S., Bernat, E., Wong, P., & Shevrin, H. (1999). Further evidence for unconscious learning: preliminary support for the conditioning of facial EMG to subliminal stimuli. *Journal of Psychiatric Research, 33*: 341–347.

Calich, J. C., & Hinz, H. (Eds.) (2007). *The Unconscious. Further Reflections. Psychoanalytic Ideas and Applications: 5*. London: International Psychoanalytic Association, Psychoanalytic Ideas and Application Series.

Carhart-Harris, R., & Friston, K. (2010). The default mode, ego functions and free energy: a neurobiological account of Freudian ideas. *Brain, 133*: 1265–1283.

Carroll, L. (1871). *Through the Looking Glass, And What Alice Found There*. New York: Dover Publishing, 1993.

Casement, P. (1991). *Learning from the Patient*. New York: Guilford Press.

Coles, R. (1965). On courage. *Contemporary Psychoanalysis, 1*: 85–98.

Coltart, N. (1992). *Slouching Towards Bethlehem*. London: Free Association Books.

Cooper, A. M., Kernberg, O. F., & Person, E. S. (Eds.) (1989). *Psychoanalysis toward the Second Century*. New Haven, CT: Yale University Press.

Damasio, A. (1999). *The Feeling of What Happens*. New York: Harvest.

Damasio, A. (2010). *Self Comes to Mind*. New York: Pantheon.

Danckwardt, J. F. (2011a). The fear of method in psychoanalysis. *Psychoanalysis in Europe Bulletin, 65*: 113–124.

Danckwardt, J. F. (2011b). Die vierstündige analytische Psychotherapie in Ausbildung und Behandlung—ein Auslaufmodell? [Four-sessions weekly psychotherapy in training and treatment—a discontinued model?] *Z Psychoanal Theorie Prax, 26*(2): 208–220.

Darwin, C. (1872). *The Expression of Emotions in Man and Animals*. London: John Murray.

De Bono, E. (1970). *Lateral Thinking: Creativity Step by Step*. New York: Harper.

de Cervantes, M. (1605). *The Ingenious Gentleman Don Quixote de la Mancha*. New York: Viking Press, 1949.

De Veer, M. W., Gallup, G. G., Theall, L. A., van den Bos, R., & Povinelli, D. J. (2003). An 8-year longitudinal study of mirror self-recognition in chimpanzees (*Pan troglodytes*). *Neuropsychologia*, *41*: 229–234.

Duncker, K. (1945). On problem solving. *Psychological Monographs*, *58*(5): i–113.

Edelman, G. (1993). *Bright Air, Brilliant Fire*. New York: Basic.

Eickhoff, F.-W. (1995). Über den Konstruktivismus im Werk Wolfgang Lochs (On constructivism in Wolfgang Loch's work). In: Eickhoff, F.-W., 2009. Primäre Identifizierung, Nachträglichkeit und 'entlehntes unbewusstes Schuldgefühl' (Primary identification, deferred action and 'borrowed unconscious guilt'). Ausgewählte Schriften zu psychoanalytischen Themen 1976–2008 (Selected writings on psychoanalytic subjects 1976–2008). Supplement 24 of the *Jahrbuch der Psychoanalyse* (pp. 171–176. Stuttgart: Frommann-holzboog.

Eifermann, R. (2007). On the inevitable neglect of the unconscious: a contemporary reminder. In: J. C. Calech & H. Hinz (Eds.), *The Unconscious: Further Reflections* (pp. 133–148). London: International Psychoanalytic Association.

Eisnitz, A. (1980). The organization of the self-representation and its influence on pathology. *Psychoanalytic Quarterly*, *49*: 361–392.

Eissler, K. (1953). Notes upon the emotionality of a schizophrenic patient and its relation to problems of technique. *Psychoanalytic Study of the Child*, *8*: 199–251.

Ellenberger, H. F. (1970). *The Discovery of the Unconscious: The History and Evolution of Dynamic Psychiatry*. New York: Basic Books.

Etchegoyen, R. H. (1991). *The Fundamentals of Psychoanalytic Technique*. London: Karnac.

Falzeder, E. (2002). *The Complete Correspondence of Sigmund Freud and Karl Abraham, 1907–1925*, C. Schwarzacher (Trans.). London: Karnac.

Falzeder, E., & Brabant, E. (1996). (Eds.). *The Complete Correspondence of Sigmund Freud and Sándor Ferenczi, 1914–1919* (Vol. 2), P. Hoffer (Trans.). Cambridge MA: Harvard University Press.

Feldman, M. (2007). Addressing parts of the self. *International Journal of Psychoanalysis*, *88*: 371–386.

Fenichel, O. (1941). *Problems of Psychoanalytic Technique*. Albany, NY: Psychoanalytic Quarterly Press.

Fenichel, O. (1945). *The Psychoanalytic Theory of Neurosis*. New York: W. W. Norton.

Ferenczi, S. (1911). On obscene words. In: *Final Contributions to the Problems and Methods of Psychoanalysis*. London: Hogarth Press.

Ferro, A. (1999). *The Bi-Personal Field: Experiences in Child Analysis*. London: Routledge.

Ferro, A. (2009). *Mind Works: Technique and Creativity in Psychoanalysis*. London: Routledge.

Fonagy, P., & Target, M. (1997). Attachment and reflective function: their role in self-organization. *Development and Psychopathology*, *9*: 679–700.

Frank, A. (1969). The unrememberable and the unforgettable: passive primal repression. *Psychoanalytic Study of the Child*, *24*: 48–77.

Frank, A. (1995). Metapsychology. In: B. Moore & B. Fine (Eds.), *Psychoanalysis: The Major Concepts* (pp. 508–520). New Haven, CT: Yale University Press.

Freud, A. (1936). *The Ego and the Mechanisms of Defense*. New York: International Universities Press.

Freud, E. L. (Ed.) (1960). *Letters of Sigmund Freud 1873–1939*, T. & J. Stern (Trans.). New York: Basic Books.

Freud, S. (1894a). The neuro-psychoses of defence. *S.E.*, *3*: 45–61. London: Hogarth.

Freud, S. (1895a). Project for a scientific psychology. *S.E.*, *1*: 281–397. London: Hogarth.

Freud, S. (with Breuer, J.) (1895d). *Studies on Hysteria*. *S.E.*, *2*. London: Hogarth.

Freud, S. (1896). Letter of January 1, 1896 [extract]. *S.E.*, *1*: 388–391. London: Hogarth.

Freud, S. (1898). Letter to Wilhelm Fliess dated March 10, 1898. In: J. M. Masson (Ed.), *The Complete Letters of Sigmund Freud to Wilhelm Fliess, 1887–1904* (pp. 301–302). Cambridge, MA: Harvard University Press.

Freud, S. (1900a). *The Interpretation of Dreams*. *S.E.*, *4–5*. London: Hogarth.

Freud, S. (1901b). *The Psychopathology of Everyday Life*. *S.E.*, *6*: 1–310. London: Hogarth.

Freud, S. (1905d). *Three Essays on the Theory of Sexuality*. *S.E.*, *7:* 125–243. London: Hogarth.

Freud, S. (1908e). Creative writers and day-dreaming. *S.E.*, *9*: 143–153. London: Hogarth.

Freud, S. (1911b). Formulations on the two principles of mental functioning. *S.E.*, *12*: 215–226.

Freud, S. (1912b). The dynamics of transference. *S.E.*, *12*: 99–108. London: Hogarth.

Freud, S. (1912e). Recommendations to physicians practising psycho-analysis. *S.E., 12*: London: Hogarth.

Freud, S. (1914c). On narcissism: an introduction. *S.E., 14*: London: Hogarth.

Freud, S. (1914g). Remembering, repeating and working-through. *S.E., 12*: London: Hogarth.

Freud, S. (1915a). Observations on transference love. *S.E., 12*: London: Hogarth.

Freud, S. (1915c). Instincts and their vicissitudes. *S.E., 14*: 109–140. London: Hogarth.

Freud, S. (1915d). Repression. *S.E., 14*: 141–158. London: Hogarth.

Freud, S. (1915e). The unconscious. *S.E., 14*: 161–215. London: Hogarth.

Freud, S. (1915f). A case of paranoia running counter to the psycho-analytic theory of the disease. *S.E., 14*: 261–272. London: Hogarth.

Freud, S. (1916–1917). *Introductory Lectures on Psycho-Analysis. S.E., 15–16*. London: Hogarth.

Freud, S. (1917d). A metapsychological supplement to the theory of dreams. *S.E., 14*: 222–235. London: Hogarth.

Freud, S. (1917e). Mourning and melancholia. *S.E., 14*: 237–260. London: Hogarth.

Freud, S. (1920g). *Beyond the Pleasure Principle. S.E., 18*: 7–64. London: Hogarth.

Freud, S. (1923b). *The Ego and the Id. S.E., 19*: 3–68. London: Hogarth.

Freud, S. (1925a). A note upon "the mystic writing-pad". *S.E., 16*: 227–232. London: Hogarth.

Freud, S. (1925d). An autobiographical study. *S.E., 20*: 7–74. London: Hogarth.

Freud, S. (1926d). *Inhibitions, Symptoms and Anxiety. S.E., 20*: 77–124. London: Hogarth.

Freud, S. (1927c). *The Future of an Illusion. S.E., 21*: 3–56. London: Hogarth.

Freud, S. (1927e). Fetishism. *S.E., 21*: 152–157. London: Hogarth.

Freud, S. (1933a). *New Introductory Lectures on Psycho-analysis. S.E., 22*. London: Hogarth.

Freud, S. (1937d). Constructions in analysis. *S.E., 23*: 255–269. London: Hogarth.

Freud, S. (1940a[1938]). *An Outline of Psychoanalysis. S.E., 23*: 139–207. London: Hogarth.

Freud, S. (1954). *The Origins of Psychoanalysis*, M. Bonaparte, A. Freud, & E. Kris (Eds.) New York: Basic Books.

Freud, S. (1987). Overview of the transference neuroses [draft of the twelfth paper on metapsychology of 1915] in: *A Phylogenetic*

Fantasy: Overview of the Transference Neuroses, edited and with an essay by Ilse Grubrich-Simitis, A. Hoffer & P. T. Hoffer (Trans.). Cambridge, MA: Belknap Press of Harvard University Press.

Friston, K. (2010). The free-energy principle: a unified brain theory? *Nature Reviews Neuroscience*, *11*: 127–138.

Galin, D. (1974). Implications for psychiatry of left and right cerebral specialization. *American Journal of Psychiatry*, *31*: 572–583.

Garlick, D., Gant, D., Brakel, L. A. W., & Blaisdell, A. (2011). Attributional and relational processing in pigeons. *Frontiers in Comparative Psychology*, *2*, article 14.

Ghorpade, A. (2009). State-dependent self-representations: a culture bound aspect of identity. *American Journal of Psychoanalysis*, *69*: 72–79.

Glover, E. (1941). *On Fear and Courage*. London: Penguin.

Glover, E. (1943). The concept of dissociation. *International Journal of Psychoanalysis*, *24*: 7–13.

Gottlieb, R. M. (1997). Does the mind fall apart in multiple personality disorder? Some proposals based on a psychoanalytic case. *Journal of the American Psychoanalytic Association*, *45*: 907–932,

Green, A. (1973). *The Fabric of Affect in the Psychoanalytic Discourse*, A. Sheridan (Trans.). London: Routledge, 1999.

Green, A. (1982). La mère morte. In: *Narcissisme de Vie, Narcissisme de Mort* (pp. 222–253). Paris: Editions de Minuit.

Green, A. (1993). *The Work of the Negative*. London: Free Association.

Green, A. (2001). *Life Narcissism, Death Narcissism*, A. Weller (Trans.). London: Free Association.

Grinberg, L., & Grinberg, R. (1976). *Identidad y cambio*. Barcelona: Ediciones Paidós Iberica.

Grotstein, J. S. (2001). *Does God Help? Developmental and Clinical Aspects of Religious Belief* (pp. 321–359). Edited by Salman Akhtar and Henri Parens. Northvale, NJ: Jason Aronson.

Grunbaum, A. (1998). A century of psychoanalysis: critical retrospect and prospect. In: M. Carrier & P. Machamer (Eds.), *Mindscapes: Philosophy, Science, and the Mind* (pp. 323–360). Pittsburgh, PA: University of Pittsburgh Press.

Guralnik, O., & Simeon, D. (2010). Depersonalization: standing in the spaces between recognition and interpellation. *Psychoanalytic Dialogues*, *20*: 400–416.

Hanly, C. (2007). The unconscious and relational psychoanalysis. In: J. C. Calich & H. Hinz (Eds.), *The Unconscious: Further Reflections* (pp. 47–62). London: International Psychoanalytic Association, Psychoanalytic Ideas and Applications Series.

Hartmann, H. (1939). *Ego Psychology and the Problem of Adaptation*, D. Rapaport (Trans.). New York: International Universities Press, 1958.

Hartmann, H. (1948). Comments on the psychoanalytic theory of instinctual drives. In: *Essays on Ego Psychology*. New York: International Universities Press.

Hartmann, H. (1950). Comments on the psychoanalytic theory of the ego. In: *Essays on Ego Psychology* (pp. 113–141). New York: International Universities Press.

Hartmann, H. (1958). *Ego Psychology and the Problem of Adaptation*, D. Rapaport (Trans). *Journal of the American Psychoanalytic Association*, Monograph Series, No. 1. New York: International Universities Press.

Hartmann, H., & Kris, E. (1945). The genetic approach in psychoanalysis. *Psychoanalytic Study of the Child*, *1*: 11–30.

Heijn, C. (2005). On foresight. *Psychoanalytic Study of the Child*, *60*: 312–334.

Holder, A. (1992). Introduction to *Sigmund Freud. Das Ich und das Es. Metapsychologische Schriften* (Sigmund Freud. The ego and the id. Metapsychological writings). Frankfurt: Fischer Taschenbuch.

Isaacs, S. (1952). The nature and function of phantasy. In: M. Klein, P. Heimann, S. Isaacs, & J. Riviere (Eds.), *Developments in Psychoanalysis*. London: Hogarth Press, 1970.

Jacobson, E. (1964). *The Self and the Object World*. New York: International Universities Press.

Joffe, W. J., & Sandler, J. (1968). Comments on the psychoanalytic psychology of adaptation with special reference to the role of affects and the representational world. *International Journal of Psychoanalysis*, *49*: 445–454.

Jung, C. (1916). *The Structure of the Unconscious*, H. Read, M. Fordham, & G. Adler (Eds.), *C.W.*, *12*. Princeton, NJ: Princeton University Press, 1967.

Kant, I. (1781–1787). *The Critique of Pure Reason*, N. Kemp Smith (Trans.). New York: Saint Martin's Press, 1965.

Kaplan-Solms, K., & Solms, M. (2000). *Clinical Studies in Neuropsychoanalysis*. London: Karnac.

Kernberg, O. (1975). *Borderline Conditions and Pathological Narcissism*. New York: Jason Aronson.

Kernberg, O. (1976). *Object Relations Theory and Clinical Psychoanalysis*. New York: Jason Aronson.

Kernberg, O. (1992). *Aggression in Personality Disorders and Perversions*. New Haven, CT: Yale University Press.

Kernberg, O. (1995). *Love Relations: Normality and Pathology*. New Haven, CT: Yale University Press.

Kinston, W., & Cohen, J. (1986). Primal repression: clinical and theoretical aspects. *International Journal of Psychoanalysis, 67*: 337–353.

Klein, G. (1976). *Psychoanalytic Theory*. New York: International Universities Press.

Klein, M. (1926). The psychological principles of early analysis. In: *Love, Guilt and Reparation and Other Works (Writings, Vol. 1,* Chap. 6). London: Hogarth, 1975.

Klein, M. (1930). The importance of symbol-formation in the development of the ego. In: *Love, Guilt and Reparation and Other Works (Writings, Vol. 1,* Chap. 12). London: Hogarth, 1975.

Klein, M. (1935). A contribution to the psychogenesis of manic depressive states. In: *Love, Guilt and Reparation and Other Works—1921–1945* (pp. 262–289). New York: Free Press, 1975.

Klein, M. (1946). Notes on some schizoid mechanisms. *International Journal of Psychoanalysis, 27*: 99–110.

Kluft, R. (1985). Childhood multiple personality disorder: predictors, clinical findings, and treatment results. In: R. P. Kluft (Ed.), *Childhood Antecedents of Multiple Personality* (pp. 167–196). Washington, DC: American Psychiatric Press.

Kluft, R. P. (1986). Personality unification in multiple personality disorder: a follow-up study. In: B. G. Braun (Ed.), *Treatment of Multiple Personality Disorder* (pp. 29–60). Washington, DC: American Psychiatric Press.

Koestler, A. (1964). *The Act of Creation*. New York: Penguin/Arkana Press.

Kohut, H. (1971). *The Analysis of the Self: A Systematic Approach to the Psychoanalytic Treatment of Narcissistic Personality Disorders*. Chicago, IL: University of Chicago Press, 2009.

Kohut, H. (1977). *The Restoration of the Self*. New York: International Universities Press.

Kohut, H. (1982). Introspection, empathy, and the semi-circle of mental health. *International Journal of Psychoanalysis, 63*: 395–407.

Kohut, H. (1985). On courage. In: C. B. Strozier (Ed.), *Self Psychology and the Humanities* (pp. 5–50). New York: W. W. Norton.

Krause, R., & Merten, J. (1999). Affects, regulation of relationship, transference, and countertransference. *International Forum of Psychoanalysis, 8*: 103–114.

Kris, E. (1952). *Psychoanalytic Explorations in Art*. New York: International Universities Press.

Lacan, J. (1953). Some reflections on the ego. *International Journal of Psychoanalysis*, *34*: 11–17.

Lacan, J. (1977). *Ecrits: A Selection*, A. Sheridan (Trans.). London: Tavistock.

Lakoff, G., & Johnson, G. (1999). *Philosophy in the Flesh: The Embodied Mind and its Challenge to Western Thought*. New York: Basic Books.

Langer, S. K. (1942). *Philosophy in a New Key*. Cambridge, MA: Harvard University Press.

Langer, S. K. (1953). *Feeling and Form*. London: Routledge and Kegan Paul.

Langer, S. K. (1988). *Mind: An Essay on Human Feeling* (abridged edn). Baltimore, MD: Johns Hopkins University Press.

Laplanche, J., & Pontalis, J.-B. (1973). *The Language of Psychoanalysis*, D. Nicholson-Smith (Trans.). New York: W. W. Norton.

Levine, S. (2006). Catching the wrong leopard: courage and masochism in the psychoanalytic situation. *Psychoanalytic Quarterly*, *75*: 533–556.

Libet, B. (1985). Unconscious cerebral initiative and the role of conscious will in voluntary action. *Journal of Behavioral and Brain Sciences*, *8*: 529–539.

Lipton, P. (1991). *Inference to the Best Explanation*. London: Routledge.

Loch, W. (1965). Übertragung und Gegenübertragung (Transference and countertransference). *Psyche*, *19*: 1–23.

Loch, W. (1980). Metapsychologie (entry on metapsychology). In: J. Ritter & K. Gründer (Eds.), *Historisches Wörterbuch der Philosophie* (Historical dictionary of philosophy) (Vol. 5) (pp. 1298–1299). Basel: Schwabe.

Loch, W. (1995). Psychische Realität—Materielle Realität. Genese—Differenzierung—Synthese (Psychic reality—material reality. Genesis—differentiation—synthesis). *Jahrbuch Psychoanalyse*, *34*: 103–141.

Loch, W. (1999). Grundriß der psychoanalytischen Theorie (Metapsychologie) [Outline of psychoanalytic theory (metapsychology)]. In: *Die Krankheitslehre der Psychoanalyse* (Psychoanalytic psychopathology) (6th edn) (pp. 13–78), H. Hinz (Ed.). Stuttgart: S. Hirzel.

Loch, W. (2010) [1995]. Psychische Realität—Materielle Realität. Genese—Differenzierung—Synthese [Psychic reality-material reality. Genesis-differentiation-synthesis]. In: Erinnerung, Entwurf und Mut zur Wahrheit im psychoanalytischen Prozess. [Memory, project and courage for truth in the psychoanalytic process.] edited and with an introduction by Cord Barkhausen and Peter Wegner. Frankfurt a. M.: Brandes&Apsel.

Loewald, H. (1978). Primary process, secondary process and language. In: *Papers on Psychoanalysis* (pp. 178–206). New Haven, CT: Yale University Press, 1980.

Loewenstein, R. M. (1951). The problem of interpretation. *Psychoanalytic Quarterly*, *20*: 1–23.

Lothane, Z. (2001). A response to Grunbaum's 'A century of psychoanalysis: critical retrospect and prospect' and other texts: requiem or reveille? *International Forum of Psychoanalysis*, *10*: 113–132.

Maclean, P. (1990). *The Triune Brain in Evolution*. New York: Plenum.

MacLeish, A. (1960). *Poetry and Experience*. London: Penguin, 1961 and Peregrine Books, 1965.

Mahler, M., Pine, F., & Bergman, A. (1975). *The Psychological Birth of the Human Infant: Symbiosis and Individuation*. New York: Basic Books.

Malloch, S., & Trevarthen, C. (2009). Musicality: communicating the vitality and interests of life. In: *Communicative Musicality: Exploring the Basis of Human Companionship* (pp. 1–9). Oxford: Oxford University Press.

Marten, K., & Psarakos, S. (1995). Evidence of self-awareness in the bottlenose dolphin (*Tursiops truncatus*). In: S. T. Parker, R. W. Mitchell, & M. L. Boccia (Eds.), *Self-Awareness in Animals and Humans: Developmental Perspectives* (pp. 361–379). New York: Cambridge University Press.

Marty, P. (1980). *L'Ordre Psychosomatique*. Paris: Payot.

Marty, P., de M'Uzan, M., & David, C. (1963). *L'Investigation Psychosomatique*. Paris: Presses Universitaires de France.

Masson, J. M. (Ed.) (1985). *The Complete Letters of Sigmund Freud to Wilhelm Fliess, 1887–1904*, J. M. Masson (Trans.). Cambridge, MA: Belknap Press of Harvard University Press.

McDougall, J. (1974). The psyche-soma and the analytic process. *International Review of Psychoanalysis*, *1*: 437–459.

McDougall, J. (1989). *Theaters of the Body*. New York: Norton.

McEwan, I. (2005). *Amsterdam*. London: Vintage Books.

Merker, B. (2009). Consciousness without a cerebral cortex: a challenge for neuroscience and medicine. *Journal of Behavioral and Brain Sciences*, *30*: 63–134.

Mesulam, M. M. (2000). Behavioral neuroanatomy: large-scale networks, association cortex, frontal syndromes, the limbic system and hemispheric lateralization. In: *Principles of Behavioral and Cognitive Neurology* (2nd edn) (pp. 1–120). New York: Oxford University Press.

Metcalfe, J., & Wiebe, D. (1987). Intuition in insight and noninsight problem solving. *Memory & Cognition*, *15*: 238–246.

Milner, B., Corkin, S., & Teuber, H-L. (1968). Further analysis of the hippocampal amnesic syndrome: 14 year follow-up study of HM. *Neuropsychologia*, *6*: 215–234.

Modell, A. (1981). Does metapsychology still exist? *International Journal of Psychoanalysis*, *62*: 391–402.

Moore, B., & Fine, B. (Eds.) (1968). *A Glossary of Psychoanalytic Terms and Concepts*. New York: American Psychoanalytic Association.

Moore, B., & Fine, B. (Eds.) (1990). *Psychoanalytic Terms and Concepts*. New Haven, CT: Yale University Press.

Moruzzi, G., & Magoun, H. (1949). Brain stem reticular formation and activation of the EEG. *Electroencephalography and Clinical Neurology*, *1*: 455–473.

Nagpal, A. (2011). A Hindu reading of Freud's "*Beyond the Pleasure Principle*". In: S. Akhtar & M. K. O'Neil (Eds.), *On Freud's "Beyond the Pleasure Principle* (pp. 230–239). London: Karnac.

Ogden, T. H. (1986). The *Matrix of the Mind. Object Relations and the Psychoanalytic Dialogue*. London: Karnac.

Ogden, T. H. (1997). Some thoughts on the use of language in psychoanalysis. *Psychoanalytic Dialogues*, 7: 21.

O'Neil, M. K. (2009). Commentary on 'Courage'. In: S. Akhtar (Ed.), *Good Feelings: Psychoanalytic Reflections on Positive Emotions and Attitudes* (pp. 55–62). London: Karnac.

Ornston, D. (1982). Strachey's influence: preliminary report. *International Journal of Psychoanalysis*, *63*: 409–426.

Osborn, A. F. (1962). Developments in creative education. In: S. J. Parnes & H. F. Harding (Eds.) *A Source Book for Creative Thinking* (pp. 19–29). New York: Scribners.

Panksepp, J. (1998). *Affective Neuroscience*. New York: Oxford University Press.

Panksepp, J., & Biven, L. (2012). *Archaeology of Mind*. New York: Norton.

Penfield, W., & Jasper, H. (1954). *Epilepsy and the Functional Anatomy of the Human Brain*. Oxford: Little, Brown.

Pessoa, F. (2002). *The Book of Disquiet*, R. Zenith (Trans.). London: Penguin Classics.

Pfeiffer, E. (Ed.) (1985). *Sigmund Freud and Lou Andreas-Salomé Letters*, W. Robson-Scott & E. Robson-Scott (Trans.) New York: W. W. Norton. Letter from Sigmund Freud to Lou Andreas-Salomé, July 30, 1915.

Piaget, J. (1970). Inconscient affectif et inconscient cognitive. Paper presented to the Fall Meeting of the American Psychoanalytic Association, New York.

Piaget, J., & Inhelder, B. (1969). *The Psychology of the Child*. New York: Basic Books.

Pine, F. (1997). *Diversity and Direction in Psychoanalytic Technique*. New Haven, CT: Yale University Press.

Pirandello, L. (1995). *Six Characters in Search of an Author and Other Plays*. New York: Penguin.

Plotnik, J. M., de Waal, F. B. M., & Reiss, D. (2006). Self-recognition in an Asian elephant. *Proceedings of the Natural Academy of Sciences, 103*: 17053–17057.

Pulver, S. (1971). Can affects be unconscious? *International Journal of Psychoanalysis, 52*: 347–354.

Ramachandran, V. (1994). Phantom limbs, neglect syndromes, repressed memories, and Freudian psychology. *International Review of Neurobiology, 37*: 291–333.

Rangell, L. (1971). The decision making process—a contribution from psychoanalysis. *Psychoanalytic Study of the Child, 26*: 425–452.

Rangell, L. (1995). Affects. In: B. Moore & B. Fine (Eds.), *Psychoanalysis: The Major Concepts* (pp. 381–391). New Haven, CT: Yale University Press.

Rapaport, D. (1960). *The Structure of Psychoanalytic Theory: Psychological Issues II Monograph 6*. New York: International Universities Press.

Rapaport, D., & Gill, M. M. (1959). The points of view and assumptions of metapsychology. *International Journal of Psychoanalysis, 40*: 153–162.

Reddy, S. (2001). Psychoanalytic reflections on the sacred Hindu text, the Bhagavad Gita. In: S. Akhtar & H. Parens (Eds.), *Does God Help? Developmental and Clinical Aspects of Religious Belief* (pp. 153–175). Northvale, NJ: Jason Aronson.

Reddy, S. (2005). Psychoanalytic process in a sacred Hindu text: the Bhagavad Gita. In: S. Akhtar (Ed.), *Freud Along the Ganges: Psychoanalytic Reflections on the People and Culture of India* (pp. 309–333). New York: Other Press.

Reith, B. (2011). The WPIP investigative process: from the anxiety of the analytic couple to that of the research team. Report of the Working Party on 'Initiating Psychoanalysis' (WPIP). *Psychoanalysis in Europe Bulletin, 65*: 57–60.

Rodrigué, E. (1969). The fifty thousand hour patient. *International Journal of Psychoanalysis, 50*: 603–613.

Rosen, J. (1947). The treatment of schizophrenia by direct analytic therapy. *Psychiatric Quarterly, 2*: 3–13.

Rosen, J. (1953). *Direct Analysis*. New York: Grune and Stratton.

Ross, J. M. (2003). Preconscious defense analysis, memory, and structural change. *International Journal of Psychoanalysis, 84*: 59–76.

Roussillon, R. (1999). *Agonie, clivage et symbolisation*. Paris: PUF.

Roussillon, R. (2008). *Le jeu et l'entre-je(u)*. Paris: PUF.

Rubin, J. B. (1996). *Psychotherapy and Buddhism: Toward an Integration*. New York: Plenum.

Rugg, H. (1963). *Imagination*. New York: Harper Row.

Rumiati, R. (2006). Creatività. In: *Psiche. Dizionario di psicologia, psichiatria, psicoanalisi, neuroscienze*. Turin: Giulio Einaudi Editore.

Rycroft, C. (1968). *Imagination and Reality*. London: Hogarth Press.

Sandler, J. (1983). Reflections on some relations between psychoanalytic concepts and psychoanalytic practice. *International Journal of Psychoanalysis, 64*: 35–45.

Sandler, J. (1992). Reflections on developments in the theory of psychoanalytic technique. *International Journal of Psychoanalysis, 73*: 189–198.

Sandler, J., & Sandler, A. M. (1983). The 'second censorship' and the 'three-box model' and some technical implications. *International Journal of Psychoanalysis, 64*: 413–425.

Searles, H. F. (1965). *Collected Papers on Schizophrenia and Related Subjects*. New York: International Universities Press.

Schafer, R. (1976). *A New Language for Psychoanalysis*. New Haven, CT: Yale University Press.

Schilder, P. (1950). *The Image and Appearance of the Human Body*. New York: International Universities Press.

Schimek, J. G. (1975). A critical re-examination of Freud's concept of unconscious mental representation. *International Review of Psycho-Analysis, 2*: 171–187.

Schore, A. N. (2002). Advances in neuropsychoanalysis, attachment theory, and trauma research: implications for self psychology. *Psychoanalytic Inquiry, 22*: 433–484.

Searle, J. (1992). *The Rediscovery of Mind*. Cambridge, MA: MIT Press.

Searles, H. F. (1973). Concerning therapeutic symbiosis. *Annual of Psychoanalysis, 1*: 247–262.

Segal, H. (1957). Notes on symbol formation. *International Journal of Psychoanalysis, 38*: 391–397.

Shengold, L. (1989). *Soul Murder: The Effect of Childhood Abuse and Deprivation*. New Haven, CT: Yale University Press.

Shevrin, H., Bond, J., Brakel, L., Hertel, R., & Williams, W. (1996). *Conscious and Unconscious Processes: Psychodynamic, Cognitive and Neurophysiological Convergences*. New York: Guildford Press.

Shewmon, D., Holmse, D., & Byrne, P. (1999). Consciousness in congenitally decorticate children: developmental vegetative state as a self-fulfilling prophecy. *Developmental Medicine & Child Neurology*, *41*: 364–374.

Slap, J. (1987). Implications for the structural model of Freud's assumptions about perception. *Journal of the American Psychoanalytic Association*, *35*: 629–645.

Slap, J., & Slap-Shelton, L. (1991). *The Schema in Psychoanalysis*. Hillsdale, NJ: Analytic Press.

Smadja, C. (2008). *Les modèles psychanalytiques de la psychosomatique*. Paris: Presses Universitaires de France.

Solms, M. (1997). What is consciousness? *Journal of the American Psychoanalytic Association*, *45*: 681–778.

Solms, M. (1998). Preliminaries for an integration of psychoanalysis and neuroscience. Presented to a meeting of the Contemporary Freudian Group of the British Psychoanalytical Society.

Solms, M. (2003). *The Brain and the Inner World: An Introduction to the Neuroscience of the Subjective Experience*. New York: Other Press.

Solms, M. (2013). The conscious id. *Neuropsychoanalysis*, *15* (in press).

Solms, M., & Panksepp, J. (2012). The id knows more than the ego admits. *Brain Science*, *2*: 147–175.

Solms, M., & Turnbull, O. (2000). London (Anna Freud Centre: Neuropsychoanalysis Project). *Neuropsychoanalysis*, *2*: 288–289.

Spitz, R. (1965). *The First Year of Life*. New York: International Universities Press.

Stern, D. (1985). *The Interpersonal World of the Infant*. New York: Basic Books.

Stern, D. (2011). *Forms of Vitality. Exploring Dynamic Experience in Psychology, the Arts, Psychotherapy, and Development*. Oxford: Oxford University Press.

Strachey, J. (1957). Editor's note to 'The unconscious'. *S.E.*, *14*: 161–165.

Strachey, J. (1961). Editor's note to *The Ego and the Id*. *S.E.*, *19*: 3–10. London: Hogarth.

Strachey, J. (1962). The emergence of Freud's fundamental hypotheses. In: *S.E.*, *3*: 62–68. London: Hogarth.

Strawson, G. (1994). *Mental Reality*. Cambridge, MA: MIT Press.

Suttie, I. (1935). *The Origins of Love and Hate*. London: Kegan Paul [reprinted London: Pelican Books, 1960; London: Peregrine Books, 1963].

Swami Chinmayananda (1977). *Discourses on Mundakopanishad*. Madras: Chinmaya Publications.

Swami Chinmayananda (2002). *The Holy Bhagavad Gita*. Mumbai: Central Chinmaya Mission Trust.

Swami Dayananda Saraswati (1975). *Om: The Light of Truth* [English translation of Satyarth Prakash], C. Bharadwaja (Trans). New Delhi: Sarvadeshik Arya Pratinidhi Sabha.

Swami Madhavananda (2000). *Vivekachudamani of Sri Shankaracharya,* text with English translation, notes, and index. Calcutta: Advaita Ashrama Publications.

Swami Nikhilananda (2002). *Atmabodha: Self knowledge of Sri Shankaracharya*. Madras: Sri Ramakrishna Math.

Swami Vireswarananda (2001). *Brahma Sutras*, with text, word-for-word translation, English rendering, comments according to the commentary of Sri Shankara, and index. Kolkata: Advaita Ashrama Publications.

Symington, N. (2009). How belief in God affects my clinical work. In: M. K. O'Neil & S. Akhtar (Eds.) *On Freud's "The Future of an Illusion"* (pp. 237–252). London: Karnac.

Talvitie, V., & Ihanus, J. (2002). The repressed and implicit knowledge. *International Journal of Psychoanalysis, 83*: 1311–1323.

Talvitie, V., & Ihanus, J. (2003). Response to commentaries. *Neuropsychoanalysis, 5*: 153–158.

Taylor, W. S., & Martin, M. F. (1944). Multiple personality. *Journal of Abnormal and Social Psychology, 39*: 281–300.

The New Shorter Oxford English Dictionary (1993). L. Brown (Ed.). New York: Oxford University Press.

Tolstoy, L. (1995). *What is Art?* R. Pevear & L. Volokhonsky (Trans.). London: Penguin.

Trevarthen, C. (1979). Communication and cooperation in early infancy: a description of primary intersubjectivity. In: M. Bullowa (Ed.), *Before Speech* (pp. 321–349). Cambridge: Cambridge University Press.

Vallabhaneni, M. R. (2005). *Advaita Vedanta*, psychoanalysis, and the self. In: S. Akhtar (Ed.), *Freud Along the Ganges: Psychoanalytic Reflections on the People and Culture of India* (pp. 359–393). New York: Other Press.

Vivona, J. M. (2012). Is there a non-verbal period of development? *Journal of the American Psychoanalytic Association, 60*: 231–265.

Volkan, V. (1987). Psychological concepts useful in the building of political foundations between nations (Track II diplomacy). *Journal of the American Psychoanalytic Association, 35*: 903–935.

Waelder, R. (1962). Psychoanalysis: scientific methodology and philosophy. *Journal of the American Psychoanalytic Association, 10*: 617–637.

Wälder, R. (1936). The principle of multiple function: observations on over-determination. *Psychoanalytic Quarterly*, *5*: 45–62.

Wallas, G. (1926). *The Art of Thought*. London: Watts, 1949.

Wegner, P. (2011). On Freud's 'The future prospects of psycho-analytic therapy'. Celebration of the Centenary of the International Psychoanalytical Association, Madrid, 4 November 2010. *Psychoanalysis in Europe Bulletin*, *65*: 234–239.

Wegner, P. (2012a). The opening scene and the importance of the countertransference in the initial psychoanalytic interview. In: B. Reith, S. Lagerlöf, P. Crick, M. Møller, E. Skale, (Eds.), *Initiating Psychoanalysis. Perspectives. Teaching Series* (pp. 225–242). London: Routledge.

Wegner, P. (2012b). Process-orientated psychoanalytic work in the first interview and the importance of the opening scene. *Psychoanalysis in Europe*, Bulletin, *66*: 23–45.

Weiskrantz, L. (1990). *Blindsight*. New York: Oxford University Press.

Weiss, J. (1988). Testing hypotheses about unconscious mental functioning. *International Journal of Psychoanalysis*, *69*: 87–95.

Weiss, J., & Sampson, H. (1986). *The Psychoanalytic Process: Theory, Clinical Observation, and Empirical Research*. New York: Guilford Press.

Werner, H., & Kaplan, B. (1963). *Symbol Formation: An Organismic Developmental Approach to the Expression of Thought*. New York: John Wiley.

Wertheimer, M. (1959). *Productive Thinking*. New York: Harper & Row.

Winnicott, D. W. (1953). Transitional objects and transitional phenomena: a study of the first not-me possession. *International Journal of Psychoanalysis*, *34*: 89–97. Reprinted in *Collected Papers: Through Paediatrics to Psychoanalysis* (1958), London: Tavistock; and also in *Playing and Reality* (1971), London: Tavistock.

Winnicott, D. W. (1955). Metapsychological and clinical aspects of regression within the psycho-analytical set-up. *International Journal of Psychoanalysis*, *36*: 16–26.

Winnicott, D. W. (1956). Primary maternal preoccupation. In: *Collected Papers: Through Paediatrics to Psychoanalysis*. London: Tavistock, 1958.

Winnicott, D. W. (1960). Ego distortion in terms of true and false self. In: *Maturational Processes and the Facilitating Environment* (pp. 140–152). New York: International Universities Press, 1965.

Winnicott, D. W. (1967). Mirror role of mother and family in child development. In: *Playing and Reality* (pp. 111–118). London: Tavistock.

Winnicott, D. W. (1971). *Playing and Reality*. London: Tavistock.

Wisdom, J. O. (1967). Testing an interpretation within a session. *International Journal of Psychoanalysis, 48*: 44–52.

Wong, P., Bernat, E., Snodgrass, M., & Shevrin, H. (2004). Event-related brain correlates of associative learning without awareness. *International Journal of Psychophysiology, 53*: 217–233.

Wright, K. (1991). *Vision and Separation: Between Mother and Baby*. London: Free Association Books.

Wright, K. (2009). *Mirroring and Attunement: Self-realisation in Psychoanalysis and Art*. Hove: Routledge.

INDEX

advaita (monism), 133, 135, 149
affect(ive), 3, 8, 15, 39–41, 84, 103–104, 106–112, 114–117, 153, 170, 190–192, 200, 207, 209–210, 214, 217, 221, 230, 237, 246, 256–257, 263–264
  accompanying, 97
  anxiety, 44, 210, 212
  conception of, 106
  conscious(ness), 108, 113, 117–118
  content, 125
  contour, 170
  development of, 40–41, 50, 112, 153, 200, 207, 210
  differentiated, 207
  impulse, 39–40, 191
  inherently, 106–107, 257
  intolerable, 225–226, 231
  latent, 1
  manifestation of, 41
  nature of, 111
  neuroscience, 103–104, 110, 256
  preconscious, 208, 263
  primitive, 15
  processes, 103
  quantum of, 10, 14
  quotas of, 109, 117
  release of, 41
  repressed, 41, 153
  resonance, 170
  response, 170
  self, 170
  signal, 115
  state, 39, 190, 192, 233
  status of, 208
  structures, 40, 106, 191–192, 198
  theory, 15
  unconscious, 14–15, 40, 108, 207, 210
  untransformed, 116
  vitality, 177
aggression, 6, 93, 146, 150, 152, 227, 250
  currents, 225
  drives, 138, 150
  internalised, 228
  nature, 172
agnana (neurosis), 141
ahankara, 141–142, 148, 152–153, 157
Aisenstein, M., 18–19, 204, 215, 263–264, 270
Akhtar, S., 7–8, 10, 18, 85, 159, 268, 270
Alexander, F., 13, 271
Amati-Mehler, J., 8, 271
Anderson, M., 103, 271
anger, 39, 129, 140, 151–152, 182
anxiety, 15, 40–41, 44–46, 88–90, 99–100, 138, 153, 157, 161, 173, 182, 191, 210, 213–214, 231, 238, 240–241, 264
  abandonment, 229
  affect, 44, 210, 212
  annihilation, 228
  castration, 6
  hysteria, 44–47, 58
  instinctual, 225
  non-, 266
  personal, 161
  release of, 46
  separation, 228
  signal, 15
  unconscious, 39
aphasia, 25, 30, 63, 68, 71, 74, 76–77
  agnostic, 77
  asymbolic, 76
  verbal, 76
Archimedes, 12
Argentieri, S., 8, 271
Arieti, S., 8, 16, 271
Aristotle, 241
Arjuna, 140, 144–145, 147, 151–152

Arlow, J. A., 16, 218, 223, 271
Asendorpf, J. B., 230, 271
atman, 133, 135, 145, 148–149, 151–152, 156–158
attachment, 151, 154, 259
 disoriented, 224
attunement, 169, 176, 178
 maternal, 165, 170, 176, 260
 structure, 172
avidya, 152

Baranger, M., 201, 271
Baranger, W., 201, 271
Bargh, J., 103, 271
Basile, G., 238
Bassanese, F. A., 232, 271
Baudonnière, P.-M., 230, 271
behaviour(al), 5, 8, 10, 16, 25, 44, 46, 62, 72, 90, 95, 98, 103–104, 110–111, 128, 151, 209, 221–222, 258
 animal, 122
 criteria, 110
 destructive, 221, 265
 human, 156, 259
 infant, 170
 initiatives, 111
 instrumental, 111
 neurology, 105
 organised, 121
 therapy, 228
 unwanted, 228
Beres, D., 216, 271
Bergman, A., 15, 224, 281
Bergmann, M. S., 86, 271
Bernat, E., 125–127, 271, 273, 288
Bernstein, W. M., 19, 271
Bettelheim, B., 139, 271
Bion, W. R., 7–8, 14, 86, 159, 178, 181, 201, 223, 263, 271–272
 alpha elements, 201
 beta elements, 201–202
 container–contained, 178
 O, 159, 201
Biven, L., 104, 282
Blaisdell, A., 123, 277
Blau, A., 15, 272
Bleuler, P., 35, 61, 227
Blos, P., 159, 272
Bollas, C., 3, 181, 237, 272
Bolognini, S., 8, 19, 201, 242, 244, 263, 266, 268, 272
Bond, J., 103, 284
Bouvet, M., 213, 272
Brabant, E., 81, 83, 274
Brahman, 134–135, 145–146, 149, 154, 156, 158, 259
Brakel, L. A. W., 103, 120, 122–123, 130, 257–258, 272, 277, 284
Brenner, C., 5, 136, 150–151, 272
Brenner, I., 6, 218, 221, 224, 227–228, 264–266, 272–273
Breuer, J., 26, 32, 35, 46, 48, 160–161, 175, 212, 223, 254, 275
Brown, L. J., 201–202, 273
Bruner, J., 164, 273
Bunce, S., 125, 273
Byrne, P., 110, 285

Calich, J. C., 86, 255, 273
Canestri, J., 8, 271
Carhart-Harris, R., 116, 273
Carroll, L., 230, 273
case studies
 Christine/Mirror Girl, 231
 Cindy/Candy, 220–222, 226
 John, 182–183, 187, 192, 196, 198, 200
 Minh/Linh, 224–227
 Mrs E, 88–89, 93
 Mrs X, 210–211
Casement, P., 13, 273
Chartrand, T., 103, 271
chitta, 141, 148
Cohen, J., 2, 279
Coles, R., 18, 273
Coltart, N., 158, 273
conscious(ness), (*passim*) *see also*: Freud
 absence of, 30
 access, 113
 activity, 36, 56
 affect(ive), 108, 111, 113, 115, 117–118, 208
 aims, 17
 aspects, 217, 255
 attention, 116
 autonoetic, 113
 awareness, 16, 113, 125–127, 137, 171, 173
 basic, 106
 cathexis, 42, 45–46, 65, 192
 co-, 228
 cognition, 115
 communications, 96, 194
 core-, 107, 111, 257
 cortical, 105
 critical, 105
 declarative, 113
 desire, 128
 dual, 32
 ego, 236, 239, 241
 events, 121
 experience, 197
 extended, 113

idea, 37–39, 51, 188–189, 195
inmost, 133
intention, 220
knowledge, 29, 102
lapses of, 110
limited, 135
memory, 4, 50, 102, 188
mentation, 121
mind, 173, 207, 236, 266
nature of, 135
object of, 27, 39
obliteration of, 106
perception, 67, 108, 113–114, 117–118, 233, 266
pre-, 13, 17, 35, 42, 49, 53–56, 65–66, 84, 94, 97, 137, 184, 192–195, 198, 200, 206–208, 222, 233, 236, 249, 251, 255, 258, 263–264, 267
presentation, 7, 63, 66, 84, 113, 153–154, 162, 198–199
primary, 113
process, 30, 34, 83, 97, 116, 120, 136, 146, 185
psychology of, 30, 35
quality of, 106
reflective, 113
representations, 84
secondary, 113–114
splitting of, 32
state of, 5–6, 99, 104, 106, 217, 219, 224
sub-, 32, 219
substitute, 153
supreme, 133, 144–146
system, 84, 103, 118
thoughts, 61, 66
understanding, 185
unimpeded, 163
Cooper, A. M., 254, 273
Cooper, J., 103, 271
Corkin, S., 102, 282
countertransference, 14, 97, 99, 212, 214
dynamics, 87
process, 263
reactions, 97

Damasio, A., 104, 107, 110, 114, 257, 273
Danckwardt, J. F., 99–100, 273
Darwin, C., 103, 273
David, C., 18, 281
death, 8, 89, 122, 132, 148–150, 156–158, 224, 229, 238
denial of, 158
drive, 150, 157
instinct, 10
De Bono, E., 243, 273
de Cervantes, M., 231, 266, 274
de M'Uzan, M., 18, 281
desire, 128–130, 142, 144–146, 151–152, 155, 159, 231, 239, 259
aesthetic, 151
egoistic, 141–142
erotic, 151
past, 141
system of, 124
unconscious, 128
undifferentiated, 152
De Veer, M. W., 230, 274
development(al), 8, 13, 52, 85–86, 88, 100, 112, 132, 137, 190–193, 200, 230, 235, 239, 241, 252, 255, 268
childhood, 57, 104, 233
circumstances, 191
early, 164, 172
emotional, 177
genetic, 85
individual, 51, 55, 112, 123
language, 164, 176
of affect, 40–41, 50, 112, 153, 191, 200, 207
of anxiety, 44–46
of dreaming, 87
process of, 52, 235, 252
professional, 242
psychical, 56
speech, 72
unconscious, 3
de Waal, F. B. M., 230, 283
Duncker, K., 243, 246, 249, 274

Edelman, G., 113, 274
ego, 2–3, 6, 9–10, 17, 31, 46, 55, 57–59, 65–66, 85–86, 95, 108–110, 116–117, 137–139, 141–142, 144, 148, 157, 162–163, 176, 195, 197, 208–209, 215, 222, 228–229, 233, 236–237, 240–241, 245–246, 248, 251, 253, 257, 265–267
body-, 138, 229, 265
capacities, 14
central, 235, 238–239, 241, 244, 246, 251–252, 268
cognitive, 242
conscious, 236, 241
control, 249
defensive, 5, 243, 252
-dystonic, 2
-environment, 86
function, 223, 225, 248
ideal, 138, 159
individual, 31, 239
process, 102

psychology, 5
reservoir, 116
self-, 93
strength, 227
-structure, 85
subject's, 238, 246–247, 251
super-, 2–3, 9–10, 86, 93, 95, 137–139, 159, 163, 171, 221, 226
-syntonic, 17, 57, 195
unconscious, 102, 194
Eickhoff, F.-W., 86–87, 94, 274
Eifermann, R., 268, 274
Eisnitz, A., 7, 274
Eissler, K., 15, 274
Ellenberger, H. F., 160, 274
energy, 9–10, 50, 58, 72, 116–118, 158, 205, 207–208, 248, 267
activating, 117
cathartic, 54
cathectic, 47, 50, 193
chemical, 25
equilibrium of, 85
expenditure of, 43, 47
free, 14, 116
Helmholtzian, 116
instinctual, 109, 111
mental, 117
nervous, 50
physical, 150
primal, 152
psychic, 9, 150, 157, 210
spiritual, 157
vital, 152
wasting of, 248–250
Etchegoyen, R. H., 86, 274

Falzeder, E., 81–83, 274
fantasy, 13, 92, 95, 204
of multiplicity, 227
unconscious, 16, 95, 203, 223
Feldman, M., 5, 274
Fenichel, O., 5, 15, 274
Ferenczi, S., 8, 81, 83, 275
Ferro, A., 201, 263, 275
Fine, B., 10, 15, 282
Fonagy, P., 8, 275
Frank, A., 2, 11, 275
Freud, A., 5, 67, 275
Freud, E. L., 203, 275
Freud, S. (*passim*)
A case of paranoia running counter to the psychoanalytic theory of the disease, 2, 276
A metapsychological supplement to the theory of dreams, 1, 54, 61, 81–82, 276
A note upon "the mystic writing-pad", 50, 114, 276
An autobiographical study, 132, 276
An Outline of Psychoanalysis, 51, 107–108, 138, 276
Anna O, 223
Beyond the Pleasure Principle, 10, 49, 85, 118, 150, 213, 276
Constructions in analysis, 15, 87, 276
Creative writers and day-dreaming, 178, 275
cs (conscious system), 3–4, 7, 9, 16–17, 34–37, 41–42, 44–47, 49–53, 55–56, 65–66, 82, 93, 99, 102, 105, 107, 109–112, 114, 117–118, 137, 149, 153, 187, 189, 191, 194–195, 208, 215, 223, 236, 243, 257
Fetishism, 6, 276
Formulations on the two principles of mental functioning, 49, 54, 64, 108, 275
Frau Emmy von N., 25
Inhibitions, Symptoms and Anxiety, 2, 9, 15, 45, 276
Instincts and their vicissitudes, 1, 9, 39, 57, 66, 81–83, 104, 157, 192, 198, 205–206, 276
Introductory Lectures on Psycho-Analysis, 16, 32, 57, 87, 276
Letter to Wilhelm Fliess, 8, 275
Mourning and melancholia, 1, 63, 81–82, 276
New Introductory Lectures on Psycho-analysis, 26, 49, 209, 276
Observations on transference love, 82, 276
On narcissism: an introduction, 49, 60, 82, 276
Overview of the transference neuroses, 82, 276
pcpt-cs (perceptual-conscious system), 105, 107, 109–111, 114, 117–118, 257
pcs (pre-conscious system), 3, 9, 14, 35–36, 41–45, 47–56, 63–66, 84, 93, 102, 107, 110, 112–118, 137, 146, 154, 162–163, 187, 192–196, 199, 215, 235–236
Project for a scientific psychology, 2, 18, 25, 116–117, 275
Recommendations to physicians practising psychoanalysis, 97, 276
Remembering, repeating and working-through, 82, 276
Repression, 1, 40, 52, 81–82, 153, 163, 173, 180, 260, 276

Studies on Hysteria, 26, 32, 35, 46, 48, 160–161, 175, 212, 223, 254, 275
The dynamics of transference, 213, 275
The Ego and the Id, 2, 6, 9, 15, 26–27, 40, 55, 65, 85, 102, 105, 109–112, 118, 137–138, 163, 206, 208–209, 215, 223, 229, 263–264, 276
The Future of an Illusion, 159, 276
The Interpretation of Dreams, 26, 30, 32–34, 36, 40, 45, 48–49, 53–54, 61, 63–64, 84, 118, 136, 160, 223, 254, 275
The neuro-psychoses of defence, 109, 117, 275
The Origins of Psychoanalysis, 132, 276
The Psychopathology of Everyday Life, 8, 43, 49, 85, 226, 254, 275
The unconscious, 1–8, 12, 14–18, 23, 26, 71, 75, 81–85, 93, 98–99, 101, 112, 117, 119–124, 127, 129–130, 132, 136–137, 139, 146–147, 149–150, 153, 155, 161–164, 167–169, 172, 174–175, 179–181, 184–186, 188–190, 193, 195, 197–199, 201, 204, 206–208, 216, 218–219, 223, 235, 243, 254–258, 261, 263–264, 268–269, 276
Three Essays on the Theory of Sexuality, 53, 150, 205, 275
ucs (unconscious system), 2–4, 7, 9, 15–17, 19, 34–37, 40–42, 44–45, 47–53, 55–59, 64–66, 82, 84, 93, 99, 102, 104, 110–113, 117, 124, 129, 137–139, 146–147, 149, 152–154, 157, 161–162, 169, 187, 189, 191–196, 199, 208, 215, 233, 235–236, 243, 256–257
Wolf Man, 57
Friston, K., 116, 273, 277

Gabrieli, J., 103, 271
Gabrieli, S., 103, 271
Galin, D., 101, 277
Gallup, G. G., 230, 274
Gant, D., 123, 277
Garlick, D., 123, 277
Garma, A., 203, 237
Ghorpade, A., 7, 277
Gill, M. M., 85, 283
Glover, E., 18, 85, 277
Glover, G., 103, 271
Gottlieb, R. M., 227, 277
Green, A., 12, 205, 212, 277
Grinberg, L., 244, 277
Grinberg, R., 244, 277
Grotstein, J. S., 158, 277
Grunbaum, A., 11, 277
Guralnik, O., 218, 277

Hanly, C., 201, 263, 277
Hartmann, H., 3, 6, 85–86, 149, 278
Heijn, C., 13, 278
Herbart, J. F., 24
Hertel, R., 103, 284
Hinduism, 19, 132–133, 146
Hinz, H., 86, 255, 273
Holder, A., 83, 278
Holmse, D., 110, 285

id, 2, 10, 86, 95, 103–104, 106–107, 117, 137–139, 149, 163, 206, 208–209, 214, 256, 263
Ihanus, J., 15, 286
Inhelder, B., 230, 283
instinct(ual), 1, 9, 14, 16, 28, 34, 39, 46, 66, 83, 85, 104, 138, 149, 153, 155, 157–158, 172, 180, 190, 198, 204–205, 215, 234–235, 238, 256, 258–259
activity, 56
affects, 104
anxiety, 225
basis, 115
cathexis, 46–47, 65
characteristics, 150
charge, 214
component, 205
concept of, 153, 205
contents, 93
danger, 46
death, 10, 150
derivatives, 5
emotions, 111
energy, 109, 111
excitation, 45
forces, 138, 149
impulse, 39–41, 46–48, 52, 121, 153, 190–191, 201, 206, 209
influence, 223
life, 56, 150
manifestation, 150
mature, 157
nature of, 205
needs, 106
of animal, 57, 104, 124, 149, 233
of protoplasm, 150
process, 103
representatives, 2, 47–48, 149, 172, 191, 193, 207
repressed, 190
response, 115

satisfaction, 152, 213
self-preservation, 150
sexual, 150, 205
substrate of the mind, 16
tension, 149, 214
unconscious, 39, 45, 190
International Psychoanalytic Association, 82, 87
Isaacs, S., 95, 172, 278

Jacobson, E., 6, 222–223, 278
Jasper, H., 105–106, 282
Jeffrey, A., 12
Joffe, W. J., 15, 278
Johnson, G., 176, 280
Joseph, E. D., 216, 271
Jung, C., 16, 61, 278

kama (desire), 151–152
Kant, I., 33, 121, 187, 219, 278
Kaplan, B., 164–165, 287
Kaplan-Solms, K., 103, 133, 155, 278
Kernberg, O. F., 7, 11–12, 15, 254, 273, 278–179
Kinston, W., 2, 279
Klein, G., 11, 279
Klein, M., 15–16, 86, 172, 201, 204, 223, 263, 279
Kluft, R. P., 6, 228, 279
Koestler, A., 12, 279
Kohut, H., 7, 11, 18, 86, 230, 247–248, 267, 279
Krause, R., 15, 279
Kris, E., 13, 85, 278–279
Krishna, 140, 144–145, 147–148, 151
krodha (anger), 151–152
Kuhl, B., 103, 271

Lacan, J., 174, 230, 280
Lakoff, G., 176, 280
Langer, S. K., 164–169, 176–177, 260, 280
Laplanche, J., 1, 16, 85, 280
Levine, S., 18, 280
Libet, B., 102, 280
libido, 42, 44, 58, 146, 150–152, 210
narcissistic, 252
life, 18, 88, 92, 115, 137, 150, 152, 154–155, 168, 176–177, 182, 210–211, 232, 239, 259, 266
after death, 8
beginning of, 204
cultural, 254
day-to-day, 154
dream-, 58
drive, 150
emotional, 166, 176
everyday, 101, 226
experience, 239, 256
human, 177
impressions of, 52, 193, 236
inner-, 67
instinctual, 56
interests of, 61
mental, 1, 13, 30–31, 50, 55, 103, 108, 120, 146, 150, 160, 185–186, 189, 196, 204–205
normal, 41
professional, 176
psychic, 139, 214, 264
real, 123, 128
secret, 221
sense of, 162
threatening, 229
Lipton, P., 120–121, 280
Loch, W., 85–87, 96, 280
Loewald, H., 164, 281
Loewenstein, R. M., 5, 281
Lothane, Z., 11, 281

Maclean, P., 103, 281
MacLeish, A., 175, 178, 281
Magoun, H., 104, 106, 282
Mahler, M., 15, 224, 281
Malloch, S., 178, 281
manas, 141, 148
Marten, K., 230, 281
Martin, M. F., 227, 286
Marty, P., 18, 281
Masson, J. M., 85, 205, 281
McDougall, J., 19, 88, 281
McEwan, I., 12, 281
Merker, B., 104–106, 110–111, 281
Merten, J., 15, 279
Mesulam, M. M., 106, 281
metaphor, 1, 7, 16, 122, 134, 151, 153, 157, 170–171, 187, 190, 238, 240, 249
aptness, 168
form, 266
language, 168
level, 248
representation, 240
spatial, 189
structure of mind, 142
temporal, 189
Metcalfe, J., 242, 267, 281
Milner, B., 102, 282
mirroring, 7, 167, 169–172, 260
Modell, A., 11, 282
Moore, B., 10, 15, 282
Moruzzi, G., 104, 106, 282

multiple personality, 218–219, 227, 265
disorder, 265

Nagpal, A., 260, 282
narcissism, 7, 49, 58–60, 65, 83, 177, 196, 199, 211, 228, 239, 251–252, 266
negative, 213
neuropsychology, 101, 103, 115, 117, 256–257
neuroscience, 114, 155
affective, 103–104, 110, 256
behavioural, 103
clinical, 103
cognitive, 103–104, 256
contemporary, 116
neurosis (*agnana*), 41, 49, 58–59, 65–66, 140–141, 196, 214
obsessional, 47, 58–59, 61–62
psycho-, 205, 209, 213
state, 93
transference, 212, 264

object, 7, 15, 33, 58, 63–66, 75–77, 84, 93, 106–107, 113, 138, 140–144, 150, 154–155, 162–165, 171–172, 176, 187, 196, 198–200, 206, 213–214, 216–217, 219, 243–247, 251, 259, 264, 267
art, 165, 175, 261
associations, 76–77
-cathexis, 58–59, 63, 84, 113, 138, 154, 162, 196, 198–200
ego-, 59, 197
external, 171
inanimate, 31
internal, 33, 171, 219, 229, 239, 244–246, 249
lost, 66
new, 58
Oedipal, 130
of attention, 167
of consciousness, 27, 35, 39, 114, 190
of construction, 212
of investigation, 96
of knowledge, 144, 146
of perception, 115, 140
of study, 104
part-, 198
paternal, 88
perceptual, 106
phantasied, 58
positive, 244, 267
presentation, 71, 75–76, 207
primary, 94, 252, 268
primitive, 59, 196
real, 58
-relations, 14, 59, 177, 188, 197, 199–200, 223, 246, 252
-representations, 3, 10, 196–199
self-, 198
separate, 173
subject–, 198
transitional, 172
true, 63
whole, 246
world, 144–145, 148, 151, 154–157, 222, 259
objective, 141, 152, 158, 165, 176, 269
aspects, 141
detection, 126
language, 169
mind, 140–141
neurophysiology, 120
system, 165
usage, 165
validation, 157
Ochsner, K., 103, 271
Oedipal, 175
autonomy, 93
objects, 130
phase, 139
pre-, 130, 175, 177, 224
Oedipus complex, 139, 159
Ogden, T. H., 168, 172, 260, 282
O'Neil, M. K., 18, 282
Ornston, D., 139, 282
Osborn, A. F., 243, 282

Panksepp, J., 103–104, 256, 282, 285
Paris School of Psychosomatics, 204, 206, 263
Penfield, W., 105–106, 282
perception, 7, 27, 33, 45–46, 56, 64, 88, 105–109, 113–118, 143, 145, 147–148, 155, 187, 194, 196, 207, 216–220, 222–223, 230, 241, 253, 259, 264–265
colour, 220, 265
conscious, 67, 108–109, 114, 233
external, 33, 56, 87, 108–109, 133, 147, 194, 208, 217, 219–220, 265
infant's, 171
internal, 33, 109, 217, 219–220, 234, 265
object of, 115, 140–141
realistic, 232
self-, 19, 107, 217–218, 224, 227–229, 232, 265–266
sense-, 64, 87, 169, 209, 241
unconscious, 147, 208, 227
world of, 106

perceptual, 106, 122, 257
  capacities, 217
  conflicts, 99
  consciousness, 113–114, 117–118
  data, 138
  input, 230
  mechanism, 107
  neurons, 117
  objects, 106
  residues, 64
  system, 118
Perrault, C., 238
Person, E. S., 254, 273
perspective, 5, 10, 27, 85–86, 133, 161, 165, 173, 180, 237, 246, 251, 268
  adaptive, 10, 85
  alternate, 159
  biologic, 127
  cognitive psychology, 176
  diverse, 244
  dynamic, 9
  economic, 9, 11, 14
  genetic, 10
  Hindu, 259
  intersubjective, 14
  metapsychological, 10
  object-relations, 223
  paternal, 173–174
  psychoanalytical, 11, 177
  relational, 14, 163–164, 260
  structural, 10
  topographic, 9, 84–85
  transcendental, 133
  Winnicottian, 228
Pessoa, F., 253, 282
Pfeiffer, E., 82–83, 282
phantasy, 3, 16, 62, 93, 177
  unconscious, 172
Piaget, J., 13, 230, 282–283
Pine, F., 8, 15, 224, 281, 283
Pirandello, L., 232–233, 266, 283
Plato, 241
Plotnik, J. M., 230, 283
Pontalis, J.-B., 1, 16, 85, 280
Povinelli, D. J., 230, 274
prakriti (primordial matter), 134–135, 144, 149
Pranas, 148
processes, 40, 48–50, 56, 96–97, 99, 108–109, 121, 124, 127, 129–130, 137, 146, 150, 155, 193, 235–236, 241–242, 244–245
  affective, 103
  conscious, 29, 34, 83, 136, 181, 185
  contiguous, 41
  cortical, 103, 117
  ego, 102
  excitatory, 54
  internal, 97
  intuitive, 243
  latent, 5–6, 32, 219
  living, 161
  mental, 5–6, 9, 13, 23–27, 30, 32–33, 35–36, 99, 101–102, 138, 147, 185, 187, 218–220, 237, 247–248, 254, 265
  nerve, 67
  neurophysiologic, 120
  of activation, 108
  of discharge, 191
  primary, 104, 123
  psychic, 241, 251
  psychical, 52–54
  psychodynamic, 103
  psychological, 119–120
  repressed, 34
  secondary, 102
  somatic, 29, 184
  splitting, 98
  thinking, 248
  thought, 64
  unconscious, 13, 25, 36, 49, 97, 101–102, 125–128, 146, 152, 187, 216, 218, 258
  verifying, 97
projection, 46, 183, 185, 249–250, 267
projective identification, 197, 223, 245–247
Psarakos, S., 230, 281
psychic(al), 29, 33–34, 69–70, 83, 98, 119, 121, 131, 136, 184, 187, 203–204, 212, 219, 245, 264
  act, 27–28, 32, 34–36, 64, 84, 113, 137, 147, 154, 163, 186–188, 190, 192, 199, 219
  agents, 163
  apparatus, 138, 203
  arrangement, 228, 236, 246
  aspect, 70
  character, 30, 147
  circumstances, 17
  conflict, 9
  content, 163
  continuities, 24, 30, 184–185
  determination, 139, 148–149
  development, 56
  elements, 68, 136–137, 153
  energy, 9, 150, 152, 157, 209
  equivalent, 246
  events, 69, 131
  expression, 138
  factor, 72

forces, 194, 209
function, 54, 209
id, 208
inheritance, 16
inter-, 201, 239, 243, 252, 263, 266
intra-, 9, 163–164, 244, 249, 252, 261
life, 139, 214, 264
locality, 6–7, 9, 36, 63, 84, 153, 162, 187, 199
material, 160
model, 262
movements, 192
organisation, 54, 56, 64, 84, 113, 154, 194, 199–200, 211
paralysis, 9
pathologies, 205
phenomena, 43, 69, 131
point of view, 70
process, 8, 29, 43, 48, 52–54, 61, 85, 146, 184, 193, 204, 241, 251
quality, 208
reality, 4, 6, 49, 87–88, 93–94, 98–99, 130, 139, 146, 156, 158, 193, 220, 222, 227, 265
representatives, 138, 150, 190, 204–205, 207
repressed, 54
somato-, 204, 263–264
space, 198
state, 5–7, 12, 29, 70, 251
structure, 99
symptom, 28
systems, 34–35, 48, 52, 59, 105, 188
topography, 35–37, 105, 187–189
truth, 196
unconscious, 29, 32, 87, 102, 137
work, 194, 214, 235
world, 87
Pulver, S., 15, 283

rajas (passion), 151
Ramachandran, V., 103, 283
Rangell, L., 13, 15, 283
Rapaport, D., 10, 85, 283
Rappoport de Aisemberg, E., 204, 270
reality, 33, 96, 98, 121, 124–127, 129–130, 133–135, 146, 156, 158, 173, 178, 187, 189–190, 219, 227, 247, 257–258
absolute, 134, 142
aspects of, 124, 257
child's, 244
complications of, 52
concrete, 93
conflict, 258
experience of, 152
external, 87–88, 98, 126–127, 152, 237
hatred of, 6
material, 87–88, 98
notions of, 187
of unconsciousness, 156
phantasy, 93
-principle, 50, 102, 107, 115–116, 138
psychic, 4, 6, 49, 87–88, 93–94, 98–99, 130, 139, 146, 156, 158, 193, 220, 222, 227, 265
sense of, 138
social, 129, 144
supreme, 140, 145
-testing, 49–50, 54
transcendental, 156
true, 156
ultimate, 133, 142, 154, 156, 158
Reddy, S., 141, 283
Reiss, D., 230, 283
Reith, B., 19, 99, 261–264, 283
repression, 4, 14–15, 17, 28, 37, 39–44, 46–48, 52–58, 64–66, 84, 102, 113, 137–138, 153–154, 162–163, 173, 176, 180–181, 188, 191–192, 195, 199–200, 207–208, 222–223, 235, 248, 258, 260, 263, 265, 267
-derived, 3
infantile, 222
metapsychology of, 233
primal, 2, 42–43, 208
primary, 14
process of, 43, 45, 58
theory, 26
Robertson, E., 103, 271
Rodrigué, E., 11, 283
Rosen, J., 4, 283
Ross, J. M., 5, 284
Roussillon, R., 200–201, 263, 284
Rubin, J. B., 158, 284
Rugg, H., 12, 284
Rumiati, R., 243, 246, 249, 284
Rycroft, C., 169, 284

Sampson, H., 13, 287
Sandler, A. M., 18, 284
Sandler, J., 15, 18, 95–96, 278, 284
Sanskrit, 132, 134, 141, 151, 154, 159
Schafer, R., 11, 284
Schilder, P., 230, 284
Schimek, J. G., 216, 284
schizophrenia, 8, 58–66, 161, 163, 198, 227, 265
Schore, A. N., 19, 284
Searle, J., 120, 130–131, 284
Searles, H. F., 8, 167, 284
Segal, H., 198, 284

self, 5–7, 15, 19, 32, 105, 139, 146, 148, 166, 170, 175, 186, 217–218, 221–222, 225, 228–233, 239, 244–246, 248–250, 252–253, 256, 260, 265–268
affective, 170
-analysis, 194
-awareness, 228
-constancy, 223, 228
-contradiction, 52
-destructive, 221, 265
-directed, 244
dissociated, 226, 229
-disturbance, 265
-ego, 93
embodied, 134, 136, 144, 152
-enrichment, 3
-evident, 187
-experience, 139
-fulfilment, 158
-hood, 139
hypersexual, 221
individual, 134–135, 141–142
infant, 170
-integration, 158
-knowledge, 169
liberated, 135
mental, 222
notion of, 139
nuclear, 246
-object, 198
-observation, 74, 217, 266
-ordained, 147
-organisation, 222–223
overall, 218
-perception, 19, 107, 217, 224, 227–229, 232, 265
-preservative, 150
professional, 250
psychology, 14, 220
rageful, 225
-realisation, 152, 158, 167, 175, 178
-reflective, 183
regular, 225
-representation, 3, 6–7, 10, 196–197, 217
sense of, 230, 244
-state, 7, 135, 225, 231
structure, 177
supreme, 134–136, 142
thing-in-, 159
transgender, 221
true, 18
sexual(ly), 93, 182
action, 93
arousal, 88, 106
attack, 229
criminal, 229
drive, 150
excitement, 93
hyper-, 221
impulse, 44
instinct, 150, 205
intercourse, 2, 16
intrusion, 229
longings, 139
nature, 172
relations, 211
torture, 231
transference, 93
trauma, 228
wish, 93
sexuality, 2, 88, 182
human, 205
Shengold, L., 228, 284
Shevrin, H., 103, 123, 125–127, 271–273, 284, 288
Shewmon, D., 110, 285
Simeon, D., 218, 277
Slap, J., 216, 220, 223, 285
Slap-Shelton, L., 220, 223, 285
Smadja, C., 204, 285
Snodgrass, M., 125–127, 271, 288
Solms, M., 19, 103–104, 114, 118, 133, 155, 256–257, 278, 285
sookshma sareera, 148
Spitz, R., 15, 285
splitting, 6, 15, 33, 63, 141, 198, 219–220, 223, 248–250, 252, 267
-brain, 101
functional, 250
mind, 227
of consciousness, 32, 219, 223
process, 98
state, 249
vertical, 6, 249
Stern, D., 15, 165, 170, 176–177, 260, 285
Strachey, J., 109, 117, 131, 139, 175–176, 202, 215, 259, 285
Straparola, G. F., 238
Strawson, G., 131, 285
subject(s), 2–8, 10, 41, 44, 102, 106, 127, 140, 143, 164–165, 198, 203, 207, 209, 213, 236, 238–239, 241–242, 244–246, 249–252, 267
intuitive, 248
-object, 198
sentient, 106
waking, 177
subjective, 97, 107, 111, 141, 157, 163, 165, 217, 269
conditioning, 33, 219

experience, 9
formulation, 243, 246–247, 249, 267
inter-, 201, 263
language, 163
mental phenomena, 120
mind, 140–142
perspective, 14
truth, 98
Suttie, I., 178, 285
Swami Chinmayananda, 134, 141–142, 147–148, 285–286
Swami Dayananda Saraswati, 133–135, 154, 286
Swami Madhavananda, 141, 286
Swami Nikhilananda, 133, 152, 286
Swami Vireswarananda, 134, 286
symbol(-ism), 4, 62, 76–77, 86, 89, 144, 154, 167, 169–170, 174, 176–178, 200, 213–214, 226, 232, 264
aesthetic, 165, 177
conventional, 165
discursive, 165, 176
equations, 198
function, 165, 172
imaginary-, 177
linguistic, 176
pre-, 202
presentational, 165, 176–177
primary, 200
primitive, 172
representations, 200
secondary, 200
solution, 221
space, 198
structure, 172
territory, 167
Symington, N., 260, 286

Talvitie, V., 15, 286
Target, M., 8, 275
Taylor, W. S., 227, 286
Teuber, H-L., 102, 282
The New Shorter Oxford English Dictionary, 216–217, 286
Theall, L. A., 230, 274
theory, 26, 30, 36, 52, 68, 95–96, 120, 130, 161, 173–174, 176, 178, 184, 256, 258
affect, 15
analytic, 178
classical, 220
dream-, 208
drive, 209
meta-, 81, 85–86, 95
object-relations, 14, 246
of anxiety, 264
of art, 164–165, 167, 175–176
of dreams, 1, 81–82
of dynamic unconscious, 161–162
of ego, 163
of memory, 36
of repression, 180
of transference, 213
of unconscious, 174, 208
psychoanalytic, 3, 10, 24, 95, 98, 169, 171, 177, 184, 254–255
psychological, 150
relational, 220
repression, 26
somatopsychic, 204
structural, 2, 15, 139, 223
topographical, 174, 223
thing-presentation, 7, 63–64, 71, 75, 84, 113, 161–167, 169, 173, 176, 182–184, 198–202, 207, 261–262
Tieck, L., 238
Tolstoy, L., 254, 269, 286
transcendental, 133–134, 149, 154, 158, 259
experience, 133
nature, 135
perspective, 133
reality, 156
transference, 58–59, 89, 93, 99, 178, 197, 212–214, 221, 223–224, 229, 263
classical, 212, 214
compulsion, 212, 264
conflict, 89
-countertransference, 94, 208, 212
dynamics, 87, 213
interpretable, 212
love, 82
manifestations, 213
neuroses, 43, 58–59, 63–65, 82, 84, 93, 162, 199–200, 212–213, 264
sexual, 93
theory of, 212–213
verbalised, 264
yearning, 5
transformation, 18, 26, 28, 87–88, 137, 164, 166, 178–182, 185, 188, 195–196, 199–202, 237, 240, 261–262
Trevarthen, C., 170, 178, 281, 286
triee vada, 133, 135, 149
Turnbull, O., 19, 285

unconscious(ness) (*passim*) *see also*: Freud
activity, 30, 33, 67, 184, 238
affects, 14–15, 39–40, 108, 207, 210
aims, 17
anxiety, 39

aspect, 138, 217
attribute, 39
biological, 124, 257
capacities, 200
cathexis, 42
cognitive, 13
collective, 16
communication, 194, 256
compartmentalisation of, 6
conditioning, 125
constellations, 3
control, 13
creativity, 12
decision making, 13
derivatives, 197–198
descriptive, 180
desire, 128
determinants, 183
development, 3
domain, 169
dynamic, 102, 160–162, 203, 220, 248, 260, 263, 265
ego, 194
elements, 3, 137, 153, 256
embarrassment, 102
emotions, 14, 39–40, 262
events, 121
experience, 184, 201
factors, 223
fantasy, 16, 95, 203, 213, 223
feelings, 39, 110
forces, 217
Freudian, 19
functioning, 217
guilt, 15
hope, 13
idea, 4, 14–15, 26, 37–40, 43–44, 46, 51, 110, 188, 192, 206
identification, 192, 201
impulse, 17, 39, 57, 190, 195
inference, 67
influences, 19, 46, 222
instincts, 39, 45
learning, 125
level, 6, 13
life, 120, 160, 189
material, 67, 206, 209
meaningful, 119
memory, 4, 37–38, 160, 188–189
mental, 31, 101
mentation, 120–121
mind, 254, 260, 268
motivation, 94, 226
operations, 122, 124, 127
perception, 208, 227
phantasy, 172, 202
phenomena, 87, 139, 156
physical, 102
plan, 13
presentation, 7, 63, 65–66, 84, 113, 153–154, 162, 199
problem solving, 3, 13, 17, 19
procedural, 252
process, 13, 23–26, 33, 36, 49, 97, 102, 114, 120, 125–128, 136, 146, 152, 187, 216, 218–219, 254, 258
psychical, 32, 101, 137
psychology of, 85
registration, 36, 187
remembering, 102
representational, 120
repressed, 206
seeing, 102
significance, 203
state, 67, 120, 142, 160
system, 84, 103, 123–124, 129, 207
transmitting, 97
urges, 142
volition, 102
work(ing), 3, 266
world, 166

Vallabhaneni, M. R., 139, 286
van den Bos, R., 230, 274
vasanas, 141–144, 147–149, 151, 153, 155, 157–158, 259
Vedic, 133
viveka, 143
Vivona, J. M., 176, 286
Volkan, V., 16, 286

Waelder, R., 10, 286
Wälder, R., 228, 287
Wallas, G., 242, 267, 287
Warkentin, V., 230, 271
Wegner, P., 82, 88, 97, 255–256, 264, 287
Weiskrantz, L., 102, 287
Weiss, J., 13, 287
Werner, H., 164–165, 287
Wertheimer, M., 243, 287
Wiebe, D., 242, 267, 281
Williams, W., 103, 284
Winnicott, D. W., 18, 86, 166–167, 169–170, 172, 201, 228, 237, 260, 263, 287–288
Wisdom, J. O., 246, 288
Wong, P., 125, 127, 273, 288
word-presentation, 63–65, 68, 71–73, 76, 84, 110, 112–113, 161–165, 169, 176, 184, 198–202, 207–208, 262
Wright, K., 167, 169–170, 173–174, 177–178, 260–261, 288

For Product Safety Concerns and Information please contact our EU representative GPSR@taylorandfrancis.com
Taylor & Francis Verlag GmbH, Kaufingerstraße 24, 80331 München, Germany

www.ingramcontent.com/pod-product-compliance
Lightning Source LLC
Chambersburg PA
CBHW050335270326
41926CB00016B/3465

* 9 7 8 1 7 8 2 2 0 0 2 7 7 *